T0305726

THE COOPERATIVE ECONOMY

Societal grand challenges have taken a toll on humanity, which finds itself at a crossroads. The concentration of wealth and economic inequality, the dominance of Big Tech firms, the loss of privacy and free choice, and the overconsumption and abuse of natural resources have been reinforced by globalization. Regulation, legislation, international treaties, and government and corporate policies have fallen short of offering sufficient remedies. This book identifies the root cause of these problems and offers a bold solution: a new economic system, free from the design flaws that have contributed to these societal grand challenges.

The proposed cooperative economy is an ethical community-driven exchange system that relies on collective action to promote societal values while accounting for resource constraints. Unlike the modern economic system that is predominantly driven by opportunistic behavior, the cooperative economy moves away from a materialistic orientation and follows a more balanced perspective that leverages prosocial behavior. The book explains how this new system adopts design principles that promote self-sufficiency of communities, sustainability, and entrepreneurship while limiting overconsumption and excessive profit-making. It enhances economic equality by leveraging price subsidization and by restricting salary differences. The book describes how the system serves the interests of consumers, vendors, and employees while preventing the accumulation of power by the platform owner who operates this system.

This book is invaluable reading for policymakers who have been searching for solutions to some of the grand challenges that our society faces, and to managers who have sought alternative ways to cope with platform ecosystems, resource shortages, and supply chain disruptions. It revisits long-held assumptions, offering a treatise and food for thought, as well as a plan for concrete action. The book is also highly relevant to scholars and students in the study of economics, strategy, innovation, and public policy and to all readers who are concerned about the future of our planet and society.

DOVEV LAVIE is a Professor of Strategic Management at Bocconi University with a PhD from the Wharton School, University of Pennsylvania. He is a Sloan Industry Studies Fellow and a recipient of the Strategic Management Society's Emerging Scholar Award and the Academy of Management Newman Award. He studies societal grand challenges, the interplay of competition and cooperation, and value creation and capture in alliances and ecosystems.

"In this book, renowned social scientist Dovev Lavie describes how our economic system reinforces our human tendencies toward opportunism. The consequences have been grave. To address grand challenges such as overconsumption and abuse of natural resources, we now need to turn to an alternative cooperative economic system in which we reinforce our prosocial inclinations. Lavie provides compelling scientific evidence that this is possible and well within our reach. If you are seeking inspiration on how to change the world, read this book!"

Anita McGahan, *Professor and Chair in Organizations & Society, University of Toronto; Past President, Academy of Management*

"This is one of those rare and ambitious books that challenges the very capitalist system that we all take for granted. Lavie carefully unpacks not only the list of problems we face as a society, but then puts forward a new way of organizing that might help us address many of them. He sets aside piecemeal tweaks to our system and instead proposes a new model that he calls the 'cooperative economy.' We all agree that our system as we know it is broken. But few have thus far imagined what a new way of organizing our economy might look like. This book opens up the possibility that there may yet be a way forward."

Ranjay Gulati, *Professor of Business Administration, Harvard Business School*

"Is a free enterprise, market economy based upon fairness and kindness a realistic alternative for one based upon greed and exploitation? Dovev Lavie's vision of a cooperative economy has convinced me that it is indeed possible."

Robert Grant, *Professor of Management, Bocconi University*

THE COOPERATIVE ECONOMY

A SOLUTION TO SOCIETAL GRAND CHALLENGES

Dovev Lavie

Routledge
Taylor & Francis Group

LONDON AND NEW YORK

Cover design: Dovev Lavie / Danielle Lavie / Sveta Designs.
Getty images: Maksym Dehil; arsenisspyros; dimdimich.

First published 2023
by Routledge
4 Park Square, Milton Park, Abingdon, Oxon OX14 4RN

and by Routledge
605 Third Avenue, New York, NY 10158

Routledge is an imprint of the Taylor & Francis Group, an informa business

British Library Cataloguing-in-Publication Data
A catalogue record for this book is available from the British Library

Library of Congress Cataloging-in-Publication Data
Names: Lavie, Dovev, author.
Title: The cooperative economy : a solution to societal grand challenges / Dovev Lavie.
Description: New York, NY : Routledge, 2023. |
Includes bibliographical references and index. | Identifiers: LCCN 2022038009 (print) |
LCCN 2022038010 (ebook) | ISBN 9781032370699 (hardback) |
ISBN 9781032370651 (paperback) | ISBN 9781003336679 (ebook)
Subjects: LCSH: Cooperation. | Community development. | Sustainable development. |
Interpersonal relations.
Classification: LCC HD2963 .L385 2023 (print) | LCC HD2963 (ebook) |
DDC 306.3/4–dc23/eng/20220810
LC record available at https://lccn.loc.gov/2022038009
LC ebook record available at https://lccn.loc.gov/2022038010

ISBN: 978-1-032-37069-9 (hbk)
ISBN: 978-1-032-37065-1 (pbk)
ISBN: 978-1-003-33667-9 (ebk)

DOI: 10.4324/9781003336679

Typeset in Minion Pro
by Newgen Publishing UK

I dedicate this book to my parents, Raphael and Maria Lavie.

CONTENTS

AUTHOR BIOGRAPHY

Dovev Lavie is Professor of Strategic Management in the Department of Management and Technology of Bocconi University in Milan. Formerly, he served as Professor and Vice Dean of MBA Programs in the Faculty of Industrial Engineering and Management at the Technion in Haifa. He earned his PhD in Management at the Wharton School of the University of Pennsylvania and served as Assistant Professor at the University of Texas at Austin. He also held visiting positions at the London Business School, Imperial College London, University College London, and BI Norway. Lavie is a Sloan Industry Studies Fellow, a recipient of the Strategic Management Society's Emerging Scholar Award, and winner of the INFORMS TMS Best Dissertation Award and the Academy of Management Newman Award. His research interests include societal grand challenges, the interplay of competition and cooperation, value creation and capture in alliance portfolios and ecosystems, and the balancing of exploration and exploitation. He has consulted with and trained executives in various sectors, mostly in technology-intensive industries. His work has been published in leading journals including the *Strategic Management Journal*, *Administrative Science Quarterly*, *Academy of Management Review*, *Academy of Management Journal*, and *Organization Science*. Lavie has served as Associate Editor of the *Academy of Management Journal* and the *Strategic Management Journal* and on the boards of other leading journals. He also served as Director-at-Large on the board of the Strategic Management Society and held leadership positions at the SMS Cooperative Strategies Interest Group and the Academy of Management STR Division.

PREFACE

In March 2020, the Lombardy region of Italy experienced the most devastating Covid-19 outbreak, with a spiking death toll, prolonged lockdowns, and desperation. I spent most of the spring semester in Vienna, but upon my return to Milan, I continued to teach online, avoided visits to the university, and barely left my tiny home office.

The solitude led me to ponder existential questions. The suffering of deprived populations and the individuals who lost their jobs amid the pandemic made me think about the challenges that our society faces and will continue to struggle with beyond the pandemic. The pandemic seemed to have drawn attention away from concerns about climate change and worsened the ramifications of economic inequality. With the transition to the virtual workspace and online shopping, the Big Tech firms have grown to dominate many spheres of life. Publishing academic articles that matter little to a few seemed detached from this unfortunate reality, so I searched for a more meaningful purpose. My exploration has evolved into spiritual development when seeking answers to ancient questions. Then, around April 2021, the answer came. In a moment I realized my purpose in life, both personally and professionally.

The answer came in the form of a model—an economic model that is quite distinct from our current economic system, but well aligned with the laws of creation and the principles that have been advocated by spiritual guides throughout the history of humankind. To my disappointment, I concluded that I have spent the past couple of decades making great strides in the wrong direction. While I have been researching and teaching about firms' value creation and capture, I may have inadvertently contributed to the societal grand challenges that I seek to resolve. This insight prompted me to reverse my research agenda and focus on the fair distribution of value rather than on strategies for its accumulation. I summarized my idea in a paragraph, which I then elaborated in a two-pager that defined the objectives and the core principles of the cooperative economy. A month later, I sketched a design for a lab experiment, but finding PhD students or postdocs with relevant expertise for developing the corresponding algorithms turned out to be challenging.

In September 2021, I started my sabbatical at Imperial College London. After clearing my desk of articles that were lingering in the review process, I decided to write a short piece about the cooperative economy, with the hope that by casting a broader net I would attract technical experts. Two hundred pages later, it became clear to me that this was likely to end up as a book rather than as an article. The work on the book was intensive. Much like the content, the format was not ordinary. The book was neither a typical academic essay nor a typical trade book. The problem and solution were anchored in research, but my purpose was not to offer a theory but to craft a proactive plan for its implementation. As I elaborated my ideas, I realized that this book not only challenges the consensus in the field of strategic management but also revisits long-held assumptions in the economics discipline. Unlike most of the research on societal grand challenges that calls for traditional remedies such as regulation and legislation that could fix the flaws in our economy, my conclusion was that our economy is unfixable. I admit that offering an alternative economic system can be perceived as radical, but as an engineer, I found it a simpler solution than tampering with the current system that was designed to support the concentration of wealth rather than its distribution.

Yet the cooperative economy does not only entail a different design but also requires us to revisit our assumptions concerning human nature. Whereas established economic models take for granted that firms maximize profit while consumers maximize utility, for the cooperative economy to function, we should all be willing to benefit others at our own expense. Not only that, but such prosocial behavior should make us more satisfied than we could be made by self-interested opportunistic behavior. This requires us to envision humans as conscious, honorable people, embedded in their communities rather than as Homo economicus who only react to economic stimuli.

Prosocial behavior is conditional rather than absolute, so for it to transpire, the system must ensure that those who are inclined to behave opportunistically are excluded and that opportunistic behavior is penalized. The proposed economic system requires social responsibility from all stakeholders. There is no free lunch. The platform owner should give up power, vendors should limit their profits, consumers should reduce their consumption and subsidize low-income peers, and employees should forgo excessive salaries. These concessions make sense only if stakeholders prioritize societal values over economic gains. By following the principles of the cooperative economy, we can promote economic equality and combat the concentration of wealth; restrain dominant platform owners and regain data privacy and free choice in consumption; reduce overconsumption and abuse of natural resources; and overcome some of the downsides of globalization. Unfortunately, all stakeholders, including vendors, consumers, and governments, have clear incentives to persist with their economic growth aspirations. Therefore, the implementation should start by changing our mindset and giving more weight not to corporations but to cohesive communities that can take the lead in the proposed transformation. This is indeed challenging, but our planet's hourglass is running out of sand, and more conventional remedies have fallen short. It is clear to me that this book will be controversial, but at least it will invoke a conversation and encourage my fellow researchers to test my ideas. My hope is that the cooperative economy would transition from theory to practice, and that you, my reader, will find interest and a way to take part in this journey.

I am indebted to the late Avi Fiegenbaum, who introduced me to the field of strategic management. I offer my gratitude to my professors and mentors at the Wharton School who provided me with the training that was needed to follow my career path. My background in strategic management uniquely positions me to raise overarching questions and to understand not only how economic models work but also why they do not work. In this book I apply an approach that is typically used for analyzing the dynamics of corporate behavior and performance to examine the overall organization of economic activities in our society. I also benefited from the interactions with my co-authors and colleagues at the University of Texas at Austin, the Technion, Bocconi University, and the institutions that I visited, including the London Business School, BI Norway, University College London, and Imperial College London. I appreciate the feedback received in the seminars in which I presented this book at Ohio State University, Purdue University, Imperial College London, the London Business School, Cambridge University, the Technion, BI Norway, and Bocconi University, which also sponsored my sabbatical. I acknowledge the support of Ranjay Gulati, who guided me in the publication process. Last but not least, I thank my parents, Raphael and Maria Lavie, whose love, devotion, and moral standards helped pave my way, as well as my kids, who challenge and inspire me.

CHAPTER ONE

Introduction

DOI: 10.4324/9781003336679-1

We live in interesting times, yet humanity is at a crossroad. Industrialization and digitalization have brought immense economic growth, but relatively few fully enjoy this prosperity. Products and services have been personalized and made available to consumers with increased accessibility and variety, but hunger and despair have become more pervasive in deprived regions. Production and distribution have been globalized and made more efficient, yet natural resources are insufficient to support overconsumption, and our warming planet shows signs of exhaustion. Capable corporations have accumulated much power at the expense of competitors, vendors, and consumers who have lost their privacy and free choice in digital platforms. The pervasive consumeristic culture has undermined traditional values and unstitched the social fabric of local communities. This transformation may be completed with the upcoming metaverse, where consumers' interactions could be monetized under the orchestration of virtual machines that study and exploit consumers in the name of profit making. This is neither a horror nor a science fiction movie. This is our reality. Is it really that bad? How have we ended up in this situation? Who is to blame for it? Most importantly, how can we fix it?

Few will disagree that the modern economic system in the Western world is imperfect. In fact, it is quite perfect in facilitating value creation and capture by the privileged few. For decades, my colleagues and I have taught generations of MBA students and executives how to strategize and gain competitive advantage, and these students have learned and applied this teaching quite well. Big Tech firms such as Amazon, Apple, Google, Meta, and Microsoft have mastered that doctrine and captured dominant market positions that cannot be easily contested. Antitrust regulation and enforcement have stood disarmed in their efforts to restrain these firms, which seem to be one step ahead of their predators. It is the Big Tech firms that have become predators, luring consumers with free apps and oppressing society. Nevertheless, they cannot be fully blamed for mastering the rules of the modern economic system. This system allows profit maximization to override societal values such as sustainability and well-being, which have been treated as constraints or distractions. Of particular interest is "techlash" and the worldwide inquiry into and prosecution of the Big Tech firms; meanwhile, these firms and their owners have proceeded full steam ahead with the accumulation of wealth and the concentration of power.

In this book, I identify four aggravated problems that our current economic system has fostered as well as a fifth problem that reinforces the other four. Clearly, these are not the only problems that our society faces, but these are interrelated problems that share a common root cause. Furthermore, despite efforts to remedy these problems, they have worsened in past decades. I will briefly explain these problems and clarify why conservative approaches to solving them have failed. These problems are:

- Wealth concentration and economic inequality
- The grip of platform owners
- Loss of privacy and private choice
- Overconsumption and abuse of natural resources
- Some drawbacks of globalization

Wealth concentration and economic inequality. In the past few decades, and especially during the Covid-19 pandemic, the rich have become richer while the poor have become poorer. For example, in the United States, three individuals possess wealth that is greater than that of half of the population. Whereas the income share of the affluent has increased, their tax liability has declined, in part due to regressive taxation and in part due to tax evasion. Economic inequality has been related to shortened life expectancy and illness as well as to corruption and political instability. The middle class in Western society has witnessed the sharpest decline in purchasing power. Although the United Nations has recognized the importance of reducing inequality and ending poverty and hunger, governments have shifted the tax burden from rich corporations to families. The international agreement on minimum corporate tax rate that was signed in October 2021 is insufficient for stopping this trend and preventing tax evasion. Some public welfare programs have only reinforced inequality by depriving the needy from opportunities to become economically independent. Labor unions have lost membership and power under flexible employment regulation, while technology development has benefited capital owners rather than employees. Thus, economic inequality persists.

The grip of platform owners. The triumph belongs to ecosystem platform owners, those Big Tech firms that possess the technological infrastructure on which we all rely. The emergence of the Internet was supposed to free us from brick-and-mortar intermediaries. Instead, it gave birth to more powerful digital gatekeepers that dominate markets at the expense of all stakeholders but their shareholders. The platform owners do not adhere to the traditional rules of competition, and since they often offer free services without restricting output, antitrust regulation is ill equipped to cope with them. They suppress competition with exclusionary practices that keep competition at bay. These practices include self-preferencing their offerings, excluding competitors or acquiring them, and penalizing vendors that seek to work with their competitors. The vendors offer value-adding complementary products and services, but do not receive their fair share of the value created. They are forced to pay high service fees to the platform owner that exploits its superior data access to compete with them. As revealed in the case of Epic Games vs. Apple, even the most powerful vendors can be excluded from the platform if they refuse to concede. For consumers, the free service comes at a high price. The dominant platform owners expand vertically and horizontally to various businesses, restrict consumers' choices while increasing their switching costs, and eventually reduce quality and increase prices. As is apparent with the case of Meta, advertising revenue has received priority over consumer welfare, leaving users struggling with fake news and unsafe content. The owners of the Big Tech firms are among the richest individuals in the world, and their computer scientists and software engineers are well compensated. However, the platform owners have exploited many other employees, who are underpaid, overworked, and silenced. Platform owners such as Uber, Lyft, and Wolt promised freedom to earn extra income at leisure but made their contractors dependent and deprived them of employee rights before doubling the platform's commissions. Employee welfare in traditional industries has worsened as well, with many struggling to maintain job security and decent working conditions. Policy making, antitrust laws, and regulation are in the works to update the outdated laws, but the slow wheels of justice are insufficient to catch up with the elusive platform owners that modify their business models at will. Severe measures such as a breakup of the Big Tech firms may not leave consumers better off, whereas lax measures such as trusting these firms to regulate themselves are naïve.

Loss of privacy and private choice. Consumers pay the platform owners for their free services with personal data, which is analyzed, dissected, and reconstructed using advanced algorithms, machine learning, and artificial intelligence that is occasionally unintelligent and biased. The purpose is not only to predict consumer behavior, but to guide or misguide it as per the profit-making interest of the platform owner. In this process, algorithmic consumers economize on effort but lose their free choice. This observation concerns not only the purchasing of products based on recommendations but also the shaping of political views and discourse. Private information is collected and integrated across numerous websites, content is analyzed, and soon emotions and facial gestures will be studied too, making us vulnerable to manipulation and psychological harm. The Cambridge Analytica scandal may be the most notorious case but is not an isolated event. The Big Tech firms have established surveillance capitalism to sophisticatedly monetize our eyeball movements. Recent legislation in Europe seeks to protect users' data and ensure privacy, but it places a greater burden on small vendors, thus reinforcing the grip of platform owners. Enforcement has concentrated on the observable rather than important violations, with negligible penalties. In the United States, lobbyists have been successful in preventing or delaying protective regulation. In fact, platform owners have used recent data protection and privacy laws to augment their competitive advantage relative to their competitors and vendors. Automated algorithms have served not only to manipulate users but also to deceive antitrust enforcement, which cannot prove the malicious intent of software code. Hence, data privacy and free choice have been compromised.

Overconsumption and abuse of natural resources. With their relentless profit-seeking, firms have not only exploited stakeholders but also abused our planet's natural resources by leveraging advertising that spurs overconsumption. In the past century, the exploitation of raw materials has increased by 650 percent, and the extraction of natural resources has increased by more than 300 percent in four decades. The population of animals declined by almost 70 percent during that period, in which the land, air, sea, and rivers have been polluted, with global warming prompting natural disasters. And while a quarter of produced food is wasted, in deprived regions, many experience hunger. Consumers have also done little to change their habits and become more mindful about the unfortunate consequences of their lifestyles. At the current rate of consumption, by 2050, 2.5 planets will be needed to supply demand. It is mostly the affluent nations and individuals that overconsume, restricting the availability of finite natural resources to others. Firms have trained us to consume to satisfy emotional desires rather than physical needs, but happiness is beyond reach for those falling into this trap. Many firms proudly exhibit their environmental peacock feathers, only to lure consumers with their greenwashing to make extra profit. Some firms have improved their production processes by incorporating alternative energy sources and recycling. But although such supply-side initiatives have been fostered by regulation, responsible consumption has not. Responsible consumption and voluntary simplicity remain slogans, and no consumption caps have been set by policymakers. Reducing consumption is likely to restrict consumers' utility and firms' profits while jeopardizing the economic growth of nations, so all stakeholders have a shared interest in enduring overconsumption. Thus, by 2030, with the exhaustion of natural resources, shortages and catastrophic weather conditions are likely to become more prevalent.

Some drawbacks of globalization. The free flow of goods, capital, and labor has many merits, but not everyone can enjoy the gains. Globalization has fostered economic inequality by increasing the return on capital while depriving the underprivileged, who have remained immobile and taxable. Multinational corporations have leveraged globalization to specialize, optimize their supply chains, reduce costs, and evade taxes, while gaining power relative to governments. National policy measures have fallen short in responding to job loss, brain drain, flux in international migration, and unemployment. Globalization has promoted consumerism and overconsumption while making financial networks and supply chains more vulnerable, as demonstrated by the tsunami in Japan, the mortgage crisis in the United States, the Covid-19 pandemic, and the war in Ukraine. Moreover, the individualistic culture promoted by globalization has challenged societal values and otherwise cohesive social structures. Attempting to transplant societal values into multinational corporations with a for-profit mission is unlikely to succeed. It seems, then, that the drawbacks of globalization have exacerbated the problems of the modern economic system.

These grand challenges have taken a toll on society, and their unfortunate consequences for humanity's well-being seem inevitable. Yet I argue that all these problems have one root cause, which is mistakenly ascribed to human nature. Observers often point to greed as the underlying motive that drives opportunistic behavior at all costs. Nevertheless, we should not blame firms for seeking profits or consumers for maximizing utility. We must blame the economic system that has prioritized these aims over societal values, and that rewards the opportunistic entrepreneurs while penalizing those who strive for cooperation. But economic theory has made some incorrect assumptions. Not all humans were born as opportunistic creatures. Some are more opportunistic than others, and the majority tend to be cooperative. So why do we mostly observe greed and opportunistic behavior in our economic system? The answer has to do with the design of this system that reinforces opportunistic behavior beyond the tipping point. When everyone around us behaves opportunistically, we cannot afford not to. A vicious cycle transpires, whereby profit seeking becomes the default, while societal values are often forgotten.

All efforts to fix the economy via regulation, legislation, innovation, and aid are doomed because they treat only the symptoms, not the disease. After decades of attempts to infuse compassion into a ruthless economic system, we must admit that we have failed. The modern economic system is unfixable. But this is not a reason for despair.

Once we realize that the failure is not due to human nature per se, and that there is merely a design flaw, we can strive for a solution. Indeed, we cannot amend the economic system that is driven by opportunistic behavior, but we can design a new system that is not. The mirror image of opportunistic behavior is prosocial behavior, whereby individuals seek to enhance the utility of others, sometimes at a personal cost, rather than maximize their own utility at the expense of others. Although this seems theoretical, perhaps even fictional, there is evidence documenting such behavior. Experiments suggest that about half of humanity is conditionally prosocial—that is, they will be kind to others if others are kind to them. Acts of kindness are, however, penalized in the current economic system, often met with exploitation and lack of reciprocity. By providing incentives and rewarding those who exploit others, this economic system intervenes and breaks the natural cycle of positive reciprocity. This is how opportunistic behavior drives out prosocial behavior. But the introduction of new design principles can reinforce prosocial behavior while shielding us from opportunistic behavior. Such an underlying force can undo the harm caused by the current economic system, and promote economic equality, redistribute wealth and power, cease exploitation of private data, and restrict overconsumption and abuse of natural resources, while giving more weight to local communities (see Figure 1.1). Unfortunately, these objectives cannot be achieved within the realm of the current economic system. My suggestion is to incorporate the new design principles in a new economic system, which I refer to as the cooperative economy.

In this book, I introduce the notion of the cooperative economy—a prosocial platform system that first and foremost serves societal values, while acknowledging natural resource constraints. The cooperative economy diverts attention away from a materialistic orientation and follows a more balanced perspective that does not mix the means (accumulation of wealth) with the ends (striving for happiness). This

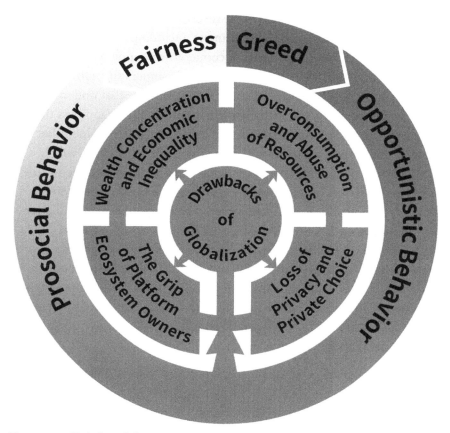

Figure 1.1 *Underlying behaviors in the economic system and their consequences.*

proposed system adopts design principles that limit consumption and
profit making while facilitating economic equality. The system serves
the interests of consumers, vendors, and employees while preventing the
accumulation of power by the platform owner who operates it. Unlike
the greed that drives the current economic system, the engine of the
cooperative economy is prosocial behavior. The system scrutinizes greedy
individuals and penalizes opportunistic behavior such as false disclosure
of information and arbitrage attempts, while motivating and rewarding
prosocial behavior. Once opportunistic behavior becomes a deviant
practice, self-reinforcing prosocial behavior can overtake it, leading to a
more just distribution of value in the system.

The main novelty of this system is the reversal of the subsidization process. Instead of having most consumers, including the poor, subsidize the rich capital owners, the cooperative economy leverages price discrimination whereby high-income consumers subsidize low-income consumers. Prosocial behavior is the principle that underlies this subsidization process, with consumers enjoying the happiness that comes with donation and influence, while leveraging the cushion that protects them from misfortune. Unlike progressive taxation in which the state steps in as a political intermediary that imposes a burden while depriving taxpayers of their discretion and sense of contributing to society, price subsidization creates a perception of unmediated donation to community members, and thus carries the benefits of prosocial behavior. The cooperative economy also provides employees with the freedom to pursue a profession of choice or start a business without worrying too much about failure or financial distress. Hence, the system encourages entrepreneurship rather than discourages it. Free riding is also discouraged by requiring low-income consumers who receive donated products and services to repay in kind.

One of the means to promote prosocial behavior is restoring a sense of community that supports face-to-face interaction and mutual support among participants in economic exchange. Switching from a global economy to a constellation of local economies minimizes transport distances and makes the value chain less vulnerable while enhancing sustainability. Another design principle is consumption per need rather than consumption per desire. This entails constraining consumption by imposing limits on consumed quantities. For their part, vendors are expected to accept reasonable profit caps, with a balancing process that redirects excess profit back to consumers. These principles represent an extension of the notion of corporate social responsibility to encompass various stakeholders' responsibilities, including vendor social responsibility, consumer social responsibility, and platform social responsibility. As part of the platform's responsibilities, and given their destructive influence, advertising and promotion are banned on the platform, and no attempt is made to influence consumer behavior within the system. The cooperative economy can be implemented as a set of digital platforms, with technologies involving sophisticated algorithms, machine learning, and artificial intelligence used not to inflate consumption and abuse consumers but to protect users from opportunistic behavior, optimize system parameters, and maximize societal values.

The cooperative economy ensures fair competition by providing new entrants with guaranteed market access and minimum order volume. In turn, stricter controls for quality of vendors, goods, and sustainability targets keep vendors at bay, ensuring consumers' welfare. Vendors with higher quality receive priority in fulfilling orders. In addition to redefining the principles of economic exchange for vendors and consumers, the cooperative economy promotes protective and respectful employment principles and promotes redistribution of income by reducing salary differences within participating vendors, thus further enhancing economic equality.

Employees, vendors, and consumers are all protected from the platform operator that accepts a restricted position in which it cannot self-preference its products or services, given that it does not engage in any business other than its platform service provision. To prevent concentration of wealth and power, the system excludes financial shareholders, whereas other stakeholders—consumers, vendors, and employees—receive equal voice in promoting their interests with the platform operator. Eventually, the platform operator would become a federation of platform operators, each serving its local community. In light of this decentralization of ownership and power, antitrust regulation and enforcement can redirect monitoring efforts to the inspection of algorithms, which would hopefully become a standard for all platforms even beyond the cooperative economy.

The cooperative economy offers a possible solution to some societal grand challenges by dismantling the persistent problems from which the modern economic system suffers. Instead of applying a band-aid to treat this bleeding system, the proposed system reengineers its DNA, replacing its greed-driven core logic with a counter-logic of prosocial behavior. To achieve that, the cooperative economy must rise from the dust. It will be a grassroots initiative for the community and by the community. It will leverage some support from government and non-government organizations, but mostly that of individuals who identify with its mission and cause.

The notion of the cooperative economy can be contrasted with alternative approaches for revising our current economic system. Some expect corporations that have benefited the most from capitalism to promote societal values while pursuing economic gains. Others call for transferring ownership of assets from corporations to society in pursuit of democratic socialism. Such approaches are neither practical nor sufficient. The cooperative economy expects communities rather than firms to take the lead and proposes a shift in mindset rather than a mere change of governance form. Its economic logic replaces opportunism with prosocial behavior, thus departing from established approaches that have taken utility and profit maximization for granted.

The theoretical ideas that I present here may seem progressive or even utopian but are in fact pragmatic. To clarify this, I elaborate in this book on the specification of the economic model and offer a practical plan for its implementation. To facilitate implementation, I call on my fellow researchers to join in refining and perfecting the proposed system. I also extend a call to private financiers who wish to see a return to society as opposed to a private return on investment, to donate in funds and kind(ness). Most importantly, I reach out to software engineers, programmers, and algorithm experts, among other professionals who wish to make a difference in this world, to join the Cooperative Economy Foundation and make this seemingly idealistic idea a reality that can change the world for the better.

This book is organized as follows. Chapter 2 elaborates on the imperfections of the modern economic system, discussing its five problems: economic inequality, the grip of platform owners, loss of privacy and private choice, overconsumption and abuse of natural resources, and some drawbacks of globalization. It provides detailed statistics and evidence on the trends and causes of these problems, with some illustrative examples. Chapter 2 concludes with an effort to isolate the common root cause, pointing to greed and the prioritization of economic gains as the underlying force behind these intertwined problems. Chapter 3 discusses past and current efforts to contain these problems, including some ambitious plans to remedy them. It then explains why each of the established and even recent approaches for fixing the problems of the economic system is either already showing signs of failure or is doomed to fail. The worsening of these problems in recent years is living proof of the insufficiency of these approaches. Chapter 3 concludes that given the deficiencies of the current economic system, there is no point in furthering efforts to fix it, thus calling for more drastic measures. Chapter 4 shifts gears from a descriptive account to a prescriptive outlook, moving from the problem space to the solution space and laying the foundations for the cooperative economy. To make strides toward a solution, this chapter challenges the established assumptions in economic theory, identifying nuances related to the heterogeneity of human nature and behavior, which leave room for an alternative system. It then introduces evidence and explains paying it forward and prosocial behaviors that depart from the assumption and observed behavior of opportunism. This chapter analyzes the conditions under which prosocial behavior is likely to emerge and persist, before providing a list of design principles for the cooperative economy. These principles undo the design faults of the current economic system, thus offering an alternative framework that serves societal values rather than the desire for profit making. The chapter explains how the cooperative economy facilitates a fair value distribution rather than value capture. Chapter 4 also highlights the unique features of the proposed economic model, clarifying how the cooperative economy differs from economies based on capitalism or communism.

Chapter 5 proceeds by translating the theoretical framework into a practical guide for implementing the proposed solution. The social responsibilities of the platform operator, vendors, and consumers are elaborated on by pointing to specific commitments. This chapter discusses practical issues concerning screening applicants and deciding whom to admit as a user of the system. It also considers algorithms that set prices for products and services based on available income that can help combat economic inequality. It then presents practices for setting purchase limits that can mitigate overconsumption. The chapter proceeds to discuss the use of vendors' quality ratings before considering the privileges and obligations of stakeholders, i.e., consumers, vendors, and the platform operator. Chapter 5 then introduces the barter and donation platforms that complement the two-sided market exchange platform by enabling participants to exchange previously purchased products and services as well as receive such goods for free in exchange for a commitment to repay in kind, even symbolically. This chapter concludes with some practical suggestions for fundraising and marketing that can help promote the implementation of the system. Chapter 6 wraps up the discussion with a proactive voice that calls for action in the face of the deteriorating moral state of the current economic system. This chapter also identifies potential pitfalls and the means for overcoming them in the process of developing the cooperative economy. Finally, further updates and supplementary information are available on the cooperativeeconomy.net website.

There are no magic solutions to the state of the current economic system. Yet taking a stab at amending this system is past due. Grave times call for drastic measures and radical ideas that challenge the conventional wisdom in economic thinking. Given the urgency of the task, my suggestion is experiment first, fine-tune later. I believe that unlike previously proposed solutions that focused on retaining a version of the current economic system, this alternative approach of starting anew can work.

CHAPTER TWO

Some imperfections of the modern economic system

DOI: 10.4324/9781003336679-2

The field of strategic management aims to promote value creation and capture and to guide managers in how to enable their firms to gain and sustain competitive advantage.[1] Since the emergence of this field of inquiry in the 1980s, much headway has been made in formalizing and advancing its agenda. After 40 years, we, business strategy professors, can proudly conclude that its mission has been accomplished. We have taught generations of business school graduates how to become skillful managers, well versed in the art of profit generation. The dominant doctrine has suggested that the primary social responsibility of firms is to increase profits and maximize shareholder value.[2] Following this idea, we have contributed, indirectly, to the emergence of some successful firms that thrive and prosper. These firms have grown, expanded, and conquered traditional industries with their emerging technologies, innovative business models, and dominant platform ecosystems, honing this effective and efficient economic machine to perfection. Firms such as Google, Amazon, Meta (aka Facebook), Apple, Netflix, Uber, and Airbnb have become household names, and many consumers cannot imagine their lives without them. By leveraging their network externalities (the benefits associated with increase in the number of users) and winner-takes-all positions in their respective domains, such leading firms have left little room for contenders.[3] These digital platforms exemplify the illnesses of the modern economic system in the Western world, which has promoted the principles of aggressive capitalism. These illnesses are pervasive also in traditional industry sectors of the global economy but are most pronounced in the context of digital platforms, which directs attention to emerging problems that have transpired throughout the economy in recent years. As strategy educators, we have repeatedly offered the examples of the Big Tech firms in the classroom, teaching the young generation of students about their success stories, so that one day these students can perhaps launch a new Facebook or Uber. I admit that I am very proud of my MBA students who started their ventures while taking my Business Strategy class. One former student recently raised funds for his firm at a market capitalization of $2 billion, and another student team sold their venture to Intel for $900 million. We all praise and admire these unicorns.

But in the past few years, we have witnessed rising public backlash, or "techlash." The Cambridge Analytica case was a wake-up call to those who trusted digital platforms to safeguard personal data and avoid its misuse. Louder concern has been voiced by stakeholders ranging from consumers and vendors to government officials and judicial institutions.[4] The "Big Tech" congressional antitrust hearings by the US House Judiciary Antitrust Subcommittee, and investigations of worldwide practices by regulators and agencies such as the Justice Department and the Federal Trade Commission, have scrutinized the anticompetitive practices of Amazon, Apple, Meta, and Google, paying increasing attention to the negative implications of their dominance in such domains as e-commerce, social media, app stores, and online search.[5] An increasing number of graduate students have refused to take lucrative positions at the Big Tech companies, which they have come to view as harmful. As one job candidate commented: "These companies go out of their way to try and woo software engineers, and I realized it would send a powerful message for me as a potential employee to tell them no."[6] The above concerns supplement complaints about firms exploiting natural resources and harming environmental sustainability.[7] Overall, these concerns suggest that the established economic system that has guided corporate and consumer behaviors may suffer from some flaws. Certain firms have thrived and prospered, but the question is: at what societal cost?

By now it is clear that the social responsibility of firms goes beyond maximizing profits and shareholder value. In fact, firms that appoint managers with a business degree have been shown to increase shareholder value at the expense of employees' wages and shares in profits, with no improvements in productivity, investments, sales growth, and profitability relative to firms with non-business managers.[8] Accordingly, strategy professors have quickly updated their course syllabi and embarked on emerging research on sustainability and corporate social responsibility (CSR), which acknowledges the importance of building relationships with various stakeholders in addition to the firm's shareholders.[9] The research findings assure managers that taking such responsibility pays off economically.[10] Firms have heard the message and jumped on the

CSR bandwagon on their road to enhanced financial performance. The most straightforward form of CSR has been corporate donations. It is intriguing that among the leading donors to environmental charities are firms that may not be necessarily identified as CSR leaders. For instance, by 2018, Microsoft had donated more than $1.4 billion in cash or kind and had engaged with more than 200,000 non-profit organizations, while in 2019 the ExxonMobil Foundation donated $253 million to various social and environmental causes.[11] In 2020, Google announced a donation of $800 million to cope with the Covid-19 pandemic,[12] while Jeff Bezos, Amazon's founder, announced his intention to donate $10 billion to battle climate change.[13] Notably, the Bill & Melinda Gates Foundation has been the only non-state donor among the top sponsors of the World Health Organization. Warren Buffett pledged to donate 99 percent of his wealth to philanthropic foundations, with several other billionaires including Bill Gates, Michael Bloomberg, Elon Musk, and Mark Zuckerberg committing to donate half of their wealth to charity. However, according to the Institute for Policy Studies, "while some pledgers earnestly intend to fulfill their promises, many are unable to because their assets are simply growing too fast."[14] Indeed, corporate donations provide tax benefits and increase shareholder value,[15] but have they managed to effectively fight climate change, save wildlife, abolish poverty, undo economic inequality, and promote well-being?

Corporate greed and wealth concentration have continued to accelerate during the Covid-19 pandemic, when one would have expected greater solidarity with humankind. Economic inequality and social divide have become more pervasive at a time that calls for compassion and mutual aid. For example, according to Oxfam, in the first six months of 2020 an estimated 400 million jobs were lost and 500 million people became impoverished. Not surprisingly, vulnerable communities such as minorities and immigrants suffered the most. In contrast, the 32 most profitable firms in the world increased their profits by $109 billion relative to their average annual figures in the previous four years (of these, Google, Apple, Meta, Amazon, and Microsoft accounted for $46 billion in extra profits). While 94 percent of these firms' profits were distributed to their wealthy shareholders (e.g., Google and Microsoft distributed $15 billion and $21 billion respectively during these six months, while Apple distributed $81 billion to its shareholders in 2019), less than 0.5 percent of their profits were donated to address the ramifications of the Covid-19 pandemic.[16] It seems, then, that firms' contributions to society have mostly benefited themselves.

Where have we been going wrong? Before attempting to answer this question and offer a remedy, let us delve deeper and gain a better understanding of some of the faults of the current economic system and their roots. Note that my purpose here is neither to offer a balanced perspective that acknowledges the many merits of the economic system nor relate every disaster to a faulty design of that system. Rather, I wish to highlight some well-known challenges that can be ascribed, at least in part, to the principles of economic exchange and to the industrious pursuit of value creation and capture. These challenges include wealth concentration and economic inequality, the grip of ecosystem platform owners, loss of privacy and private choice, overconsumption and abuse of natural resources, and some drawbacks of globalization that reinforce the former caveats.

2.1   WEALTH CONCENTRATION AND ECONOMIC INEQUALITY

Inequality refers to the case whereby access to resources and opportunities is unevenly distributed across a population.[17] An important aspect of inequality concerns the uneven distribution of wealth and income in an economic system. In particular, wealth, defined as the value of households' financial and real assets net of debt, is essential for the functioning of the economy. This is because it serves not only for consumption, entrepreneurship, and retirement, but also for coping with natural disasters, job loss, and health crises, such as the Covid-19 pandemic. In 2020, in the midst of the pandemic, the 1 percent wealthiest individuals in the world owned 45.8 percent of the world's wealth, with 0.002 percent of the population owning more than 6 percent of that wealth. In contrast, 55 percent of the world's poorest adults owned only

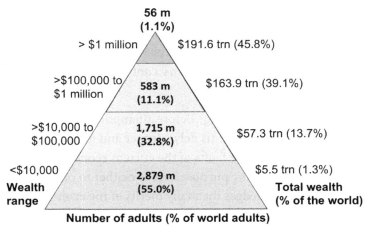

Figure 2.1 *The world's wealth distribution.*

Source: Shorrocks, Davies, and Lluberas[a]

a Shorrocks, A., Davies, J., & Lluberas, R. (2021), *Global wealth report*, Credit Suisse Research
   Institute, June, www.credit-suisse.com/media/assets/corporate/docs/about-us/research/publicati
   ons/global-wealth-report-2021-en.pdf.

1.3 percent of the wealth (see Figure 2.1). Wealth inequality is associated
with ethnicity. For instance, according to the 2016 Consumer Finance
Survey, in the United States, the median wealth of Blacks was 10.1 percent
of that of whites. The wealth is also concentrated geographically, with
57 percent of global wealth held in North America and Europe despite
their being populated by only 17 percent of the world's adults in 2020.
In addition to North America and Western Europe, economic wealth is
concentrated in rich countries in East Asia, the Pacific, and the Middle
East, with the list of wealthy countries led by Switzerland, the United
States, Australia, and New Zealand. The wealth in these countries is 100
times that in central African and central Asian countries. The distribution
of wealth is even more pronounced within countries.[18]

With an economic system that benefits the rich, wealth inequality has
worsened in the past decade. Whereas in 2009, the 380 richest individuals
had a wealth equal to that of the poorest half of the world's population,
by 2018, it took only 26 billionaires to match the wealth of that bottom
half (Figure 2.2).[19] The Covid-19 pandemic accelerated this trend: even
though the global stock market fell by 13.2 percent on average during the

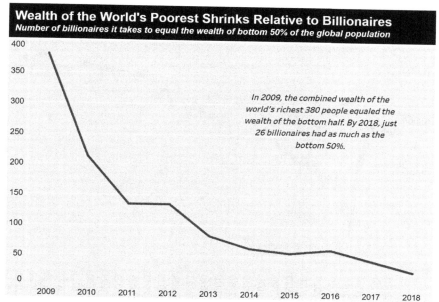

Figure 2.2   *Number of billionaires to match wealth of bottom 50 percent of the population.*

Source: Inequality.org[a]

a Inequality.org. (2021), "Global wealth inequality," https://inequality.org/facts/global-inequality/#glo bal-wealth-inequality, accessed October 10, 2021.

first quarter of 2020, it bounced back swiftly. Between February 14 and February 20, 2020, the Dow Jones Index fell from 29,398 points to 19,174 points, but by August 13, 2021, it hit 35,515 points (see Figure 2.3). While the world's market capitalization increased by $14 trillion between March 2020 and March 2021, 25 firms captured 40 percent of this gain, with an average increase of $231 billion (Apple, Amazon, and Tesla led this list).[20] Not surprisingly, between mid-March and the end of June 2020, the top 1,000 billionaires increased their wealth by 21 percent on average, with top earners being the founders of the previously mentioned firms. For example, Jeff Bezos's wealth rose from $113 billion to $165 billion, and Mark Zuckerberg's wealth increased from $55 billion to $84 billion. During that time, the poor experienced loss of wealth, despite having little to lose in the first place, with minorities suffering most. For instance, in the United States, 7.5 percent of white employees lost their jobs, compared to 12.3 percent of Hispanics and 11.5 percent of Blacks.[21] In

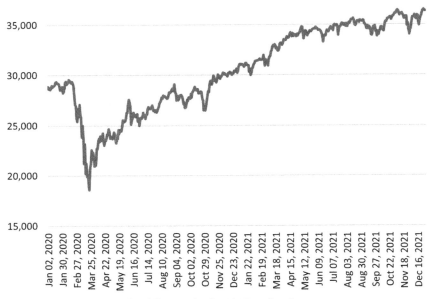

Figure 2.3   *Dow Jones Index following the Covid-19 outbreak.*

a survey of American adults conducted in mid-August 2020, 15 percent of the respondents reported that they had lost their jobs or were laid off because of the Covid-19 outbreak.[22] The inequality continued to increase, and by March 2021, Jeff Bezos's wealth reached $177 billion, followed by Elon Musk ($151 billion), Bill Gates ($124 billion), and Mark Zuckerberg ($97 billion).[23] Whereas billionaires gained $2.5 billion per day in 2018, about half of humanity were living on less than $5.50 per day during that year, which is 11 percent lower than a decade earlier.[24] During 2020, the worldwide number of people living in such poverty was estimated to have increased by at least 200 million.[25] By the end of 2021, the ten richest individuals had doubled their fortune since the start of the pandemic from $700 billion to $1.5 trillion, while the average income of 99 percent of the population fell, with 160 million people falling into poverty, reaching a 20-year record. Overall, the wealth of billionaires has increased from $8.6 trillion to $13.8 trillion during the pandemic. According to Oxfam, during that period, the death of 21,000 people per day could be ascribed to economic inequality.[26] Billionaires had tripled their wealth since 1995, with the top 1 percent of the population gaining 38 percent of the accumulated wealth compared to the 2 percent gained by the bottom 50 percent of the population, leading to "extreme concentration of the economic power in the hands of a very small minority of the super-rich."[27] The disproportional accumulation of wealth by rich countries and individuals has made it difficult to serve the urgent needs of vulnerable and poor communities, which could have benefited from a more egalitarian distribution of wealth.[28]

Economic inequality has been reinforced by the tax evasion of the affluent, another fault of the current economic system. Unfortunately— or fortunately, for them—between 2010 and 2019, the Big Tech firms avoided $155.3 billion in tax payments,[29] with Amazon paying 1.2 percent federal tax in 2019 after avoiding federal tax completely for three consecutive years. Overall, the wealth share of the top 0.1 percent of individuals in the United States has increased from 2.3 percent in 1980 to 9.3 percent in 2018, while their share of taxes paid has increased from 2.2 percent to only 4.9 percent during that period (Figure 2.4).[30] Governments, meanwhile, have shifted the tax burden from firms to families. Corporate tax levels have declined from 49 percent to 23 percent between 1985 and 2019, while the highest bracket of personal income tax has been halved to 37 percent during that period.[31] Data from the Organization for Economic Cooperation and Development (OECD) reveal that between 2007 and 2017, personal income tax and payroll taxes in 105 countries increased by 13 percent, while taxes on goods increased by 10 percent on average, together accounting for 86 percent of the tax revenue compared to 13 percent of revenue from corporate income tax.[32]

Although many associate inequality and poverty with developing countries, such impediments are also prevalent in developed nations. For example, the United States has the largest share of richest individuals in the world, with 52 percent of the world's millionaires and four times more individuals with wealth greater than $50 million than in China, the second ranked country.[33] Whereas in 1982, the average inflation-adjusted wealth of the richest 400 Americans as ranked by *Forbes* was $0.6

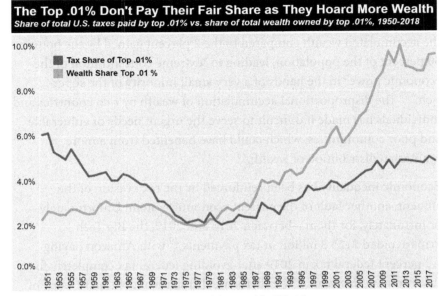

Figure 2.4 *Share of taxes paid versus wealth owned by US richest.*

Source: Lord and Collins[a]

a Lord, B., & Collins, C. (2021), *No, the rich are not paying their fair share*, Institute for Policy Studies, March 17, https://inequality.org/great-divide/no-the-rich-are-not-paying-their-fair-share/.

billion, by 2020, that figure had reached $8 billion. And while the average household wealth of the top 1 percent increased from $10.57 million to $26.4 million between 1983 and 2016, National Bureau of Economic Research (NBER) data suggest an average decline from a wealth of $6,900 to –$8,900 debt for the bottom 40 percent of households in the United States during that period. Interestingly, according to Inequality. org, whereas in 1962 the top 1 percent and the bottom 90 percent of Americans both owned a third of the national wealth, the NBER data indicate that by 2016, the top 1 percent increased their share to 39.6 percent of the wealth, while the bottom 90 percent of Americans owned only 21.6 percent of the wealth.[34] Based on Federal Reserve Distributional Financial Accounts, by 2021, the top 1 percent held 53.3 percent of the value of stocks and mutual funds and 4.7 percent of the debt, whereas the bottom 90 percent owned only 11.4 percent of the stocks and mutual funds, but 74.8 percent of the debt. This growing divide and economic inequality are also prevalent across ethnic groups within nations. Based on the Survey of Consumer Finances and Institute for Policy Studies, there is racial divide in the United States, with 27.9 percent of the Blacks and 25.8 percent of the Hispanics having no wealth, compared to 13.9 percent of the whites.[35]

Wealth inequality is reinforced by income inequality. Income encompasses earnings from salaries, interest, dividends, and rent. Whereas in 1980, the top 10 percent of earners in North America held 34.23 percent of the national income, by 2016 their share had reached 46.96 percent. Between 1980 and 2016, the share of the top 1 percent in US national income increased from 11 percent to 20 percent.[36] The top 0.1 percent earned almost 200 times more than the bottom 90 percent (average annual income of $7.2 million versus $36,797 in 2018), and while the proportion of families below the poverty line remained at 10 percent over 40 years, the income share of the top 1 percent increased from 10 percent to 22 percent during that period.[37] Indeed, between 1979 and 2019, the inflation-adjusted average income of the top 0.1 percent increased from $648,725 to $2.9 million, while that of the bottom 90 percent increased only slightly, from $30,880 to $38,923.[38] According to the Bureau of Labor Statistics, in 2021, the median white earned 27 percent more than the median Black, while the unemployment rate was 65 percent higher among Blacks. Similar ratios are reflected in the comparison to the Hispanic population. With such inequality in income, it is unlikely that the wealth distribution will be reversed.

The disparity in wealth and income has implications for public health. According to Inequality.org, while it is not surprising that life expectancy is correlated with income level, analysis of World Bank and World Health Organization data also reveals a negative association between economic inequality as captured by the Gini coefficient (a measure of the degree of economic inequality in a country) and life expectancy across countries. Income inequality is associated with higher infant mortality, higher heart failure rate,[39] and higher mortality overall.[40] In the United States, the life expectancy of the top 5 percent of individuals based on household income increased from 85.3 years to 88.5 years between 2001 and 2014, while that of the bottom 5 percent remained almost unchanged at 76.6 years.[41] On average, men in the top 1 percent income level live 15 years longer than those in the bottom 1 percent, with individuals living longer in states that maintain higher economic equality.[42] Despite the launch of the Affordable Care Act, more than two-thirds of low-income individuals in the United States fail to obtain health insurance through their employer, compared to about 40 percent of high-income individuals. The majority of uninsured Americans are low-income individuals, who are less likely to receive medical care.[43] Research has found a negative association between economic inequality and public health and well-being.[44]

Although I focused on comparing the high earners to the poor, it is also important to consider the middle class, which has experienced the sharpest decline in relative income. For instance, in the United States, between 1970 and 2018, the upper class (income more than double the median) has increased its share of national income from 29 percent to 48 percent, the lower class (income less than two-thirds of the median) has seen a slight decline from 10 percent to 9 percent share, while the middle class (income between two-thirds and double the median) has witnessed a fall from 62 percent to a 43 percent share (see Figure 2.5). Indeed, income inequality has been rising in the United States. Between

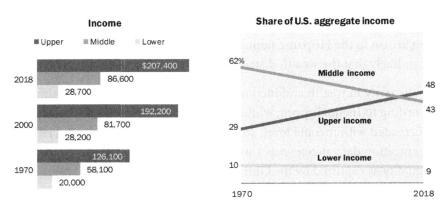

Figure 2.5 *Share of aggregate income by classes.*

Source: Horowitz, Igielnik, and Arditi[a]

a Horowitz, J., Igielnik, R., & Arditi, T. (2020), *Most Americans say there is too much economic inequality in the U.S., but fewer than half call it a top priority*, Pew Research Center, January 9, www.pewresearch.org/ social-trends/wp-content/uploads/sites/3/2020/01/PSDT_01.09.20_economic-inequailty_FULL.pdf.

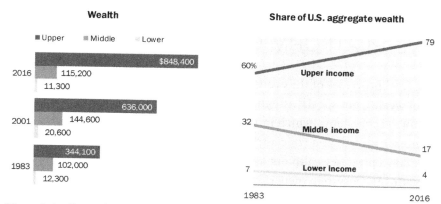

Figure 2.6 *Share of aggregate wealth by classes.*

Source: Horowitz, Igielnik, and Arditi[a]

a Horowitz, J., Igielnik, R., & Arditi, T. (2020), *Most Americans say there is too much economic inequality in the U.S., but fewer than half call it a top priority*, Pew Research Center, January 9, www.pewresearch.org/social-trends/wp-content/uploads/sites/3/2020/01/PSDT_01.09.20_economic-inequailty_FULL.pdf.

1980 and 2018, the ratio of income at the 90th percentile to that at the 10th percentile has grown from 9.1 to 12.6. When considering disparity in wealth, the trends become even clearer. Between 1983 and 2018, the wealth of the upper class in the United States increased from a share of 60 percent to 79 percent, the lower class suffered a loss from 7 percent to a 4 percent share, while the middle class declined from 32 percent to a 17 percent share[45] (Figure 2.6). Hence, the economic divide between the upper class and the middle and lower classes has been growing sharply, restricting the purchasing power and opportunities of most consumers.

The descriptive statistics tell a story of worsening economic divide. The rich got richer and the poor got poorer, while the middle class has been eroded because of an unbalanced economic system that benefits the privileged. Privileged individuals and firms with their rich owners have leveraged the principles of value creation and capture to increase their wealth, while many are left struggling to unsuccessfully maintain their standard of living. Besides the ramifications for the poor, there is the question of whether wealth and the economic power that accompanies it should be concentrated in the hands of a few influential billionaires who were not elected to such positions of power.

2.2 THE GRIP OF ECOSYSTEM PLATFORM OWNERS

Several processes of the economic system facilitate the concentration of wealth, but special attention should be paid to the emergence of platform ecosystems, which in the past couple of decades have fueled economic growth and concentration of wealth. Ecosystems have not only concentrated wealth but also redistributed power, to the benefit of platform ecosystem owners. An ecosystem can be defined as "the alignment structure of the multilateral set of partners that need to interact in order for a focal value proposition to materialize,"[46] with a platform ecosystem concerning parties that organize around a technological platform.[47] Although not every ecosystem has a leader, firms that successfully develop, launch, and own a platform often become leaders that set the rules and orchestrate their platform's interaction with complementors,[48] as in the case of Amazon, Google, Apple, Meta, Uber, Netflix, and Airbnb, among other platforms. The question is how these platform owners have managed to dominate stakeholders such as competitors, complementors, employees, and users.

Although the Internet enabled start-up firms to introduce innovative platforms and create and capture value at the outset, the centralized nature of their business models made it difficult for contenders to thrive, while the platform owners have abused their economic power.[49] The Internet prompted disintermediation of traditional industries in the early 2000s, e.g., making travel agents redundant, but platform owners such as Amazon and Uber have leveraged the Internet to emerge as powerful new intermediaries in two-sided markets that bring together vendors and consumers.[50] By maintaining exclusive ownership and control of platform infrastructure, these platform owners enjoy the power to prohibit, compel, and coerce.[51] The Digital Markets Act proposed by the European Union (EU) Commission in May 2021 confirms that "a few large platforms increasingly act as gateways or gatekeepers between business users and end users and enjoy an entrenched and durable position, often as a result of the creation of conglomerate ecosystems around their core platform services, which reinforces existing entry barriers."[52] Indeed, the Internet Davids have become Goliaths.

Strategy researchers have studied how platform owners conquer their respective industry sectors and outperform competition.[53] To dominate, these firms differentiate their solutions to meet specific needs of diverse groups of complementors and users, and then leverage network externalities, e.g., by using penetration pricing, offering incentives to early adopters, and making the platform's service free to users to quickly build an installed base of users that grants these firms a winner-takes-all position.[54] Once such a position has been reached, even competitors with technically superior solutions fail to challenge the incumbent platform owners.[55] By bringing together different complementors, the platform owners also drive out traditional vertically integrated competitors.[56] Accordingly, Amazon has reached almost 50 percent market share in e-commerce sales in the United States, which is seven times Walmart's market share. According to eMarketer, although Walmart managed to grow its e-commerce business by 11.6 percent in 2020, Amazon grew it by 43.3 percent that same year, when many brick-and-mortar retailers such as JCPenney were closing stores or filing for bankruptcy.

In digital markets, platform owners can suppress competition or prevent it from ever emerging by leveraging data as their source of market power. Platform owners effortlessly capture real-time data to analyze consumer behavior, offer personalized services, and thus increase switching costs and barriers to entry.[57] The predominant antitrust law cannot effectively combat these emerging natural monopolies:[58] legislation that aims to protect consumers from increasing prices may fail to scrutinize platform owners that offer their services for free; and market share ceases to serve as a useful indicator of market power when the market boundaries become blurry. For example, given network externalities and high switching costs, Meta's 60 percent market share in social networking would be much more challenging to contest than in traditional markets.[59] Indeed, "competition law enforcement and merger control are inadequate or insufficient to deal with competition issues in the digital sector ... [they] rest on strong hypotheses about the organization of economic activities."[60]

Platform owners also rely on exclusionary practices to drive out competition, as in the case of Google making its search engine the preinstalled default on Android smartphones, while paying Apple to make it the default on iPhones. Google has also biased its search engine results to favor its own services or those of paying vendors. Similarly, Apple leveraged its market power to exclude some of its competitors from its App Store. Platform owners have also neutralized emerging competitors by acquiring them. This has been the case, for instance, with Meta's acquisitions of rivals Instagram and WhatsApp, and with Google's acquisition of Waze. Thus, even when a new contender offers an innovative solution that can challenge the platform owner, such contender is likely to be acquired, with antitrust authorities paying less attention to such transactions given their focus on narrowly defined markets.[61] Hence, in October 2021, after 16 months of investigation of the anticompetitive practices of the Big Tech firms, the US House Judiciary Subcommittee on Antitrust reached the conclusion that "companies that once were scrappy, underdog start-ups that challenged the status quo have become the kinds of monopolies we last saw in the era of oil barons and railroad tycoons."[62] Indeed, the Big Tech firms disrupted the market, captured dominant positions, and leveraged their market power to prevent subsequent entry by others—a classic Blue Ocean strategy by the book.[63]

One would expect that complementors, i.e., vendors that provide complementary products or services to joint customers and that pledge allegiance to the platform owner, would gain a fair share of the value, but they have suffered as well from the dominance of platform owners. The latter have either dictated unfavorable terms to complementors, favored their own competing products and services on the platform, or offered their substitutes to users free of charge. For instance, Amazon used private data of vendors selling on its platform to offer competing products, and thus compete unfairly with these vendors. Indeed, platform owners can leverage information asymmetry by virtue of their structural position in the platform in order to gather data on the complementors' products and on their interactions with platform users,[64] and then acquire successful complementors or integrate their offerings.[65] Amazon has also leveraged its market power to exploit complementors and increase the fees it charges from vendors—of whom 37 percent rely on Amazon as their primary or only marketing channel[66]—while penalizing vendors that offered their merchandise for lower prices on their own retail sites. Similarly, Apple forced app developers to sell their products to iPhone users exclusively on their App Store, charging a 30 percent commission. When Epic Games sought to avoid paying this commission by allowing gamers to purchase its virtual currency directly, its game was banned from the App Store, which led it to submit a complaint against Apple. Likewise, Meta conditioned app developers' access to its application program interface (API) on their commitment to not interconnect with Meta's competitors.[67] Moreover, following Meta's acquisition of Instagram, small third-party app developers experienced declining demand.[68] Finally, the offering of Google's own apps on its Play Store restricted the development efforts of complementors while increasing the prices of apps.[69] The European Commission has concluded that platform owners such as Google and Meta operate as gatekeepers that stand between vendors and their clients and make the platform owners' services, such as online advertising, unavoidable.[70] Hence, while the size and variety of a complementor network contribute to the dominance of the platform,[71] this dominance attracts more complementors and, with the entry of the platform owner to the complementors' businesses, restricts the value that the complementors capture. The complementors may be encouraged to offer their products and services on multiple platforms, but such multi-homing may come at the expense of product quality.[72] In sum, although the dominance of platform owners is tied to the ability of complementors to create value, the complementors' share of that value suffers from this dominance.

But do consumers gain from the dominance of platform owners? To be sure, platform owners have made certain products and services more accessible, affordable, and personalized. For example, Amazon has increased the variety of available products compared to brick-and-mortar retail shops, tailored product offerings to meet specific customer preferences, and spoiled customers with same-day delivery and easy payment processing. Consumers usually find the depth and breadth of offerings an attractive feature of platform ecosystems,[73] and are often dazzled by these offerings' seemingly low prices. Nevertheless, the House Judiciary Subcommittee on Antitrust concluded that the dominant platforms "diminished consumer choice, eroded innovation and entrepreneurship in the US economy, weakened the vibrancy of the free and diverse press, and undermined Americans' privacy."[74] Similarly, the European Commission concluded that "unfair practices and lack of contestability lead to inefficient outcomes in the digital sector in terms of higher prices, lower quality, as well as less choice and innovation to the detriment of European consumers."[75] Hence, digital platforms not only trade off the interests of various stakeholders such as competitors and complementors for the convenience that their consumers enjoy,[76] but also jeopardize their consumers' long-term interests.

Indeed, platform owners often increase consumers' switching costs while limiting their choices, with most users adopting the default choices that were preset by the platform owners. Consumers' switching costs have been increased, for instance, by the limiting of user data portability across platforms, with about 90 percent of consumers purchasing new mobile devices with the same operating system, iOS or Android, as they had installed on their previous devices.[77] Apple has also increased switching costs by preventing users from downloading apps from anywhere other than its App Store, while Google made this overly complicated, so users rarely download apps from sources other than its Play Store. Both firms self-preferenced their own apps, while charging 30 percent commission from third-party app developers, thus increasing prices and diminishing innovation. Indeed, in November 2021, Google lost its appeal contesting the $2.4 billion fine set by the EU for its self-preferencing violation. Another example of a practice that limits consumer choice and reduces quality of service is the blurred distinction between organic results and paid listings on Google's search engine, which has prevented users from finding the most relevant results while compelling vendors to purchase Google ads. There are also numerous fake listings on Google Maps that are not located in the stated location and disadvantage legitimate local businesses. Similarly, using its "Buy Box" feature, Amazon has given preference to its private-label products and fulfillment services, even when alternative offers and self-fulfillment by the vendor were cheaper, faster, and more reliable.[78] Whereas these business practices have mostly limited consumer choice and increased switching costs, other practices have led more directly to reduced quality and increased prices. For example, while Meta has been focusing on increasing its advertising revenue, it has limited the features, functionality, and variety that it offers to users.[79] As another example, after Amazon concluded that Diapers.com was its primary competitor in the diaper and baby care domain, it initiated an aggressive price war, and when Diapers.com struggled, Amazon acquired its parent, and eventually shut down the firm's operations. This practice has been pursued in various other vertical markets.[80] The limited choice and higher prices have also been reinforced by Amazon's requirements that vendors offer their lowest price on its platform, which has forced them to increase prices on competing marketplaces. Similarly, Apple's 30 percent commission and pricing policy for its App Store has led to price increases. Thus, platform owners have not only increased switching costs and limited consumer choices, but also undermined the quality of service while facilitating price increases.

In addition to increasing price and reducing quality, the profit-driven mission of platform owners has failed to protect consumers from undesirable content and unsafe, prohibited, or counterfeit products sold on their platforms.[81] These practices, among many others, have harmed consumer welfare by giving priority to corporate greed. This can be added to concerns about the role of the Big Tech firms in shaping political power and fostering polarized perspectives and violence, while imposing social and psychological pressure on consumers. For instance, a recent report reveals that Meta was well aware of the harmful effects of Instagram, with 40 percent of users reporting that they felt "unattractive" after using this app. Moreover, among teenage girls with suicidal thoughts, 13 percent in the United Kingdom and 6 percent in the United States were linked to the use of Instagram.[82] In a US Senate hearing, Senator Richard Blumenthal, who chaired the Senate's Consumer Protection Subcommittee, noted that platforms such as Instagram created addictive products "that can exploit children's insecurities and anxieties."[83] Indeed, digital media platforms are as addictive as tobacco and prescription drugs but have not been regulated to protect consumer welfare.[84] Another example is the UN Human Rights Council investigation of the genocide in Myanmar that determined in 2018 that Facebook played a significant role in spreading hate and fake news, which facilitated violence against the Rohingya minority.[85] In December 2021, Rohingya refugees in the United States filed a $150 billion class action against Meta.

Not surprisingly, 75 percent of Americans consider the power of platform owners a moderate to major problem.[86] The fact that profit-seeking platform owners influence so many important aspects of life, their entry into the vertical markets that their vendors serve, and their occupation of successive stages of the value chain, from content production to fulfillment services, together create an inherent conflict of interest. The platform owners' market power has placed their business partners, vendors, and consumers at a disadvantage and has not served these stakeholders' interests well. It has incurring costs that go beyond the loss of economic welfare to also include harm to well-being.

Among the richest individuals in the world are the founders of ecosystem platforms. Jeff Bezos, Bill Gates, Mark Zuckerberg, Larry Page, and Sergey Brin are among the *Forbes* top ten richest individuals.[87] But what about the employees of these platform owners? Have they received their fair share of the value pie? Some of them certainly did. The Big Tech firms are paying the most generous salaries to their employees, with Google (#1), Meta (#2), Microsoft (#3), Amazon (#5), and Apple (#8) offering the best pay packages.[88] These are considered superstar firms that increased some of their employees' salaries, while the remaining firms in various sectors have fallen behind, which has fostered income inequality.[89] Interestingly, none of the Big Tech firms is currently listed among *Fortune*'s Top 10 Best Companies to Work for, although until 2017, for eight times in 11 years, Google led this list. Apparently, Google unlawfully underpaid temporary workers and failed to comply with some labor laws in the

EU, United Kingdom, and Asia.[90] Google has also faced employee activism related to harassment, discrimination, and abuse of power, and dismissed employees who attempted to unionize[91] or identified flaws in its technology and complained about Google's silencing of marginalized voices.[92] Employee mistreatment, surveillance, and silencing have also been common at Amazon, which faced three times as many charges at the National Labor Relations Board in 2020 as in 2019.[93] Amazon's employees also complained about the unsafe work environment in which they were treated like robots:

> It took my body two weeks to adjust to the agony of walking 15 miles a day and doing hundreds of squats. … Every single thing I did was monitored and timed. After I completed a task, the scan gun not only immediately gave me a new one but also started counting down the seconds I had left to do it. … At my warehouse, you were expected to be off task for only 18 minutes per shift—mine was 6:30 a.m. to 6 p.m.—which included using the bathroom, getting a drink of water or just walking slower than the algorithm dictated. … I felt an incredible amount of pressure.[94]

A virtual e-commerce platform cannot abstain from physical strain.

Apple has also witnessed employee complaints about harassment, racism, discrimination, lack of privacy, and abuse of power.[95] At Meta, employees complained about the "cult-like" high-pressure culture that failed to prevent fake news and data privacy problems.[96] Employees also raised concerns about a conflict between Meta's profit-making interest and the public interest, regarding Meta's role in facilitating hate, violence, and misinformation on its platform.[97] While Meta has employed more than 30,000 employees and contractors to enforce its safety and security policies, many post moderators have felt emotionally overwhelmed, with some diagnosed with post-traumatic stress disorder.[98] Employee welfare has also been a concern on other platforms. Uber drivers complained that they felt poor and powerless when Uber increased its commission from 20 percent up to 60 percent of the rider fare. Many of them had to increase their number of hours on the road and, after accounting for car maintenance and fuel expenses, barely earned minimum wage.[99] Only in 2021, following a ruling of the Supreme Court in the United Kingdom, was it determined that Uber should treat its drivers as employees and provide them with vacation pay, rest breaks, and the minimum wage.[100] Uber Eats workers have further struggled after Uber cut their delivery fees, which forced them to work longer hours amid rising maintenance costs.[101] Similarly, delivery platform Wolt, which was recently acquired by DoorDash, has become an exclusive channel for many restaurants, charging a 31 percent order fee. Chef Eyal Shani commented: "there is one restaurant in this country, named Wolt. We are one entry on the menu of that restaurant. It humiliates me, it hurts me. The pandemic of the restaurant business is not Covid, but the blue color of Wolt."[102] In turn, Wolt's delivery freelancers have complained about reduced payments, arbitrary and unfair algorithm decisions, and lack of employee rights such as social benefits and insurance, as they spend 12 hours a day on the road, engaging in reckless driving. In sum, platform owners have offered perks and good pay for employees in high demand but have underpaid less skilled employees who were left without social benefits and struggled to make a living. The Big Tech firms have created a new class of employees who perform "ghost work" that is essential for the functioning of digital platforms. This invisible workforce is responsible for flagging undesirable content, training algorithms, and translating and editing material, among other tasks, while being overworked, underpaid, and deprived of health benefits.[103]

In this regard, it is important to acknowledge that the work conditions of many employees outside the Big Tech firms are even less desirable. Since the 1980s, the economy has created numerous low-paying positions without job security, social benefits, and promotion prospects. The shift from manufacturing to a service economy has worsened the employment conditions of many employees who work in part-time unprotected jobs, such as supermarket cashiers, customer support, and delivery. The bankruptcies of established corporations such as Chrysler, Eastman Kodak, and Borders, which provided job security, stable career paths, and pensions, has given way to underpaid temporary freelance jobs that foster economic inequality.[104] In the United States, the minimum wage has not been updated for 15 years, and unions have been weakened by legislation. As a result, productivity has improved while the salaries of these low-paying positions have not. This is unfortunate given that factory, farm, and delivery workers, drivers, and healthcare support personnel, who are treated as dispensable, are vital for the functioning of the economy. In 2021, we have witnessed the effects of shortages not only because of layoffs related to the Covid-19 measures, but also because of massive employee strikes and resignations. According to the US Bureau of Labor Statistics, in August 2021, 2.9 percent of the labor force—4.3 million Americans—quit their jobs. This is the highest number since December 2000. It was estimated that in 2021, more than 30 million employees would quit, 15 percent more than in 2019,[105] and this was in a year when, according to the National Association of Manufacturers, more than half of employers were struggling to staff 10 million open positions. Resignations have been prevalent, mostly among women and in sectors such as hotels, restaurants, and childcare. The discontent of employees with unsatisfactory compensation and work conditions has also been voiced in demonstrations and strikes, as in the cases of the 40,000 network rail employees in the United Kingdom,[106] the 60,000 employees in the film and television production industry in the US, 1,100 coalmine workers at Warrior Met Coal in Alabama, and 1,400 workers at Kellogg's factories in Michigan, Nebraska, Pennsylvania, and Tennessee.[107] These workers join Uber, Lyft, and Instacart workers, among other employees of the Big Tech firms and platform owners, who have complained about their low-paying positions and work conditions. By now, the inevitable conclusion is that with their Taylorism, surveillance, and high-pressure culture, the platform owners have undermined employee welfare in the quest for profits. Regardless of whether employees are placed in a golden cage or a rusty cage, much like other stakeholders, they are firmly in the platform owners' grip.

2.3 LOSS OF PRIVACY AND PRIVATE CHOICE

Big Tech firms, among other firms with central network positions, know more about us than we know about ourselves. The human mind is cognitively constrained and thus cannot effectively process big data, which these firms can analyze using their sophisticated algorithms, machine learning, and artificial intelligence.[108] Indeed, automated data science can predict human behavior, such as purchasing decisions, better than humans can.[109] Firms and platform owners can gather personal data as well as real-time data on consumer choices, on the products and services that consumers consider or purchase, and on their reactions to them, and then store and analyze this data using artificial intelligence algorithms.[110] Most users of social media in the United States indicate that they believe that it is very easy or somewhat easy for social media platforms to figure out their ethnicity (84 percent of respondents), hobbies and interests (79 percent), political affiliation (71 percent), and religious beliefs (65 percent).[111] But in fact, platform owners know much more. For example, Facebook gathers information about users' social networks and connections, demographics, political views, personal events, hobbies, and dietary and entertainment choices. It also links this information to users' discussions and purchases on numerous other websites, so that advertisers can target particular user groups. A consumer report revealed that about 80 percent of Americans are concerned about the excessive personal data that platform owners collect and use to build user profiles.[112] It seems, then, that platform owners have a clear idea about who we are, how we think, and how we are likely to behave, and that the free services that platform owners often offer to consumers come at a price.

The dominant platforms have not served the data privacy interests of users, and instead have monitored and leveraged their personal data to monetize it beyond the economic value of their consumed services. For example, platforms such as Facebook and Instagram have enabled users to connect and share glimpses of their lives. Every day in 2018, Facebook users sent 216 million messages and 1.44 billion friend requests, uploaded 350 million photos, watched 100 million hours of video, and made 55 million status updates.[113] However, 74 percent of Facebook users were unaware of the data Meta collected on their interests and traits, with 51 percent feeling uncomfortable about Meta's analysis of this data.[114] Furthermore, platform owners often use manipulations to extract personal data, price discriminate, and prompt the purchasing of products that are not aligned with consumers' preferences or interests.[115] Well-known cases of breach of privacy involve Google's employees and subcontractors reading the personal emails of Gmail users and Apple's collection of sensitive user information, including interactions with its voice assistant, to improve its products in a way that grants it a competitive advantage. These instances illustrate how private personal information can be used not only to take advantage of consumers but also to gain an advantage relative to competitors.[116] A less known case of breach of data privacy was revealed in a recent study that found that all the popular video conference apps, such as Zoom, Microsoft Teams, Slack, Cisco Webex, and Google Meet, continue to record voice data and transfer it to the providers even after users mute their computer microphones, without their awareness and consent.[117] Unfortunately, the misuse of personal data and breach of privacy are mostly discovered when a scandal is exposed, as in the Cambridge Analytica case, in which users were deceived to think that their private information would remain private, whereas in reality it was shared and made public.[118]

The emergence of the Internet in the late 1990s gave power to users who could access rich information on products and vendors. However, because digital personal data is persistent and easy to store and repurpose, the emergence of artificial intelligence and big data mining has reversed this information asymmetry in favor of the platform owners.[119] Using deep learning and artificial intelligence analytics, they can predict consumer behavior quite accurately and leverage their inferences to increase profits.[120] Hence, aside from the question of privacy, there is the question of how personal data is being used. Users can, to an extent, decide about the personal information they share on platforms, but they have limited control over how algorithms use this information to make inferences.[121] Early applications of e-commerce algorithms helped users identify products that they were interested in and recommended other products based on past purchases and the purchases of other consumers with similar preferences. However, these algorithms have become more sophisticated and can now predict more nuanced behavior, not without amplification of inherent persistence biases as well as gender and racial biases, as a result of predictive data selection and algorithmic design flaws.[122]

By surveilling users, platform owners reconstruct their users' psychological profiles not only to predict consumer behavior but also to guide it. For example, firms have applied algorithms to shape promotional campaigns and personalize them to reduce consumer attrition.[123] Algorithms have driven more than 30 percent of the purchasing decisions on Amazon and 80 percent of the content consumed on Netflix. Algorithms often determine what news we read, where we eat, and whom we date,[124] with some consumers fully delegating decision making to such algorithms.

Unfortunately, algorithms often fail. For example, with the lockdowns and tendency to switch from public transportation to cars during the Covid-19 pandemic, travel patterns have changed, making Google's Waze algorithm, which relies on historical patterns, suggest routes that were unsafe or unnecessarily extend trips while failing to accurately predict the expected travel time. Users who have been relying on Waze for years were unable to navigate to their destination.[125] This illustrates how algorithmic users who economize on search and transaction costs also give up on autonomy and free choice, replacing human judgment with non-transparent algorithm code. This enables algorithms powered by machine learning to facilitate collusion and set supra-competitive prices,[126] as well as expose consumers to various vulnerabilities such as cyberattacks, manipulations by algorithm designers, and psychological harm.[127] For example, an experiment on Facebook has revealed that algorithms can influence users' feelings. The researchers identified massive-scale contagion of emotional content via the social network: when positive expressions in the news feed were reduced, users created fewer positive posts and more negative posts.[128] Another study has revealed that loss of autonomy on such platforms can undermine consumers' sense of well-being.[129]

The misuse and abuse of private data in the name of profit making adversely affects not only individual consumers, but society at large. Platform owners constantly run tests and experiments with new features and user data to examine what works well and to refine their algorithms,[130] most often without users' awareness. These experiments shape the behavior and interactions of users on the platform and influence social patterns and attitudes.[131] The limited exposure of algorithms to diverse information reinforces prevalent attitudes, encouraging users to adopt extreme perspectives, which lead to polarization. This has been the case with Facebook's recommendation algorithm, which, according to internal documents, feeds users "more divisive content in an effort to gain user attention and increase time on the platform." In fact, 64 percent of Facebook users who joined extremist groups did so following a recommendation made by that algorithm.[132] Despite this internal study, Meta executives shut down attempts to make the algorithm less divisive. Additionally, it has been revealed that on Twitter, false news spread six times faster than true news, and even faster in the case of false political news.[133] In another case, Meta provided Cambridge Analytica, a private firm, access to 87 million Facebook accounts, without its users' consent. This data was then used for personality analysis and for influencing public opinion during the 2016 presidential campaign in the United States. In a related incident, the Russian Internet Research Agency was accused of intervening in the presidential election by purchasing Facebook ads and building a network of fake accounts to distribute fake news.[134] These incidents mark the weakening of traditional news media, which has been overtaken by social media platforms that shape public opinion, behavior, and actions, while facilitating social divisions. In 2018, Facebook changed its algorithm to give more weight to friends' posts at the expense of journalism news. Although it claimed that the purpose was to enhance interaction, this only contributed to the spread of fake news and hate speech. There are even cases of human rights violations facilitated by the platforms. In 2021, CNN revealed ongoing advertising and coordination of human trafficking and slavery using the Facebook and Instagram platforms, despite Meta being aware of such instances since 2018.[135]

What we are witnessing is the hegemony of "surveillance capitalism,"[136] whereby the Big Tech firms attempt to monetize all reachable data, codifying human experience and expression into data that help construct a personal model of each user. This model then serves to predict, influence, and manipulate the user's choices and behavior. With the development of hardware and software apps, the reach of data has been expanding from instant messaging, searches, and website browsing to financial transactions, social interaction, personal health checks, and location data, which are tracked, processed, and sold. The advent of artificial intelligence and machine learning has made the analysis of such data more sophisticated, thus further improving business performance at the expense of users' well-being. Battling this surveillance capitalism, regulatory agencies find themselves ill equipped to defend private choice. The Big Tech firms act as a de facto government that rules in the name of profit making. The Covid-19 pandemic has given more power to the owners of digital platforms, making users more vulnerable to their design. Users may have not only lost their privacy but also their independent thought and free choice as individuals and as a collective society.

2.4   OVERCONSUMPTION AND ABUSE OF NATURAL RESOURCES

A supply-side explanation of the accumulated power of platform owners is incomplete without an understanding of the demand. Firms have not only played a role in fulfilling demand, but also in fostering it. The modern economic system enables firms to promote consumption, replenishing, and replacement of goods, which contribute to overconsumption of natural resources beyond the sustainable carrying capacity of the system. Between 1980 and 2005, the volume of natural resources extracted for producing goods increased by 50 percent to about 60 billion tons per year,[137] with this trend continuing to date. According to the Center for Sustainable Systems at the University of Michigan,[138] the average daily calorie consumption of Americans increased from 2,054 in 1970 to 2,501 in 2010, with a 66 percent increase in consumed fat during this period and 330 percent increase in consumed soft drinks between 1947 and 2003 (see Figure 2.7). Similarly, the latest World Health Organization report reveals that obesity has reached epidemic proportions in Europe, with 59 percent of adults experiencing overweight or obesity.[139] The University of Michigan report further notes that raw material consumption has increased from 2 metric tons per person per year in 1900 to 13 metric tons in 2006.[140] In 2019, greenhouse gas emissions in the United States were 6.6 billion metric tons of CO_2-equivalent, 34 percent more than in 1990.

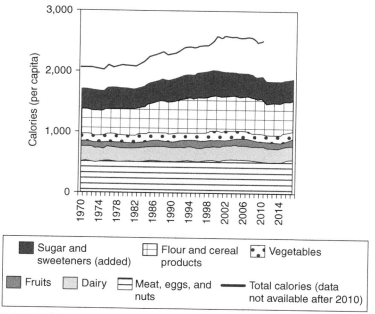

Figure 2.7   *US daily per capita caloric intake by food type, 1970–2017.*

Source: Center for Sustainable Systems at University of Michigan[a]

a   Center for Sustainable Systems, University of Michigan (2021), *US environmental footprint factsheet*, Pub. No. CSS08-08, https://css.umich.edu/factsheets/us-environmental-footprint-factsheet.

The Michigan report indicates that in 2018 the average American wasted 22 percent of food, more than any other type of waste, equivalent to a $450 loss per person per year. This is 50 percent more wasted food than in 1970. Globally, 820 million people experience hunger, while food loss and waste incur $1 trillion in economic costs, $700 billion in environmental costs, and $900 billion in societal costs. A quarter of the food produced globally is lost in the supply chain or wasted by retailers, restaurants, and consumers.[141]

Overall, the extraction of natural resources in the world has increased by 318 percent between 1970 and 2010, from 22 billion tons to 70 billion tons, with richer countries consuming ten times more than poor countries and twice the average.[142] This is despite technological developments and efficiency improvements that resulted in a 30 percent decline over 30 years in the volume of resources needed to produce one dollar of gross domestic product (GDP).[143] This exploitation of natural resources supersedes the volume of resources that can be regenerated by 20 percent per year (see Figure 2.8). As a result, by 2030 the world's standard of living is expected to start declining, and by 2050 we would need 2.5 planets to supply our needs at the current rate of consumption. Meanwhile, the monitored population of animals such as fish and birds has declined by 68 percent on average since 1970 (Figure 2.9),[144] and 33 percent of the world's soil has been moderately to highly degraded,[145] with the erosion of fertile soil leading to increasing prices of agriculture produce.

Part of the overconsumption is due to growth in population, which has doubled in size since 1970 to eight billion people to date, with a current annual population growth rate of 1.1 percent. But overconsumption is mostly a problem in developed nations, which account for only 3 percent of the population growth. According to Stephen Pacala, Director of the Princeton Environmental Institute, the world's 7 percent richest people account for 50 percent of the world's greenhouse gas emissions, while 50 percent of the population account for about 7 percent of the emissions. It is estimated that 20 percent of the world's population consume 80 percent of the world's resources, with 17 percent of the world energy consumed by Americans, who account for less than 5 percent of the

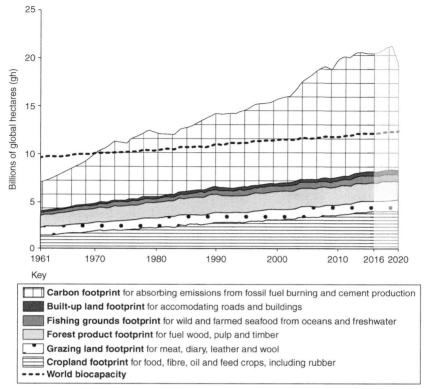

Figure 2.8 *Humanity's ecological footprint against Earth's biocapacity (from 2016—an estimate).*

Source: World Wildlife Fund[a]

a WWF (2020), *Living planet report 2020—bending the curve of biodiversity loss*, Almond, R.E.A., Grooten, M. and Petersen, T. (eds.), WWF, Gland, Switzerland. © 2020 WWF All rights reserved.

population. While the population of the United States has increased by 60 percent since 1970, consumer spending has monotonously increased by 400 percent after adjusting for inflation,[146] so this trend cannot be attributed to the population's growth or to inflation. It is rich countries and affluent individuals who consume more than their fair share, beyond their actual needs and above sustainable levels. A recent study confirms that affluent consumers drive overconsumption and are responsible for its environmental ramifications (see Figures 2.10 and 2.11),[147] with overconsumption being the catalyst of unsustainable growth and depletion of natural resources. Firms and governments have facilitated

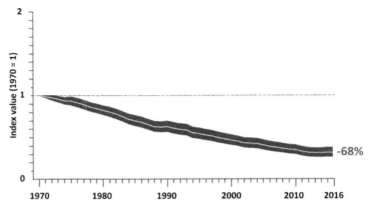

Figure 2.9 *The Living Planet Index (LPI) tracks the abundance of 21,000 populations of mammals, birds, fish, reptiles, and amphibians around the world.*

Source: World Wildlife Fund[a]

a WWF (2020), *Living planet report 2020—bending the curve of biodiversity loss*, Almond, R.E.A., Grooten, M. and Petersen, T. (eds.), WWF, Gland, Switzerland,. © 2020 WWF All rights reserved.

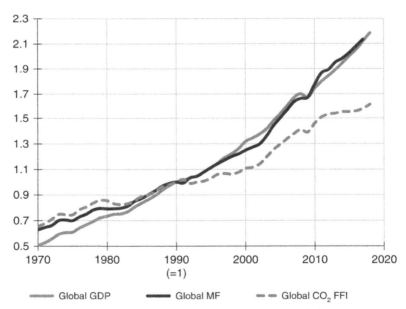

Figure 2.10 *Change in economic and environmental indicators: global GDP (in constant 2010 $); global MF (material footprint—global raw material extraction); global CO_2 FFI (emissions from fossil fuel combustion and industrial processes).*

Source: Wiedmann, Lenzen, Keyßer, and Steinberger[a]

a Wiedmann, T., Lenzen, M., Keyßer, L.T., & Steinberger, J.K. (2020), "Scientists' warning on affluence," *Nature Communications*, 11, p. 3107, https://doi.org/10.1038/s41467-020-16941-y.

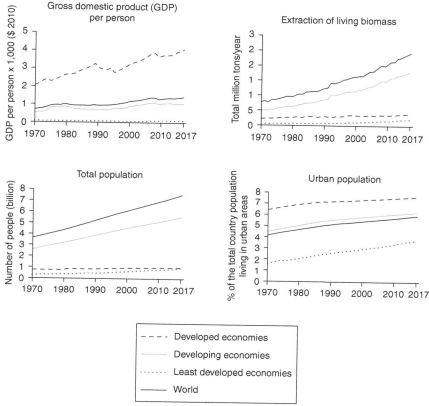

Figure 2.11 *Cross-country comparison of consumption versus population.*
Source: World Wildlife Fund[a]

a WWF (2020), *Living planet report 2020—bending the curve of biodiversity loss*, Almond, R.E.A., Grooten, M. and Petersen, T. (eds.), WWF, Gland, Switzerland,. © 2020 WWF All rights reserved.

this trend, with consumer spending reaching about 70 percent of GDP in the United States.

But why do we overconsume? There is a physical limit to how much we can eat and what we need to maintain ourselves. It is the psychology linking material goods to emotional desires that prompts us to continuously seek satisfaction in consumption, and advertisers have reinforced this linkage and capitalized on it.[148] Much of the overconsumption is driven not by physical needs but by emotional needs and the search for happiness. From that standpoint, overconsumption concerns the excessive acquisition and use of goods under the false assumption that such behavior can promote happiness, social status, and national prosperity.[149] This assumption can be falsified or at least shown to hold only up to a point based on research that reveals that in 2018 the ideal income point was $95,000 for life satisfaction (how one fares relative to higher goals and in comparison to others) and $60,000 to $75,000 for emotional well-being (relating to emotions such as feeling happy).[150] This research has also found that in some countries, income beyond the satisfaction point is associated with lower life evaluations, that is, thoughts that people have about their life. Most studies also find no association between income and happiness in cross-country comparisons.[151] Perhaps this is so because consumption of material goods can make us content for a short while rather than happy for the long term. Nevertheless, consumers in developed countries often behave in line with the consumeristic cultural orientation that relates consumption to personal satisfaction and happiness. For example, the culture in the United States has associated economic success with consumption of nonessential goods.[152] This is probably because even though happiness does not relate to absolute income, it does relate to relative income, so that comparing ourselves to others fosters a rat race in which all individuals in a group strive to consume, without much improvement in happiness.[153] Hence, it is quite difficult to challenge the perception that consumption leads to happiness.

Overconsumption also introduces a social dilemma, given that self-interested consumers tend to consume more than their fair share of the common resource pool, which reduces this pool and restricts future consumption.[154] This is especially the case with natural resources that are seemingly abundant, so that one can overconsume without being detected and penalized for taking more than the fair share. In fact, there is also a perceptual bias, whereby even consumers who are willing to settle for a fair share of the resource pool overconsume because they are unable to accurately judge what an equal share is in a large consumer group. This may explain why individuals given an equal share of the resource pool in experiments felt that they were allocated less than their equal share.[155] Hence, overconsumption can be unintended not only because of consumers' cultural orientation but also because of perceptual biases.

This problem calls for specifying consumption limits in developed countries, but unfortunately, the notion of environmental justice and equal sharing of natural resources has not been prevalent there.[156] Moreover, the United Nation's Sustainable Development Goals (SDG) 12, which calls for sustainable consumption, offers only general guidelines, and falls short of specifying quotas. It focuses on improving the efficiency of production and waste management processes rather than on calling for systemic change in consumption.[157] Although technology development and process amelioration are within the institutional consensus, they are inefficient for achieving sustainable consumption goals. Why have the United Nations and developed nations failed to specify limits for consumption? Some attribute this to moral corruption, whereby decision makers avoid taking actions to cope with long-term challenging problems that have ramifications for future generations.[158] However, the more likely explanation for this overconsumption of natural resources is the "tragedy of the commons."[159] According to this explanation, when it is not possible to completely exclude consumers of common-pool resources, such as natural resources, which provide finite benefits, rational utility-maximizing consumers (who seek to extract the most benefits for themselves) are expected to fully exploit these resources instead of conserving them for the benefit of all consumers. It has been shown that central governance of such common-pool resources fails as a result of corruption and inefficient control, although voluntary institutions with open communication may be able to conserve resources under certain conditions. Unfortunately, the latter has not been commonly practiced for the world's natural resources.

After considering the roles of consumers and institutions in driving overconsumption, it is important to acknowledge a key actor that fuels this trend. Firms not only produce goods to meet demand, but also prompt such demand. Global spending on advertising has seen an annual increase of about 5 percent in the past decade, up to $586.5 billion in 2020. While spending on TV and newspaper ads declined between

2015 and 2019, Internet advertising increased from $156 billion to $299 billion, with the average American spending 11 hours per day in front of screens[160] and hence continuously exposed to such advertising. US firms spend 20 percent of their budget on advertising, which translates to about $1,200 per citizen and accumulates to 2.2 percent of the national GDP. A recent study found that children are exposed to 683 advertisements per day on average.[161] An analysis of advertising spending between 1970 and 2007 demonstrates how advertising spurs consumption and increases its share of the GDP.[162] Over the years, the focus of advertising has shifted from needs to desires, leveraging psychology to convince consumers to purchase products that they do not necessarily need. Hence, advertising has implicitly advanced a consumeristic culture.[163] Besides prompting immediate desires, advertising has also shaped youngsters' attitudes toward consumption and materialism, reinforcing continued consumption, while negatively impacting their well-being.[164]

The overconsumption prompted by firms is subsequently met by overproduction that extracts resources at an exorbitant environmental cost. Although in recent years more corporate attention has been paid to sustainability goals, many firms' production processes still harm the environment and exhaust natural resources. For example, since 1960, agriculture production has tripled. Seventy-two percent of farms are small and use only 8 percent of the world's land, but the 1 percent largest industrial farms use 65 percent of the land.[165] Agriculture and food production consume 70 percent of the water used by humans and account for 26 percent of greenhouse gas emissions, with deforestation accounting for 10 percent of the emissions. Of this, livestock farming accounts for 14.5 percent of the emissions and correspondingly generates 65 percent and 37 percent of the world's nitrous oxide and methane emissions.[166] Industrial farming relies on toxic pesticides, pollutes the soil, air, and water, destroys wildlife, and facilitates antimicrobial resistance, with an estimated annual environmental cost of $3 trillion.[167] For example, a 2-acre fish farm produces waste equivalent to that of a 10,000-people town, with 5 kilos of ocean fish needed to produce 1 kilo of farmed fish, aside from the bycatch which is terminated by longline fishing. Industrial fishing accounts for 95 percent of the global ocean damage and 85 percent of the plastic pollution in the sea.[168]

Agriculture is not a deviant. Most industries have evolved at the expense of the environment. As another example, fast fashion has transformed the apparel industry, shifting from two seasons to more than 50 micro-seasons. By 2014, consumers bought 60 percent more clothing and kept each clothing item for half the time they did in 2000. The production of polyester for this industry released 0.68 trillion kilograms of greenhouse gas in 2015, which is equivalent to the annual emission of 185 coal-fired power plants. Given that the production of one cotton shirt consumes 2,700 liters of water, the fashion industry is responsible for drying rivers and for 20 percent of water pollution in the most needy parts of the world.[169]

The electronics industry is no better. In 2012, consumers spent $206 billion on electronics products, with only 29 percent of the resulting waste being recycled. Product life cycle has been artificially shortened for products such as smartphones, laptops, monitors, and TVs. The proportion of defective appliances that needed to be replaced increased from 3.5 percent to 8.3 percent between 2004 and 2012, while the proportion of large appliances replaced in less than five years increased from 7 percent to 13 percent during that time. Firms are actively promoting continuous consumption, upgrading and replacing their products, with the resulting electronic waste polluting the soil, air, and water.[170] These are but a few examples of the overall trend that undermines environmental sustainability, with vehicle production, metal products, livestock farming, mineral extraction, and meat processing having the most impact on the environment.[171]

In the past couple of decades, a counter-trend of environmental policies, CSR, and corporate sustainability initiatives has emerged. In the September 2015 United Nations summit, the member countries agreed on 17 SDGs, which include plans for protecting the planet, combating pollution, and promoting reasonable consumption. This forward-looking perspective of responsibility for future generations is broader than the

CSR initiative. In December 2015, the Paris Agreement on Climate Change was signed, followed by the European Green Deal that was adopted by the European Commission in December 2019, with the aim of making Europe environmentally sustainable. This deal included 50 policy measures and a binding target of reaching net zero emissions in Europe by 2050 as per the Paris Agreement, which the United States rejoined in January 2021. Some firms have voluntarily adopted sustainability policies, engaged various stakeholders, and leveraged sustainability matrices, which have also been tied to superior financial performance.[172] These sustainability policies aim to produce environmentally friendly products, prevent pollution, promote recycling and waste management, and leverage clean energy.

However, in implementing these policies, many firms have taken an instrumental approach under the assumption that such policies would help improve their financial performance.[173] Some firms have engaged in greenwashing—that is, overstating and advertising their symbolic environmentally friendly initiatives while using misleading and false claims in order to disguise their unfavorable activities and improve their stakeholders' perceptions. Such practices have become pervasive.[174] Some well-known examples include the discovery by the Environmental Protection Agency in 2015 that in order to meet US standards, Volkswagen used software to activate the diesel engine's emission control only when undergoing regulatory testing. Another example is BP rebranding itself as Beyond Petroleum and advertising the solar panels that they installed in gas stations, while ClientEarth complained in December 2019 that BP still spends more than 96 percent of its budget on oil and gas products. In fact, BP spent more on its new logo and campaign than on its investment in alternative energy. Similarly, in 2019, H&M launched a "green" line of clothing branded "Conscious," which uses "organic" cotton and recycled polyester, yet the Norwegian Customer Authority identified this as misleading marketing, since no concrete information was provided about the environmental benefits of this collection. In 2021, Apple was sued for excluding the charger from the iPhone 12 box, supposedly for environmental reasons. But its actual aim was not to save the planet but to save money and make profit from selling MagSafe—a higher energy consuming battery pack.[175] Apple saved $35 by excluding the charger and earphones from the iPhone package, which translated to $6.5 billion extra profit.[176] Although greenwashing has become the norm for many firms, more alarming is the fact that the overconsumption and abuse of natural resources have progressively worsened in the past couple of decades despite the various international, national, and corporate policies instituted with the aim of minimizing them. In the next 50 years, one-third of plant and animal species could be extinct,[177] with climate change contributing to shortages and increases in commodity prices. According to the International Monetary Fund, in 2021 alone, primary commodity prices have increased by 53 percent, with food prices showing a 28 percent increase on average. As a result of the compromised supply chain, shortages in commodities including plastic, paper, and metals have forced European countries such as Germany to shift to local production. This required the hiring of a high-salary local workforce, which together with the increasing energy prices (e.g., the price of gas increased by 170 percent in 2021) has contributed to inflation. Hence, overconsumption and abuse of natural resources carry a high price to society.

2.5 SOME DRAWBACKS OF GLOBALIZATION

One final caveat reinforces each of the four previous problems. The past four decades witnessed increasing globalization of the economy, which has contributed to growth in many countries, but not without undesirable consequences. Globalization of the world economy refers to increased international flows of goods, capital, and labor as a result of economic exchange and integration of national markets into an open global market.[178] Although this process has been ongoing since the late 19th century, it has been accelerated since the 1980s with the advancement of computing, communication, and information technologies, which eased cross-border transactions. Between 1950 and 2010, the inflation-adjusted value of global exports increased by 3,277

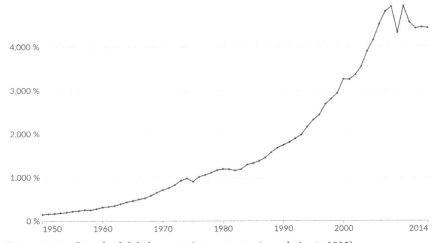

Figure 2.12 *Growth of global exports (at constant prices relative to 1913).*

Source: Ortiz-Ospina and Beltekian[a]

a Ortiz-Ospina, E., & Beltekian, D. (2018), "Trade and globalization," *Our World in Data*, https://our worldindata.org/trade-and-globalization, Chart 7, accessed October 17, 2021.

percent[179] (see Figure 2.12). During that period, the contribution of worldwide exports to the global GDP also increased, from 7.8 percent to 23.5 percent, suggesting a net increase in global trade relative to the economic growth.[180] Trade (combined imports and exports) as a share of GDP has increased from 38.6 percent in 1990 to 58.2 percent in 2019, with trade in data-driven services accounting for half of the trade in services that year (see Figure 2.13).[181] Between 1990 and 2017, the share of foreign inputs in exported goods also increased from 24 percent to 30 percent, suggesting further increase in international trade and interconnectedness of nations (see Figure 2.14).[182] The effect of globalization on efficiency gains and economic growth has been demonstrated in several cross-country studies.[183] Other studies show how firms that were most exposed to imports consequently increased their innovation and productivity.[184] In my own research, I revealed that the entry of multinational corporations to Israel in the mid-1990s pressured local firms to reposition themselves in the global market and become more competitive, collaborate with foreign competitors, or be acquired by them, while less adaptive firms went out of business.[185] Many Israeli

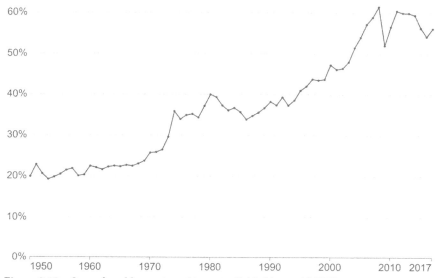

Figure 2.13 *Sum of world exports and imports divided by world GDP.*

Source: Ortiz-Ospina and Beltekian[a]

a Ortiz-Ospina, E., & Beltekian, D. (2018), "Trade and globalization," *Our World in Data*, https://our
worldindata.org/trade-and-globalization, Chart 6, accessed October 17, 2021.

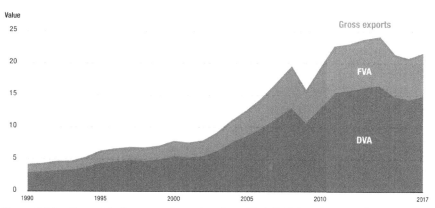

Figure 2.14 *Gross global exports: domestic value added (DVA) vs. foreign value
added (FVA).*

Source: UNCTAD[a]

a United Nations Conference on Trade and Development (UNCTAD) (2018), *World investment
report*, United Nations, New York and Geneva, https://unctad.org/system/files/official-document/
wir2018_en.pdf.

firms managed to adopt a global mindset, and a new generation of firms has been born global.[186] Among developing countries, China, India, Mexico, and Brazil were the most successful in leveraging globalization to expand trade. Globalization has enabled firms to reach global markets and specialize by leveraging their countries' comparative advantages, while locating operations in or importing inputs from countries with lower costs of production. Such outsourcing has created employment opportunities in developing countries, which offered cheap labor. The specialization and accumulation of economies of scale explain the efficiency gains from globalization.[187] Moreover, by intensifying international competition, globalization has contributed to increased availability, variety, and quality of goods at lower prices, thus enhancing consumer welfare.[188] Therefore, globalization has benefited consumers and provided capable countries and individuals with better access to international resources, investments, and employment opportunities. The average wage in most countries has increased in the past 30 years. For example, the average annual wage in OECD countries in current prices increased from $36,941 in 1990 to $49,165 in 2020. As someone who grew up in the Middle East, studied in the United States, and has been working in Europe, I am personally indebted to globalization.

That being noted, a careful examination would reveal that the benefits of globalization have not been equally shared, leaving some disadvantaged. In particular, globalization has transferred some jobs and investments from developed countries to less developed countries, increasing the return on capital in rich countries such as the United States, while eliminating low-skill jobs elsewhere. In developed countries, the capital's share of GDP increased, while that of labor decreased.[189] Indeed, exposure to foreign competition in disadvantaged sectors, such as labor-intensive manufacturing and service industries, has led to the closing of businesses, downward pressure on wages, job insecurity, and increased unemployment, given that some tasks could be performed at a lower cost elsewhere.[190] Globalization has also weakened labor unions, which could not react as strongly as in the past. Although some firms managed to reorganize and diversify to compensate for the loss of jobs with the creation of new jobs in the exposed country,[191] the creation of new jobs has not caught up with their elimination, and in any case, this has not been a remedy to those losing their jobs.[192] Unemployment benefits cannot compensate for job loss, which is often accompanied by loss of self-esteem and social respect when individuals become reliant on the social system and their relatives. Moreover, the jobs transferred to developing countries were often not accompanied by assimilation of worker rights and employment standards, so unskilled employees in countries such as China and India have been often facing unsafe, challenging work conditions, and exploitation. Although China gained most in income per capita as a result of globalization,[193] between 1995 and 2021, wealth inequality has soared in China, with the share of the top 10 percent increasing from 41.4 percent to 68 percent of the national wealth, while the share of the bottom 50 percent declined from 15.9 percent to 6.3 percent of the wealth. Similarly, income inequality rose in China, with the top 1 percent earners increasing their income share from 9.4 percent to 13.7 percent, while the share of the bottom 50 percent earners declined from 18.5 percent to 14.4 percent.[194] The most vulnerable to globalization were rural areas in poor countries that did not participate in international trade, where the population had limited opportunities for relocation or professional development and thus remained in poverty.[195] Hence, globalization has contributed to income inequality both across and within nations, with rising Gini coefficients for disposable household income in rapidly globalizing countries.[196] Even in rich countries with mature industrial economies, globalization has increased income inequality, so despite the average gain in income per capita, the perceived inequality and discontent with job loss as a result of foreign imports and international migration in these countries has intensified nationalistic and populistic views. This has led to heated political demonstrations not only in African and Latin American countries that have not seen much gain from globalization, but also in developed economies that have benefited most from globalization and that witnessed the weakening of international treaties as exemplified by Brexit. As Kofi Annan predicted: "globalization has produced three dangerous reactions: nationalism, illiberal solutions, and populism."[197]

This raises the question of social injustice: why have some been excluded from the gains associated with globalization? Indeed, globalization has been implemented in a way that has not bridged the gap between developed and developing countries. Globalization has also facilitated income inequality within countries by allowing for the free movement of capital while imposing a tax burden on immobile labor. Moreover, it has limited the ability of governments to intervene in the redistribution of wealth.[198] Rich countries such as Norway have attracted large populations of immigrants, which imposed pressure on their welfare systems. In contrast, other countries have been challenged by outward migration of skilled labor, as in the case of Romania, where 30 percent of the doctors have left for other European countries.[199] Thus, while benefiting mobile individuals, migration has also imposed challenges for origin and host nations, which have correspondingly responded with regulation to restrict immigrants' employment or to prevent brain drain.

The clear winners in globalization are multinational corporations, whose revenues increased with outsourcing of expensive labor and insourcing of cheap materials. The top 50 firms in 2020 had a combined market capitalization equal to 28 percent of the world's GDP.[200] A comparison with the Fortune Global 500 list reveals that in that year, Walmart generated more revenue than Belgium, Royal Dutch Shell was about the size of Sweden based on revenue, Amazon earned more than Finland, and Apple earned more than Chile. This illustrates the increasing bargaining power of multinational corporations that have leveraged globalization to influence policy making and exploit local policies, relocate operations in order to receive government subsidies for their investments, negotiate favorable provisions in trade agreements, and avoid taxation. For instance, US multinational corporations exploited the base erosion and profit shifting, known as the Double Irish practice, to avoid taxation of foreign profits and build an estimated untaxed reserve of $1 trillion between 2004 and 2018.[201] The result has been the concentration of wealth, economic inequality, and the shifting of the tax burden from firms to individuals and families.

Increasing international trade can also in part be blamed for the overconsumption of natural resources and its damaging environmental impact. Globalization has been associated with economic growth in industrialized nations, with China, South Korea, Poland, Hungary, and Chile leading that trend.[202] GDP growth is a primary driver of overconsumption, as can be illustrated by the 264.62 percent increase in China's coal consumption after it joined the World Trade Organization in 2001. China reached 54.3 percent of the world's coal consumption in 2020, contributing to an increase in carbon dioxide emissions.[203] According to the International Organization of Motor Vehicle Manufacturers (oica.net), in 2005, 3.97 million cars were sold in China, about half the number sold in the United States. By 2020, however, Chinese consumers bought 20.2 million cars, six times more than in the United States. This trend has been accompanied by a corresponding increase in oil consumption, which facilitates greenhouse gas emissions. Globalization has also increased greenhouse gas emissions as a result of the international transportation of goods. The overall implications can be illustrated by the 400 percent increase in the personal carbon footprint of the top 10 percent wealthiest in China between 1995 and 2021.[204] Unfortunately, globalization has limited the ability of governments to counter such trends with independent macroeconomic policies, as regulation in one country diverts production and pollution to another. A related side effect of globalization has been the increase in illegal trade of drugs, weapons, diamonds, counterfeit products, and human trafficking. For instance, counterfeit goods accounted for 3 percent of the world's GDP in 2019, with money laundering by criminal networks accounting for another 2.7 percent. Additionally, human trafficking has been estimated at $32 billion in 2005 and since then has been on the rise, with 95 percent of the irregular migration in Europe in 2016 facilitated by smugglers.[205] Thus, the easing of cross-border trade had some undesirable consequences.

Moreover, the increased reliance on international trade has exposed many countries and societies to ripple effects related to the fragile global supply chains and increasingly complex and interconnected financial network. The share of global supply chains in global trade increased from 27 percent in 1970 to more than 50 percent in 2010 (see Figure 2.15).

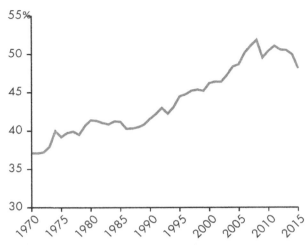

Figure 2.15 *Global supply chain trade share in global trade.*

Source: World Bank[a]

a World Bank (2020), *World development report 2020: trading for development in the age of global value chain*, World Bank, https://openknowledge.worldbank.org/handle/10986/32437. License: CC BY 3.0 IGO FIGURE.

The specialization and concentration of production in a limited number of countries has left international trade dependent on the weakest link. Further vulnerability has been introduced by products incorporating components that are produced in different countries. The emergence of artificial intelligence and the tendency of algorithms to mimic investment patterns has been the final nail in the coffin. The resulting vulnerability was evidenced in the financial crisis in 2008, which impacted many countries in Europe and South Asia that faced price cuts on real estate and exported goods as well as increased interest rates following the subprime mortgage crisis in the United States. The United Bank of Switzerland alone lost $38 billion as a result of this crisis. Another example is the decline in production of cars and electronics in the United States and Europe following the 2011 tsunami in Japan that affected not only Japanese firms but also those dependent on their exported components.[206] Interference with production and trade following the preventive measures taken by governments and the increase in online purchases because of the Covid-19 pandemic has led to major global delays in seaports and local deliveries, and hence to product shortages in various countries. A shortage of truck drivers and extreme weather conditions left 584 container ships queued for unloading outside ports by October 15, 2021, twice as many as at the beginning of that year.[207] This led to a worldwide shortage in merchandise and to price increases, with the shipping cost for a container reaching $12,000, almost ten times more than before the pandemic. The restrictions and sanctions resulting from the recent war between Russia and Ukraine were expected to triple the container shipping cost on affected routes. Aside from the increased frequency of financial crises associated with globalization, the increased interdependence of financial markets since the financial crisis in 2008, which was contained, may generate an unrecoverable ripple effect across countries if a major bank or trading company collapses. Unfortunately, it is the poor economies and individuals that are most susceptible to economic shocks and fluctuations and thus most vulnerable at times of global crisis. For instance, the price of agriculture commodities increased by 35 percent during 2021, with further increase in 2022 following the war between Russia and Ukraine, major exporters of wheat, corn, and sunflower oil. The ramifications for nutrition security and social unrest are expected to impact mostly countries in the Middle East, North Africa, and Central Asia. Hence, in the short term, when operating smoothly, the efficient global supply chain eliminates idle merchandise and capital and reduces production costs. Nevertheless, it facilitates global contagion and imposes increasing risks and costs in times of crisis.

A final concern relates to culture and identity. With the advance of communication technologies such as fast Internet and smartphones that enhance virtual proximity, globalization has facilitated the dispersion of global brands and the adoption of a common consumeristic culture that has displaced cultural diversity and national identity. Although international travel and the exchange of ideas were expected to expose individuals to various cultures and promote pluralism, globalization may have promoted a narrower, more capitalistic and individualistic perspective, especially among youngsters who adopted the global identity encapsulated by the international brands they consume. The global culture has led to social divergence by advocating personal freedom, which has weakened established social structures and challenged the legitimacy of societal and community values.[208] In addition, some immigrant groups have not been successfully integrated into their host countries and thus remained isolated. Overall, these trends have undermined social integration, mutual support, and generosity toward those in need within societies. For example, research reveals a negative association between willingness of above-median earners to economically support below-median earners as the proportion of immigrants in society increases.[209] In addition, globalization has facilitated emotions such as helplessness and alienation in communities that have been adversely affected by globalization, such as small business owners, who not only lost their business to multinational corporations, but also lost a sense of attachment to society. These phenomena are in line with the notion of anomia, which explains how individual freedoms undermine cohesion in society and hence morality.[210] Globalization has promoted a culture that underscores competitiveness and the pursuit of capital gain at the expense of moral values and ethical standards. In that regard, global integration of the economy has led to disintegration of societies and lack of appreciation for various native customs that are not aligned with a global lifestyle. Although the advance of a global mindset was initially expected to undermine ethnocentrism,[211] in the end, the backlash from globalization may have prompted nationalistic movements.[212]

In conclusion, studies of globalization have praised the virtues of multinational corporations that managed to effectively configure their subsidiary networks across the globe. But by optimizing value chains and enhancing cost efficiencies, these multinational firms annihilated local businesses while making countries vulnerable to geographical concentration of expertise and raw materials as well as weakening local governments and cultures. Multinational corporations have certainly benefited from globalization, but it is questionable that societies benefit from it. Globalization has facilitated economic development and wealth generation but has done so in a way that can be considered unfair to many. Although the drawbacks of globalization are mostly due to its failed implementation and governance by national and international institutions, one cannot deny that it has evolved into "a perverse malign force hurting millions,"[213] especially in underdeveloped and developing countries.

2.6 PUTTING THE PROBLEMS IN PERSPECTIVE: IT COMES DOWN TO GREED

Our economic system has generated immense wealth but not without faults. I have discussed the concentration of wealth and economic inequality, the rise of dominant platforms and their exploitation of power, the loss of data privacy and consumers' independent choice, the overconsumption and abuse of natural resources, and some drawbacks of globalization (see Figure 2.16). These seem to be an unrelated set of societal grand challenges, but they are in fact interdependent. Furthermore, as I explain next, the roots of these seemingly unrelated grand challenges can all be traced to one common catalyst, namely the design of our modern economic system. This means that, unfortunately, these problems are not that straightforward to resolve.

Although I focused on digital platforms such as those owned by Amazon, Meta, Google, and Apple, the system's problems have transpired throughout all traditional industry sectors of the economy. In seeking to identify root causes, we can see an emerging common theme relating to the pursuit of profit maximization as a guiding principle of the economic system that overrules all other objectives, regardless of whether they concern equality, well-being, or sustainability. This can be illustrated with government policies that support continued growth and wealth concentration while weakening labor unions and shifting the tax burden to families; with corporate practices such as Meta's promotion of its Facebook and Instagram platforms that increases advertising income while knowingly harming users and polarizing society, or with Amazon's exploitation of warehouse employees and its predatory acquisition and substitution practices that harm vendors; with the profiling and targeting of users based on personal data that enable platform owners to shape purchasing decisions and opinions; with the relentless extraction of natural resources disguised by greenwashing, which causes irrecoverable damage to the environment and deprives future generations; and with the optimization of the global supply chain that enables multinational

Figure 2.16   *The faults of the modern economic system.*

corporations that leverage trade agreements to profit by relocating operations while avoiding taxation and undermining the resilience of our fragile economy. Indeed, the current economic system not only allows for self-interested pursuit of gains at all costs, it glorifies it. In the words of Gordon Gekko's character in the movie *Wall Street*—"greed is good." If you ask youngsters whom they admire and strive to become, besides their favorite athlete or singer, they are more likely to mention Elon Musk and Mark Zuckerberg than Greta Thunberg.

However, one cannot blame successful entrepreneurs for working the system to their advantage. They simply managed to create and capture value and outperform others in striving to accomplish the mission that we, business strategy professors, taught in our classes. One should blame the economic system that has enabled them to do so. This intricate system is not easy to tamper with given its complexity and interdependent elements, which self-reinforce the primary goal of profit making. There are too many reinforcing forces against too few restraining forces in the form of governance structures and regulation that are supposed to prevent or penalize discriminatory business practices.

One may wonder whether the profit-making DNA is inherent to the system or to individuals. Greed is certainly a human trait, but it should not overshadow societal norms and values. Welfare and well-being are not less important than doing well financially. Unfortunately, the economic system has failed to provide sufficient safeguards and incentives to promote sustainability, respect data privacy, and serve the interests of various stakeholders. Instead, it has fostered and rewarded opportunistic behavior driven by greed.

A related theme that emerges from the discussion of the economic system's problems concerns concentration. But the concentration of wealth is only a consequence of system dynamics that reinforce economic inequality. The economic system benefits the privileged, increasing returns to those who are economically fortunate. More concerning, however, is the concentration of power that comes with concentration of wealth and is wired to the logic of the system, especially for platform ecosystems. The idea of network externalities that is well demonstrated in this context facilitates the concentration of power. Still, it all comes down to exploitation in the name of profit generation. Unfortunately, the system not only allows for exploitation of the disadvantaged but provides the moral basis for such behavior. Value creation and capture at all costs is the modus operandi.

What distinguishes the modern economic system from its traditional predecessor is its sophistication and digitalization. Information has become the new currency that benefits those who possess it. As discussed, the advancement of the Internet, big data analytics, artificial intelligence, and questionably intelligent algorithms, which have fallen into the hands of firms and platform owners, have enabled them to monetize frequently and extensively, to conquer and pollute the mind and the soil, to exploit human cognitive and psychological weaknesses, all for the sake of profit generation. The current economic system has prompted the concentration of information, wealth, and power in the hands of those who adhere to the rules of the system but not to the unwritten rules of society. We cannot fully blame ourselves, society, for accepting this system, because built into it are processes that disintegrate society and promote its division. When the Internet was commercialized in the late 1990s, the hope was that it would connect distant individuals and help them break free from intermediaries and information asymmetries. Instead, it has concentrated power and divided our society. The metaverse vision of platform owners such as Meta is a more sophisticated technology-enabled scheme for introducing an artificial medium that further distances users from each other and from reality, gathers and analyzes personal data using advanced sensors, and leaves users exposed to hazards and the manipulations of platform owners.

Much like artificial intelligence offers an efficient alternative to independent choice, global brands and advertising appeal to our desire for happiness, while globalization reinforces inequality, weakens labor unions, and undermines traditional social structures, thus leaving us divided and easy to conquer. We strive to survive as the economic pressures mount, losing sight of the broader picture. The modern economy lets the machine take the lead, and humans follow. More importantly, the same principles of self-interest and profit maximization work at all levels, from individuals to countries, leading to the tragedy of the commons[214] with the exhaustion of the planet's finite vital resources. While the economic system has become more interdependent and global, it has left communities less self-reliant and more vulnerable, economically and socially. As societies become less cohesive, identities fade, and long-held values are forgotten, this has turned into an end game. Policymakers, activists, and many others who recognize some of the problems have attempted to rectify them. They have sought to figure out a way to retain wealth creation while addressing the various grand challenges that I have highlighted. Unfortunately, this is not an attainable goal. I will next refer briefly to some of the proposed solutions and their implementations and explain why they are unlikely to be sufficient in the face of the onslaught.

NOTES

1 Barney, J.B., Hesterly, W.S., & Mishkin, F.S. (2018), *Strategic management and competitive advantage*, 6th edn., Pearson Education; Grant, R.M. (2021), *Contemporary strategy analysis*, 11th edn., Wiley & Sons.
2 Friedman, M. (1970), "A Friedman doctrine—the social responsibility of business is to increase its profits," *New York Times*, September 13, section SM, p. 17, www.nytimes.com/1970/09/13/archives/a-friedman-doctrine-the-soc ial-responsibility-of-business-is-to.html; Jensen, M.C., & Meckling, W.H. (1976), "Theory of the firm: managerial behavior, agency costs and ownership structure," *Journal of Financial Economics*, 3(4), pp. 305–360.
3 Cennamo, C., & Santalo, J. (2013), "Platform competition: strategic trade-offs in platform markets," *Strategic Management Journal*, 34, pp. 1331–1350; Lee, E., Lee, J., & Lee, J. (2006), "Reconsideration of the winner-take-all hypothesis: complex networks and local bias," *Management Science*, 52, pp. 1838–1848.
4 Riedel, G.A., & Knoop, C-I. (2019), *Facebook—can ethics scale in the digital age?*, Harvard Business School Case 9-319-030.
5 Nadler, J., & Cicilline, D.N. (2020), Investigation of competition in digital markets—majority staff report and recommendations, Subcommittee on Antitrust, Commercial and Administrative Law of the Committee on the Judiciary, US House of Representatives, United States.
6 Goldberg, E. (2020), "'Techlash' hits college campuses," *New York Times*, January 15.
7 Bansal, P. (2002), "The corporate challenges of sustainable development," *Academy of Management Executive*, 16, pp. 122–131.

8 Acemoglu, D., He, X., & le Maire, D. (2022), *Eclipse of rent-sharing: the effects of managers' business education on wages and the labor share in the US and Denmark*, NBER Working Paper 29874, www.nber.org/papers/w29874.

9 Freeman, E.R. (1984), *Strategic management: a stakeholder approach*, Cambridge University Press.

10 Flammer, C. (2015), "Does corporate social responsibility lead to superior financial performance? A regression discontinuity approach," *Management Science*, 61(11), pp. 2549–2824; Orlitzky, M., Schmidt, F.L., & Rynes, S.L. (2003), "Corporate social and financial performance: a meta-analysis," *Organization Studies*, 24(3), pp. 403–441.

11 GiveForms (2021), *25 companies that donate to nonprofits*, www.giveforms. com/blog/25-companies-that-donate-to-nonprofits, accessed October 4, 2021.

12 Iyengar, R. (2020), "Google is donating $800 million to help with the coronavirus crisis," CNN Business, March 27, https://edition.cnn.com/2020/03/27/tech/google-800-million-coronavirus-response/index.html.

13 Cohen, A. (2020), "Jeff Bezos commits $10 billion to new Bezos Earth Fund," *Forbes*, February 24, www.forbes.com/sites/arielcohen/2020/02/24/jeff-bezos-commits-10-billion-to-new-bezos-earth-fund/.

14 Albrecht, L. (2020), "The Giving Pledge turns 10: these billionaires pledged to give away half their wealth, but they soon ran into a problem," *Market Watch*, August 10, www.marketwatch.com/story/giving-away-money-well-is-very-hard-the-giving-pledge-turns-10-and-its-signers-are-ric her-than-ever-2020-08-08.

15 Hao, L., & Renneboog, L. (2017), "Corporate donations and shareholder value," *Oxford Review of Economic Policy*, 33(2), pp. 278–316.

16 Gneiting, U., Lusiani, N., & Tamir, I. (2020), "Power, profits and the pandemic: from corporate extraction for the few to an economy that works for all," *OXFAM Briefing Paper*, http://hdl.handle.net/10546/621044.

17 Amis, J., Brickson, S., Haack, P., & Hernandez, M. (2021), "Taking inequality seriously," *Academy of Management Review*, 46(3), pp. 431–439.

18 Shorrocks, A., Davies, J., & Lluberas, R. (2021), *Global wealth report*, Credit Suisse Research Institute, June, www.credit-suisse.com/media/assets/corpor ate/docs/about-us/research/publications/global-wealth-report-2021-en.pdf.

19 Lawson, M., Chan, M.-K., Rhodes, F., Butt, A.P., Marriott, A., Ehmke, E., Jacobs, D., Seghers, J., Atienza, J., & Gowland, R. (2019), "Public good or private wealth?," *OXFAM Briefing Paper*, https://oxfamilibrary.openreposit ory.com/bitstream/handle/10546/620599/bp-public-good-or-private-wealth-210119-summ-en.pdf.

20 Bradly, C., & Stumpner, P. (2021), *The impact of COVID-19 on capital markets, one year in*, McKinsey & Co., March 10.

21 Shorrocks, A., Davies, J., & Lluberas, R. (2020), *Global wealth report*, Credit Suisse Research Institute, www.credit-suisse.com/media/assets/corporate/ docs/about-us/research/publications/global-wealth-report-2020-en.pdf.

22 Parker, K., Minkin, R., & Bennet, J. (2020), *Economic fallout from Covid-19 continues to hit lower-income Americans the hardest*, Pew Research Center, September 24, www.pewresearch.org/social-trends/2020/09/24/economic-fall out-from-covid-19-continues-to-hit-lower-income-americans-the-hardest/.

23 Dolan, K.A., Wang, J., & Peterson-Withorn, C. (2021), "Forbes' world billionaires list—the richest in 2021," *Forbes*, www.forbes.com/billionaires/ #549ef44e251c.

24 Lawson, M., Chan, M.-K., Rhodes, F., Butt, A.P., Marriott, A., Ehmke, E., Jacobs, D., Seghers, J., Atienza, J., & Gowland, R. (2019), "Public good or private wealth?," *OXFAM Briefing Paper*, https://oxfamilibrary.openreposit ory.com/bitstream/handle/10546/620599/bp-public-good-or-private-wealth- 210119-summ-en.pdf.

25 Lakner, C., Yonzan, N., Mahler, D.G., Castaneda Aguilar, R.A., Wu, H., & Fleury, M. (2020), "Updated estimates of the impact of COVID-19 on global poverty: the effect of new data," *Data Blog*, October 7, https://blogs.worldb ank.org/opendata.

26 Ahmed, N., Marriott, A., Dabi, N., Lowthers, M., Lawson, M., & Mugehera, L. (2022), "Inequality kills: the unparalleled action needed to combat unprecedented inequality in the wake of COVID-19," *OXFAM Briefing Paper*, January 17, https://policy-practice.oxfam.org/resources/inequality-kills-the- unparalleled-action-needed-to-combat-unprecedented-inequal-621341/.

27 Chancel, L., Piketty, T., Saez, E., & Zucman, G. (2022), "World inequality report 2022," *World Inequality Lab*, 3, https://wir2022.wid.world/www-site/ uploads/2021/12/Summary_WorldInequalityReport2022_English.pdf.

28 Robeyns, I. (2017), *Wellbeing, freedom and social justice: the capability approach re-examined*, Open Book Publishers.

29 Sherman, E. (2019), "A new report claims big tech companies used legal loopholes to avoid over $100 billion in taxes. What does that mean for the industry's future?," *Fortune*, December 6, https://fortune.com/2019/12/06/ big-tech-taxes-google-facebook-amazon-apple-netflix-microsoft/.

30 Lord, B., & Collins, C. (2021), *No, the rich are not paying their fair share*, Institute for Policy Studies, March 17, https://inequality.org/great-divide/no- the-rich-are-not-paying-their-fair-share/.

31 Clausing, K., Saez, E., & Zucman, G. (2020), *Ending corporate tax avoidance and tax competition: plan to collect the tax deficit of multinationals*, UCLA School of Law, Law-Econ Research Paper No. 20-12, https://papers.ssrn.com/sol3/papers.cfm?abstract_id=3655850.

32 Berkhout, E., Galasso, N., Lawson, M., Morales, P.A.R., Taneja, A., & Pimentel, D.A.V. (2021), "The inequality virus," *OXFAM Briefing Paper*, January 25, https://oxfamilibrary.openrepository.com/bitstream/handle/10546/621149/bp-the-inequality-virus-250121-en.pdf.

33 Shorrocks, A., Davies, J., & Lluberas, R. (2021), *Global wealth report*, Credit Suisse Research Institute, June, www.credit-suisse.com/media/assets/corporate/docs/about-us/research/publications/global-wealth-report-2021-en.pdf.

34 Inequality.org (2021), "Public good or private wealth?," https://inequality.org/facts/global-inequality/#global-wealth-inequality, accessed October 10, 2021.

35 Collins, C., & Ocampo, O. (2021), *Financial reserves and the racial wealth gap*, Institute for Policy Studies, February 26, https://inequality.org/great-divide/financial-reserves-and-the-racial-wealth-gap/.

36 Alvaredo, F., Chancel, L., Piketty, T., Saez, E., & Zucman, G. (2018), *World inequality report*, World Inequality Lab.

37 Saez, E. (2018), "Striking it richer: the evolution of top incomes in the United States," in Grusky, D.B., & Hill, J. (eds.), *Inequality in the 21st century*, Routledge, pp. 39–41.

38 Mishel, L., & Kandra, J. (2020), *Wages for the top 1% skyrocketed 160% since 1979 while the share of wages for the bottom 90% shrunk*, Economic Policy Institute, December 1.

39 Dewan, P., Rørth, R., Jhund, P.S., Ferreira, J.P., Zannad, F., Shen, L., Køber, L., Abraham, W.T., Desai, A.S., Dickstein, K., Packer, M., Rouleau, J.L., Solomon, D., Swedberg, K., Zile, M.R., & McMurray, J.J.V. (2019), "Income inequality and outcomes in heart failure: a global between-country analysis," *Journal of the American College of Cardiology*, 7(4), pp. 336–346.

40 Murray, C., Lopez, A., & Alvarado, M. (2013), "The state of US health, 1990–2010: burden of diseases, injuries, and risk factors," *Journal of the American Medical Association*, 310(6), pp. 591–606.

41 Chetty, R., Stepner, M., Abraham, S., Lin, S., Scuderi, B., Turner, N., Bergeron, A., & Cutler, D. (2016), "The association between income and life expectancy in the United States, 2001–2014," *Journal of the American Medical Association*, 315(16), pp. 1750–1766.

42 Murray, C., et al. (2018), "The state of US health, 1990–2016: burden of diseases, injuries, and risk factors," *Journal of the American Medical Association*, 319(14), pp. 1444–1472.

43 Khullar, D., & Chokshi, D.A. (2018), *Health, income, & poverty: where we are & what could help*, Health Affairs Health Policy Brief, October 4.

44 Pickett, K.E., & Wilkinson, R.G. (2015), "Income inequality and health: a causal review," *Social Science & Medicine*, 128, pp. 316–326.

45 Horowitz, J., Igielnik, R., & Arditi, T. (2020), *Most Americans say there is too much economic inequality in the U.S., but fewer than half call it a top priority*, Pew Research Center, January 9, www.pewresearch.org/social-trends/wp-content/uploads/sites/3/2020/01/PSDT_01.09.20_economic-inequailty_FULL.pdf.

46 Adner, R. (2017), "Ecosystem as structure: an actionable construct for strategy," *Journal of Management*, 43(1), pp. 39–58, p. 40.

47 Jacobides, M., Cennamo, C., & Gawer, A. (2018), "Towards a theory of ecosystems," *Strategic Management Journal*, 39(8), pp. 2255–2276.

48 Cennamo, C. (2021), Competing in digital markets: a platform-based perspective. *Academy of Management Perspective*, 35(2), pp. 265–291; Cennamo, C., & Santalo, J. (2013), "Platform competition: strategic trade-offs in platform markets," *Strategic Management Journal*, 34, pp. 1331–1350.

49 Gawer, A. (2021), "Digital platforms and ecosystems: remarks on the dominant organizational forms of the digital age," *Innovation: Organization & Management*, September, pp. 1–15.

50 Armstrong, M. (2006), "Competition in two-sided markets," *RAND Journal of Economics*, 37, pp. 668–691.

51 Boudreau, K.J. (2017), "Platform boundary choices & governance: opening-up while still coordinating and orchestrating," in Furman, J., Gawer, A., Silverman, B.S., & Stern, S. (eds.), *Entrepreneurship, innovation, and platforms*, Advances in Strategic Management 37, Emerald, pp. 227–298.

52 European Commission (2020), *Proposal for a regulation of the European Parliament and of the Council on contestable and fair markets in the digital sector (Digital Markets Act)*, December 15, https://eur-lex.europa.eu/legal-content/EN/TXT/HTML/?uri=CELEX:52020PC0842&rid=8, p. 1.

53 E.g., Gawer A., & Cusumano, M.A. (2008), "How companies become platform leaders," *MIT Sloan Management Review*, 49(2), pp. 28–35; Rietveld, J., & Schilling, M.A. (2021), "Platform competition: a systematic and

interdisciplinary review of the literature," *Journal of Management*, 47(6), pp. 1528–1563.

54 Cennamo, C., & Santalo, J. (2013), "Platform competition: strategic trade-offs in platform markets," *Strategic Management Journal*, 34, pp. 1331–1350; Parker, G.G., & Van Alstyne, M. (2018), "Innovation, openness, and platform control," *Management Science*, 64, pp. 3015–3032.

55 Suarez, F.F. (2004), "Battles for technological dominance: an integrative framework," *Research Policy*, 23, pp. 271–286.

56 Schilling, M.A. (2000), "Toward a general modular systems theory and its application to interfirm product modularity," *Academy of Management Review*, 25, pp. 312–334.

57 Santesteban, C., & Longpre, S. (2020), "How big data confers market power to Big Tech: leveraging the perspective of data science," *Antitrust Bulletin*, 65(3), pp. 459–485.

58 Katz, M.L. (2019), "Platform economics and antitrust enforcement: a little knowledge is a dangerous thing," *Journal of Economics & Management Strategy*, 28, pp. 138–152.

59 Hovenkamp, H. (2021), "Antitrust and platform monopoly," *Yale Law Journal*, 130(8), pp. 1952–2050.

60 Jenny, F. (2021), "Changing the way we think: competition, platforms and ecosystems," *Journal of Antitrust Enforcement*, 9, pp. 1–18, p. 2.

61 Jenny, F. (2021), "Changing the way we think: competition, platforms and ecosystems," *Journal of Antitrust Enforcement*, 9, pp. 1–18.

62 Nadler, J., & Cicilline, D.N. (2020), Investigation of competition in digital markets—majority staff report and recommendations, Subcommittee on Antitrust, Commercial and Administrative Law of the Committee on the Judiciary, US House of Representatives, United States, p. 6.

63 Kim, W.C., & Mauborgne, R. (2004), *Blue Ocean strategy: how to create uncontested market space and make the competition irrelevant*, Harvard Business School Press.

64 Eckhardt, J.T., Ciuchta, M.P., & Carpenter, M. (2018), "Open innovation, information, and entrepreneurship within platform ecosystems," *Strategic Entrepreneurship Journal*, 12(3), pp. 369–391.

65 Wen, W., & Zhu, F. (2019), "Threat of platform-owner entry and complementor responses: evidence from the mobile app market," *Strategic Management Journal*, 40, pp. 1336–1367; Zhu, F., & Liu, Q. (2018),

"Competing with complementors: an empirical look at Amazon.com," *Strategic Management Journal*, 39(10), pp. 2618–2642.

66 JungleScout (2020), *The state of the Amazon seller*, www.junglescout.com/wp-content/uploads/2020/02/State-of-the-Seller-Survey.pdf.

67 Hovenkamp, H. (2021), "Antitrust and platform monopoly," *Yale Law Journal*, 130(8), pp. 1952–2050.

68 Li, Z.X., & Agarwal, A. (2017), "Platform integration and demand spillovers in complementary markets: evidence from Facebook's integration of Instagram," *Management Science*, 63, pp. 3438–3458.

69 Wen, W., & Zhu, F. (2019), "Threat of platform-owner entry and complementor responses: evidence from the mobile app market," *Strategic Management Journal*, 40, pp. 1336–1367.

70 European Commission (2020), *Proposal for a regulation of the European Parliament and of the Council on contestable and fair markets in the digital sector (Digital Markets Act)*, December 15, https://eur-lex.europa.eu/legal-content/EN/TXT/HTML/?uri=CELEX:52020PC0842&rid=8.

71 Anderson, E.G., Parker, G.G., & Tan, B. (2014), "Platform performance investment in the presence of network externalities," *Information Systems Research*, 25, pp. 152–172; Boudreau, K.J. (2010), "Open platform strategies and innovation: granting access versus devolving control," *Management Science*, 56, pp. 1849–1872.

72 Cennamo, C., Ozalp, H., & Kretschmer, T. (2018), "Platform architecture and quality trade-offs of multihoming complements," *Information Systems Research*, 29(2), pp. 461–478.

73 Rietveld, J., Schilling, M.A., & Bellavitis, C. (2019), "Platform strategy: managing ecosystem value through selective promotion of complements," *Organization Science*, 30, pp. 1125–1393.

74 Nadler, J., & Cicilline, D.N. (2020), Investigation of competition in digital markets—majority staff report and recommendations, Subcommittee on Antitrust, Commercial and Administrative Law of the Committee on the Judiciary, US House of Representatives, United States, p. 12.

75 European Commission (2020), *Proposal for a regulation of the European Parliament and of the Council on contestable and fair markets in the digital sector (Digital Markets Act)*, December 15, https://eur-lex.europa.eu/legal-content/EN/TXT/HTML/?uri=CELEX:52020PC0842&rid=8, p. 1.

76 Jacobides, M.G., & Lianos, I. (2021), "Regulating platforms and ecosystems: an introduction," *Industrial and Corporate Change*, 30(5), pp. 1131–1142.

77 Consumer Intelligence Research Partners, LLC (2018), "Mobile operating system loyalty: high and steady," March 8, http://files.constantcontact.com/150f9af2201/4bca9a19-a8b0-46bd-95bd-85740ff3fb5d.pdf.

78 Nadler, J., & Cicilline, D.N. (2020), Investigation of competition in digital markets—majority staff report and recommendations, Subcommittee on Antitrust, Commercial and Administrative Law of the Committee on the Judiciary, US House of Representatives, United States.

79 Hovenkamp, H. (2021), "Antitrust and platform monopoly," *Yale Law Journal*, 130(8), pp. 1952–2050.

80 Nadler, J., & Cicilline, D.N. (2020), Investigation of competition in digital markets—majority staff report and recommendations, Subcommittee on Antitrust, Commercial and Administrative Law of the Committee on the Judiciary, US House of Representatives, United States.

81 Nadler, J., & Cicilline, D.N. (2020), Investigation of competition in digital markets—majority staff report and recommendations, Subcommittee on Antitrust, Commercial and Administrative Law of the Committee on the Judiciary, US House of Representatives, United States.

82 Gayle, D. (2021), "Facebook aware of Instagram's harmful effect on teenage girls, leak reveals," *The Guardian*, September 14, www.theguardian.com/technology/2021/sep/14/facebook-aware-instagram-harmful-effect-teenage-girls-leak-reveals.

83 Sangal, A., Duffy, C., Fung, B., & Kelly, S. (2021), "Instagram head testifies before Congress," CNN Business, December 8, https://edition.cnn.com/business/live-news/instagram-adam-mosseri-congress-teens-12-08-21/h_0010f172a79b0d5cb89aadf80b8280d2.

84 Rosenquist, J.N., Scott Morton, F.M., & Weinstein, S.N. (2022), "Addictive technology and its implications for antitrust enforcement," *North Carolina Law Review*, 100(2), pp. 431–486.

85 United Nations Human Rights Council (2018), *Report of the independent international fact-finding mission on Myanmar*, Session 39, 10–28, September, www.ohchr.org/Documents/HRBodies/HRCouncil/FFM-Myanmar/A_HRC_39_64.pdf.

86 Digital Lab (2020), *Platform perceptions: consumer attitudes on competition and fairness in online platforms*, CR Survey Research Department and Advocacy Division, September 24.

87 Dolan, K.A., Wang, J., & Peterson-Withorn, C. (2021), "Forbes' world billionaires list—the richest in 2021," www.forbes.com/billionaires/#549ef44e251c.

88 Ranosa, R. (2020), "Top 50 companies with the best pay packages—according to employees," *Human Resources Director*, October 14.

89 De Loecker, J., Obermeier, T., & Van Reenen, J. (2022), "Firms and inequality," *Institute for Fiscal Studies: Deaton Review of Inequalities*, pp. 1–41, https://ifs.org.uk/uploads/Firms-and-inequalities-IFS-Deaton-Review-Inequalities.pdf.

90 Wong, J.C. (2021), "Revealed: Google illegally underpaid thousands of workers across dozens of countries," September 10, www.theguardian.com/technology/2021/sep/10/google-underpaid-workers-illegal-pay-disparity-documents.

91 Bond, S. (2020), "Google illegally fired and spied on workers who tried to organize, labor agency says," National Public Radio, December 3, https://text.npr.org/941860802.

92 BBC News (2021), "Margaret Mitchell: Google fires AI ethics founder," February 20, www.bbc.co.uk/news/technology-56135817.

93 Chan, J. (2021), "Amazon workers detail disturbing work conditions in complaint filed to the National Labor Relations Board," *Entrepreneur*, March 31, www.entrepreneur.com/article/368286.

94 Guendelsberger, E. (2019), "I worked at an Amazon fulfillment center; they treat workers like robots," *Time*, July 18, https://time.com/5629233/amazon-warehouse-employee-treatment-robots/.

95 Agustin, F. (2021), "Apple employees want the company to re-investigate complaints of harassment, racism and abuse," *Business Insider*, September 4, www.businessinsider.com/apple-employees-want-the-company-to-re-investigate-complaints-of-harassment-racism-2021-9?r=US&IR=T.

96 Elias, J. (2019), "Facebook employees earn top dollar but describe a 'cult-like' and 'ruthless' company culture," *Silicon Valley Business Journal*, January 15, www.bizjournals.com/sanjose/news/2019/01/14/facebook-culture-performance-reviews-fb-median-pay.html.

97 Pelley, S. (2021), "Whistleblower: Facebook is misleading the public on progress against hate speech, violence, misinformation," CBS News, October 4, www.cbsnews.com/news/facebook-whistleblower-frances-haugen-misinformation-public-60-minutes-2021-10-03/.

98 Newton, C. (2019), "Bodies in seats: at Facebook's worst-performing content moderation site in North America, one contractor has died, and others say they fear for their lives," *The Verge*, June 19, www.theverge.com/2019/6/19/18681845/facebook-moderator-interviews-video-trauma-ptsd-cognizant-tampa.

99 Sainato, M. (2019), " 'They treat us like crap': Uber drivers feel poor and powerless on eve of IPO," *The Guardian*, May 7, www.theguardian.com/tec hnology/2019/may/07/uber-drivers-feel-poor-powerless-ipo-looms.

100 Milligan, E., Thomson, A., & Drozdiak, N. (2021), "Uber's U.K. court loss spells a reckoning for gig work in Europe," Bloomberg, February 19, www. bloomberg.com/news/articles/2021-02-19/uber-s-u-k-court-loss-spells-a-reckoning-for-gig-work-in-europe.

101 Hughes, M. (2021), "UberEats drivers claim they are struggling to earn a living after company makes cuts to delivery fees," Wales Online, February 10.

102 Calcalist (2021), "Woltzilla: how Wolt completely changed our lives, and why it is problematic," December 23, https://newmedia.calcalist.co.il/magazine-23-12-21/m01.html?ref=ynet.

103 Gray, M.L., & Suri, S. (2019), *Ghost work: how to stop Silicon Valley from building a new global underclass*, Houghton Mifflin Harcourt.

104 Davis, G.F. (2016), *The vanishing American corporation: navigating the hazards of a new economy*, Berrett-Koehler Publishers.

105 Bureau of Labor Statistics (2021), *State job openings and labor turnover*, US Department of Labor, October 22, www.bls.gov/news.release/pdf/jltst.pdf.

106 *The Guardian* (2022), "What are the UK rail strikes about and how long will they go on?," June 21, www.theguardian.com/uk-news/2022/jun/21/uk-rail-strikes-what-is-happening-today.

107 Associated Press (2021), "Film industry workers agree to strike if deal can't be made over 'basic needs,' " *The Guardian*, October 13, www.theguardian. com/us-news/2021/oct/13/film-industry-workers-authorize-strike-negot iations; Associated Press (2021), "Hundreds rally for striking coal miners in Alabama," ABC News, August 4, https://abcnews.go.com/US/wireStory/hundreds-rally-striking-coal-miners-alabama-79269683; Associated Press (2021), "Workers at all of Kellogg's U.S. cereal plants go on strike," Associated Press News, October 5, https://apnews.com/article/kelloggs-cereal-plants-str ike-d9185eb8fa9054d34a078063c3db6c33.

108 George, G., Haas, M.R., & Pentland, A. (2014), "Big data and management," *Academy of Management Journal*, 57(2), pp. 321–326.

109 Kanter, J.M., & Veeramachaneni, K. (2015), "Deep feature synthesis: towards automating data science endeavors," *Proceedings of the IEEE Data Science and Advanced Analytics Conference*, pp. 1–10.

110 Jenny, F. (2021), "Changing the way we think: competition, platforms and ecosystems," *Journal of Antitrust Enforcement*, 9, pp. 1–18.

111 Hitlin, P., Rainie, L., & Olmstead, K. (2019), *Facebook algorithms and personal data*, Pew Research Center, January 16. www.pewresearch.org/inter net/2019/01/16/facebook-algorithms-and-personal-data/.

112 Digital Lab (2020), *Platform perceptions: consumer attitudes on competition and fairness in online platforms*, CR Survey Research Department and Advocacy Division, September 24.

113 Riedel, G.A., & Knoop, C-I. (2019), *Facebook—can ethics scale in the digital age?*, Harvard Business School Case 9-319-030.

114 Hitlin, P., Rainie, L., & Olmstead, K. (2019), *Facebook algorithms and personal data*, Pew Research Center, January 16. www.pewresearch.org/inter net/2019/01/16/facebook-algorithms-and-personal-data/.

115 Ezrachi, A., & Stucke, M. (2016), *Virtual competition: the promise and perils of the algorithm-driven economy*, Harvard University Press; Luguri, J., & Strahilevitz, L.J. (2021), "Shining a light on dark patterns," *Journal of Legal Analysis*, 13(1), pp. 43–109.

116 Montes, R., Sand-Zantman, W., & Valletti, T. (2019), "The value of personal information in online markets with endogenous privacy," *Management Science*, 65(3), pp. 1342–1362.

117 Yang, Y., West, J., Thiruvathukal, G.K., Klingensmith, N., & Fawaz, K. (forthcoming), "Are you really muted? A privacy analysis of mute buttons in video conferencing apps," *Proceedings on Privacy Enhancing Technologies*, pp. 1–21.

118 Riedel, G.A., & Knoop, C-I. (2019), *Facebook—can ethics scale in the digital age?*, Harvard Business School Case 9-319-030.

119 Abrardi, L., Cambini, C., & Rondi, L. (2021), "Artificial intelligence, firms and consumer behavior: a survey," *Journal of Economic Surveys*, pp. 1–23.

120 Protiviti (2019), *Competing in the cognitive age: how companies will transform their businesses and drive value through advanced AI*, www.protiviti.com/ sites/default/files/united_states/insights/ai-ml-global-study-protiviti.pdf.

121 Acquisti, A., Brandimarte, L., & Loewenstein, G. (2015), "Privacy and human behavior in the age of information," *Science*, 347(6221), pp. 509–514.

122 Tucker, C. (2019), "Privacy, algorithms and artificial intelligence," in Agrawal, A., Gans, J., & Goldfarb, A. (eds.), *The economics of artificial intelligence: an agenda*, University of Chicago Press, pp. 423–438.

123 Jahromi, A.T., Stakhovych, S., & Ewing, M. (2014), "Managing B2B customer churn, retention and profitability," *Industrial Marketing Management*, 43(7), pp. 1258–1268.

124 Hosanagar, K. (2019), *A human's guide to machine intelligence*, Penguin Random House.

125 Smith, C. (2021), "Waze's algorithm 'went crazy' and started sending people the wrong way," BGR, November 1, https://bgr.com/tech/wazes-algorithm-went-crazy-and-started-sending-people-in-the-wrong-direction/.

126 Calvano, E., Calzolari, G., Denicolò, V., & Pastorello, S. (2020), "Artificial intelligence, algorithmic pricing and collusion," *American Economic Review*, 110(10), pp. 3267–3297.

127 Gal, M.S., & Elkin-Koren, N. (2017), "Algorithmic consumers," *Harvard Journal of Law & Technology*, 30(2), pp. 309–353.

128 Kramer, A.D.I., Guillory, J.E., & Hancock, J.T. (2014), "Experimental evidence of massive-scale emotional contagion through social networks," *Proceedings of National Academy of Science*, 111(24), pp. 8788–8790.

129 André, Q., Carmon, Z., Wertenbroch, K., Crum, A., Frank, D., Goldstein, W., Huber, J., van Boven, L., Weber, B., & Yang, H. (2018), "Consumer choice and autonomy in the age of artificial intelligence and big data," *Customer Needs and Solutions*, 5, pp. 28–37.

130 Athey, S., & Luca, M. (2019), "Economists (and economics) in tech companies," *Journal of Economic Perspectives*, 33(1), pp. 209–230.

131 Marres, N., & Stark, D. (2020), "Put to the test: for a new sociology of testing," *British Journal of Sociology*, 71, pp. 423–443.

132 Horwitz, J., & Seetharaman, D. (2020), "Facebook executives shut down efforts to make the site less divisive," *Wall Street Journal*, May 26.

133 Vosoughi, S., Roy, D., & Aral, S. (2018), "The spread of true and false news online," *Science*, 359(6380), pp. 1146–1151.

134 Riedel, G.A., & Knoop, C-I. (2019), *Facebook—can ethics scale in the digital age?*, Harvard Business School Case 9-319-030.

135 Duffy, C. (2021), "Facebook has known it has a human trafficking problem for years. It still hasn't fully fixed it," CNN Business, October 25.

136 Zuboff, S. (2019), *The age of surveillance capitalism: the fight for a human future at the new frontier of power*, Profile Books.

137 Giljum, S., Hinterberger, F., Bruckner, M., Burger, E., Frühmann, J., Lutter, S., Pirgmaier, E., Polzin, C., Waxwender, H., Kernegger, L., & Warhurst, M. (2009), *Overconsumption? Our use of the world's natural resources*, Sustainable Europe Research Institute, September 9, https://cdn.friend softheearth.uk/sites/default/files/downloads/overconsumption.pdf?_ga= 2.196529449.48826011.1633979826-654500657.1633979826.

138 Center for Sustainable Systems, University of Michigan (2021), *US environmental footprint factsheet*, Pub. No. CSS08-08, https://css.umich.edu/factsheets/us-environmental-footprint-factsheet.

139 World Health Organization (2022), *WHO European regional obesity report 2022*, https://apps.who.int/iris/bitstream/handle/10665/353747/9789289057738-eng.pdf.

140 Center for Sustainable Systems, University of Michigan (2021), *US environmental footprint factsheet*, Pub. No. CSS08-08, https://css.umich.edu/factsheets/us-environmental-footprint-factsheet.

141 Almond, R.E.A., Grooten, M., & Petersen, T. (eds.) (2020), *Living planet report 2020—bending the curve of biodiversity loss*, WWF, www.zsl.org/sites/default/files/LPR%202020%20Full%20report.pdf.

142 Kirby, A. (2016), "Human consumption of Earth's natural resources has tripled in 40 years," EcoWatch Climate News Network, July 25, www.ecowatch.com/humans-consumption-of-earths-natural-resources-tripled-in-40-years-1943126747.html#toggle-gdpr.

143 Giljum, S., Hinterberger, F., Bruckner, M., Burger, E., Frühmann, J., Lutter, S., Pirgmaier, E., Polzin, C., Waxwender, H., Kernegger, L., & Warhurst, M. (2009), *Overconsumption? Our use of the world's natural resources*, Sustainable Europe Research Institute, September 9, https://cdn.friendsoftheearth.uk/sites/default/files/downloads/overconsumption.pdf?_ga=2.196529449.48826011.1633979826-654500657.1633979826.

144 Almond, R.E.A., Grooten, M. and Petersen, T. (eds.) (2020), *Living planet report 2020—bending the curve of biodiversity loss*, WWF.

145 United Nations Food and Agriculture Organization (2015), *Status of the world's soil resources*, www.fao.org/3/i5199e/I5199E.pdf.

146 Waters, J. (2021), "Overconsumption and the environment: should we all stop shopping?," *The Guardian*, May 30, www.theguardian.com/lifeandstyle/2021/may/30/should-we-all-stop-shopping-how-to-end-overconsumption.

147 Wiedmann, T., Lenzen, M., Keyßer, L.T., & Steinberger, J.K. (2020), "Scientists' warning on affluence," *Nature Communications*, 11, p. 3107, https://doi.org/10.1038/s41467-020-16941-y.

148 Foyster, G. (2013), *Changing gears: a pedal-powered detour from the rat house*, Affirm Press.

149 Elkins, P. (1991), "The sustainable consumer society: a contradiction in terms?," *International Environmental Affairs*, Fall.

150 Jebb, A.T., Tay, L., Diener E., & Oishi, S. (2018), "Happiness, income satiation and turning points around the world," *Nature Human Behavior*, 2, pp. 33–38.

151 E.g., Easterlin, R. (1974), "Does economic growth improve the human lot: some empirical evidence," in David, P.A., & Reder, M.W. (eds.), *Nations and households in economic growth: essays in honor of Moses Abromowitz*, Academic Press, pp. 89–126; Easterlin, R., & O'Connor, K.J. (2020), *The Easterlin Paradox*, IZA Discussion Papers 13923, Institute of Labor Economics (IZA).

152 Cushman, P. (1990), "Why the self is empty," *American Psychology*, 45, pp. 599–611.

153 E.g., Wachtel, P. (1983), *The poverty of affluence*, Free Press; Easterlin, R., & O'Connor, K.J. (2020), *The Easterlin Paradox*, IZA Discussion Papers 13923, Institute of Labor Economics (IZA).

154 Brown, P.M., & Cameron, L.D. (2000), "What can be done to reduce overconsumption?," *Ecological Economics*, 32, pp. 27–41.

155 Herlocker, C.E., Allison, S.T., Foubert, J.D., & Beggan, J.K. (1997), "Intended and unintended overconsumption of physical, spatial, and temporal resources," *Journal of Personality and Social Psychology*, 73(5), pp. 992–1004.

156 Schlosberg, D. (2007), *Defining environmental justice: theories, movements, and nature*, Oxford University Press.

157 Bengtsson, M., Alfredsson, E., Cohen, M., Lorek, S., & Schroeder, P. (2018), "Transforming systems of consumption and production for achieving the sustainable development goals: moving beyond efficiency," *Sustainability Science*, 13, pp. 1533–1547; Vladimirova, K. (2020), "Justice concerns in SDG 12: the problem of missing consumption limits," in McNeill, L. (ed.), *Transitioning to responsible consumption and production*, Transitioning to Sustainability Series 12, MDPI, pp. 187–224.

158 Gardiner, S.M. (2011), *A perfect moral storm: the ethical tragedy of climate change*, Oxford University Press.

159 Hardin, G. (1968), "The tragedy of the commons," *Science*, 162(3859), pp. 1243–1248; Ostrom, E. (2008), "Tragedy of the commons," in Durlauf, S.N., & Blume, L.E. (eds.), *The new Palgrave dictionary of economics*, 2nd edn., Palgrave Macmillan.

160 Wood, T. (2020), "Visualizing the evolution of global advertising spend (1980–2020)," *Visual Capitalist*, November 10, www.visualcapitalist.com/evolution-global-advertising-spend-1980-202.

161 Watkins, L., Aitken, R., Gage, R., Smith, M.B., Chambers, T.J., Barr, M., Stanley, J., & Signal, L.N. (2019), "Capturing the commercial world of children: the feasibility of wearable cameras to assess marketing exposure," *Journal of Consumer Affairs*, 3(4), pp. 1396–1420.

162 Molinari, B., & Turino, F. (2018), "Advertising and aggregate consumption: a Bayesian DSGE assessment," *Economic Journal*, 128(613), pp. 2106–2130.

163 Smart, B. (2010), *Consumer society: critical issues and environmental consequences*, Sage Publications.

164 Buijzen, M., & Valkenburg, P.M. (2003), "The effects of television advertising on materialism, parent–child conflict, and unhappiness: a review of research," *Journal of Applied Developmental Psychology*, 24, pp. 437–456.

165 United Nations Environment Programme (2020), "10 things you should know about industrial farming," July 20, www.unep.org/news-and-stories/story/10-things-you-should-know-about-industrial-farming.

166 Food and Agriculture Organization of the United Nations (2013), *Livestock's long shadow: environmental issues and options*, www.fao.org/3/a0701e/a07 01e.pdf.

167 Food and Agriculture Organization of the United Nations (2013), *Livestock's long shadow: environmental issues and options*, www.fao.org/3/a0701e/a07 01e.pdf.

168 Johnson, K. (2019), "4 ways the fishing industry is destroying the planet," September 30, https://animalequality.org/blog/2019/09/30/fishing-industry-destroying-environment/.

169 Drew, D., & Yehounme, G. (2017), *The apparel industry's environmental impact in 6 graphics*, World Resources Institute, July 5, www.wri.org/insig hts/apparel-industrys-environmental-impact-6-graphics.

170 Brown, T. (2021), "The environmental impact of electronics manufacturing," *The Manufacturer*, June 9, www.themanufacturer.com/articles/the-enviro nmental-impact-of-electronics-manufacturing/.

171 Hertwich, E.G., van der Voet, E., Suh, S., & Tukker, A. (2010), Assessing the environmental impacts of consumption and production, United Nations Environment Programme, pp. 1–112, www.resourcepanel.org/reports/assess ing-environmental-impacts-consumption-and-production.

172 Eccles, R.G., Ioannou, I., & Serafeim, G. (2014), "The impact of corporate sustainability on organizational processes and performance," *Management Science*, 60(11), pp. 2835–2857.

173 Gao, J., & Bansel, P. (2013), "Instrumental and integrative logics in business sustainability," *Journal of Business Ethics*, 112, pp. 241–255.

174 Walker, K., & Wan, F. (2012), "The harm of symbolic actions and green-washing: corporate actions and communications on environmental performance and their financial implications," *Journal of Business Ethics*, 109, pp. 227–242.

175 Roth, E. (2021), "Chinese students sue Apple for not including a charger with the iPhone 12," *The Verge*, October 27, www.theverge.com/2021/10/27/22748474/chinese-students-sue-apple-including-charger-iphone-12.

176 Jones, D. (2022), "Apple makes an EXTRA £5billion by no longer providing chargers and earphones with its new iPhones," *Daily Mail*, March 13, www.dailymail.co.uk/news/article-10607077/Apple-makes-EXTRA-5billion-no-longer-providing-chargers-earphones-new-iPhones.html.

177 Román-Palacios, C., & Wiens, J.J. (2020), "Recent responses to climate change reveal the drivers of species extinction and survival," *Proceedings of the National Academy of Sciences*, 117(8), pp. 4211–4217.

178 Albrow, M., & King, E. (1990), *Globalization, knowledge and society*, Sage Publications.

179 Federico, G., & Tena-Junguito, A. (2019), "World trade, 1800–1938: a new synthesis," *Revista de Historia Económica—Journal of Iberian and Latin America Economic History*, 37(1), https://doi.org/10.1017/S0212610918000216.

180 Fouquin, M., & Hugot, J. (2016), *Two centuries of bilateral trade and gravity data: 1827–2014*, CEPII Report, May 14, www.cepii.fr/cepii/en/bdd_modele/presentation.asp?id=32.

181 World Bank (2021), *World development report 2021: data for better lives*, World Bank, www.worldbank.org/en/publication/wdr2021; Feenstra, R.C., Inklaar, R., & Timmer, M.P. (2015), "The next generation of the Penn World Table," *American Economic Review*, 105(10), pp. 3150–3182.

182 United Nations Conference on Trade and Development (UNCTAD) (2018), *World investment report*, United Nations, New York and Geneva, https://unctad.org/system/files/official-document/wir2018_en.pdf.

183 E.g., Alcalá, F., & Ciccone, A. (2004), "Trade and productivity," *Quarterly Journal of Economics*, 119(2), pp. 613–646; Frankel, J.A., & Romer, D.H. (1999), "Does trade cause growth?," *American Economic Review*, 89(3), pp. 379–399.

184 E.g., Bloom, N., Draca, M., & Van Reenen, J. (2016), "Trade induced technical change? The impact of Chinese imports on innovation, IT and productivity," *Review of Economic Studies*, 83(1), pp. 87–117.

185 Lavie, D., & Fiegenbaum, A. (2000), "The strategic reaction of domestic firms to foreign MNC dominance: the Israeli experience," *Long Range Planning*, 33, pp. 651–672.

186 Hashai, N., & Almor, T. (2004), "Gradually internationalizing 'born global' firms: an oxymoron?," *International Business Review*, 13(4), pp. 465–483.

187 Evenett, S.J., & Keller, W. (2002), "On theories explaining the success of the gravity equation," *Journal of Political Economy*, 110(2), pp. 281–316; Porter, M.E. (1990), *The competitive advantage of nations*, Free Press.

188 E.g., Berlingieri, G., Breinlich, H., & Dhingra, S. (2018), "The impact of trade agreements on consumer welfare—evidence from the EU common external trade policy," *Journal of the European Economic Association*, 16(6), pp. 1881–1928.

189 Rose, S. (2007), *Does productivity growth still benefit working Americans?*, Information Technology and Innovation Foundation, Washington, DC; Thirlwell, M.P. (2007), *Second thoughts on globalization*, Lowy Institute Paper No. 18, Lowy Institute for International Policy.

190 E.g., David, H., Dorn, D., & Hanson, G.H. (2013), "The China syndrome: local labor market effects of import competition in the United States," *American Economic Review*, 103(6), pp. 2121–2168.

191 Magyari, I. (2017), *Firm reorganization, Chinese imports, and US manufacturing employment*, US Census Bureau, Center for Economic Studies.

192 Stiglitz, J.E. (2017), *Globalization and its discontents revisited: anti-globalization in the era of Trump*, Penguin Books.

193 Sachs, A., Funke, C., Kreuzer, P., & Weiss, J. (2020), *Globalization report 2020: who benefits the most from globalization?*, BertelsmannStiftung, www.bertelsmann-stiftung.de/fileadmin/files/user_upload/GlobalizationReport 2020_2_final_en.pdf.

194 Chancel, L., Piketty, T., Saez, E., & Zucman, G. (2022), "World inequality report 2022," *World Inequality Lab*, 3, https://wir2022.wid.world/www-site/ uploads/2021/12/Summary_WorldInequalityReport2022_English.pdf.

195 E.g., Topalova, P. (2010), "Factor immobility and regional impacts of trade liberalization: evidence on poverty from India," *American Economic Journal: Applied Economics*, 2(4), pp. 1–41.

196 Baten, J., & Fraunholz, U. (2004), "Did partial globalization increase inequality? The case of the Latin American periphery, 1850–2000," *CESifo Economic Studies*, 50(1), pp. 45–84; Das, D.K. (2008), "Contemporary phase

of globalization: does it have a serious downside?," *Global Economic Review*, 37(4), pp. 507–526; Milanovic, B. (2002), "True world income distribution, 1988 and 1993: first calculations based on household surveys alone," *Economic Journal*, 112(476), pp. 51–92.

197 Annan, K.A. (1999), "The backlash against globalism," *The Futurist*, March, p. 27.

198 Stiglitz, J.E. (2017), *Globalization and its discontents revisited: anti-globalization in the era of Trump*, Penguin Books.

199 Collier, P. (2018), "The downside of globalisation: why it matters and what can be done about it," *The World Economy*, 41(4), pp. 967–974.

200 Orlik, T., Jimenez, J., Sam, C. (2021), "World-dominating superstar firms get bigger, techier, and more Chinese," Bloomberg, May 21, www.bloomberg.com/graphics/2021-biggest-global-companies-growth-trends/.

201 Wikipedia, Double Irish arrangement, https://en.wikipedia.org/wiki/Double_Irish_arrangement, accessed October 17, 2021.

202 Sachs, A., Funke, C., Kreuzer, P., & Weiss, J. (2020), *Globalization report 2020: Who benefits the most from globalization?*, BertelsmannStiftung, www.bertelsmann-stiftung.de/fileadmin/files/user_upload/GlobalizationReport 2020_2_final_en.pdf.

203 BP (2021), *Statistical review of world energy*, July, www.bp.com/content/dam/bp/business-sites/en/global/corporate/pdfs/energy-economics/statistical-review/bp-stats-review-2021-full-report.pdf.

204 Chancel, L., Piketty, T., Saez, E., & Zucman, G. (2022), "World inequality report 2022," *World Inequality Lab*, 3, https://wir2022.wid.world/www-site/uploads/2021/12/Summary_WorldInequalityReport2022_English.pdf.

205 Global Initiative Against Transnational Organized Crime (2021), *The global illicit economy: trajectories of transnational organized crime*, March, https://globalinitiative.net/wp-content/uploads/2021/03/The-Global-Illicit-Economy-GITOC-Low.pdf.

206 Prestowitz, C. (2011), "Japan rules the global supply chain," *Foreign Policy*, March 22, https://foreignpolicy.com/2011/03/22/japan-rules-the-global-supply-chain/.

207 Fresh Plaza (2021), "There are almost twice as many ships detained outside ports as there were at the beginning of the year," Fresh Plaza, October 20, www.freshplaza.com/article/9365557/there-are-almost-twice-as-many-ships-detained-outside-ports-worldwide-as-there-were-at-the-beginning-of-the-year/.

208 Murray, C. (2012), *Coming apart: the state of white America, 1960–2010*, Crown Forum; Williams, J.C. (2017), *White working class: overcoming class cluelessness in America*, Harvard Business Review Press.

209 Rueda, D. (2017), "Food comes first, then morals: redistribution preferences, parochial altruism and immigration in Western Europe," *Journal of Politics*, 80(1), pp. 225–239.

210 Merton, R.K. (1957), "Social structure and anomie," *American Sociological Review*, 3, pp. 672–682; Srole, L. (1956), "Social integration and certain corollaries: an exploratory study," *American Sociological Review*, 21, pp. 709–716.

211 Pieterse, J. 1994. "Globalisation as hybridization," *International Sociology*, 6, pp. 161–184.

212 Caruana, A., & Chircop, S. (2001), "The dark side of globalization and liberalization: helplessness, alienation and ethnocentrism among small business owners and managers," *Social Marketing*, pp. 63–74.

213 Stiglitz, J.E. (2003), "We have to make globalization work for all," *Yale Global*, 17.

214 Hardin, G. (1968), "The tragedy of the commons," *Science*, 162(3859), pp. 1243–1248; Ostrom, E. (2008), "Tragedy of the commons," in Durlauf, S.N., & Blume, L.E. (eds.), *The new Palgrave dictionary of economics*, 2nd edn., Palgrave Macmillan.

CHAPTER THREE

Insufficient attempts to contain the problems

DOI: 10.4324/9781003336679-3

In the past few decades, efforts to cope with grand challenges have been extensive, but the problems are still prevalent and have worsened during this period, thus attesting to the insufficiency of such efforts. My purpose here is not to offer a comprehensive review of these remedial actions. Rather, I will briefly highlight some of the most promising recent efforts, including efforts to promote economic equality, restrain platform owners, regulate data protection and privacy, enhance environmental sustainability, and revisit globalization. I will, however, explain why these efforts are unlikely to effectively resolve the problems associated with our economic system. One of the most promising efforts was the 2015 UN resolution that identified 17 SDGs to be implemented by 2030. Meeting these goals would solve societal grand challenges by generating positive externalities while mitigating negative ones.[1] For each goal, the resolution specifies quantitative targets.[2] Although the SDG Compass[3] and the SDG Action Manager[4] detail measurement and reporting tools, they do not explain how these should be adopted by firms and integrated into their corporate objectives and strategies.[5] The broad scope and complexity of the SDGs, with their 169 targets and 232 indicators, do not facilitate concrete actions, which led some to contend that they are merely rhetoric.[6] Moreover, no specific policies and means for implementation were outlined, leaving governments to devise and pursue their own policies for implementation. I will next refer to the relevant SDGs that aim to address each problem as well as discuss other specific efforts to amend the economic system, which have been fruitful to a limited extent.

3.1   PROMOTING ECONOMIC EQUALITY

Some of the SDGs aim to battle economic inequality, including ending poverty and hunger (SDGs 1 and 2), promoting inclusive and sustainable economic growth, with employment and decent work for all (SDG 8), and reducing inequality within and among countries (SDG 10). Nevertheless, economic inequality persists. To restrict economic inequality and abolish poverty, measures should break the vicious cycle whereby the rich become richer while the poor become poorer. One of the most promising means to reverse that trend is progressive taxation. Because of the self-reinforcing concentration of wealth, some economists suggested applying progressive global tax on financial assets or instituting a regional wealth tax.[7] But over the past four decades, corporate tax and personal tax at the highest brackets have been halved, thus contributing to inequality.[8] Governments avoid raising taxes in fear that such a policy may disincentivize work and reduce productivity and economic growth. Instead, they rely more on regressive indirect taxes that increase poverty. Interestingly, the International Monetary Fund has shown that rising economic inequality is somewhat negatively associated with economic growth.[9] Nonetheless, during the Covid-19 pandemic, large firms have received relief and recovery funds at the expense of taxpayers, allowing these firms to increase their profits and earning distributions to shareholders, while small businesses and the poor have struggled.[10] Nevertheless, even if affluent individuals and firms are subject to higher taxes, it is unclear whether the extra income would reach the needy given that the elite firms and individuals have louder voices in setting priorities for public spending. Indeed, a study of political influence in the United States revealed that whereas the preferences of the average citizen do not influence the probability of enacting a public policy, a policy with high support from the economic elites and business interest groups has a 45 percent probability of adoption as opposed to 18 percent probability for policies that gain low support from the rich.[11] This finding is more typical of an oligarchy than a democracy. Accordingly, two-thirds of the population do not trust political institutions as far as the tax system is concerned.[12] Many governments have not been effective in protecting the vulnerable, and they are unlikely to become effective in doing so during a period in which the wealthy have become more influential.

Furthermore, wealthy firms and their owners have mastered the art of tax avoidance and evasion, and there is no reason to believe that they will forget this art if tax levels are increased. The globalized economy and digitalization limit governments' capacity to tax international firms that shift their economic activities and capital across countries, thus creating a disincentive for governments to increase the tax burden on such firms. For more than a decade, the OECD has led discussions for limiting competition for corporate investments among countries and agreeing on corporate tax rates. In October 2021, 136 countries agreed on a minimum tax rate of 15 percent and on a system that taxes profits where they are earned, with the expected extra tax income of about $150 billion per year.[13] It is yet to be seen if this income will reach individuals at the bottom of the income distribution, whose minimum income tax thresholds have not been increased.

Another approach for coping with economic inequality involves public services and transfers. Assisted by charities, foundations, and private donations, governments that seek to support the needy have offered social welfare programs, including unemployment and disability benefits, child support and pensions, stipends, and subsidies as well as nutrition, health services, educational programs, and shelter to the poor. Some government programs and corporate community development initiatives have been fruitful.[14] However, despite their obvious merits, these programs have not always served those who need them most. Whereas social protection programs cover 90 percent of Europeans, they reach less than 15 percent of the population in Africa.[15] Even in the Western world, the provision of public services and social protection is often misaligned with governments' privatization efforts, which seek to transfer responsibility to more efficient providers in the private sector. Most importantly, most public services tend to reinforce the economic divide in society because they do not provide individuals with opportunities to increase their income and purchasing power. To the contrary: they make the needy more dependent. Hence, public services do not "bring true freedom,"[16] but rather create an illusion of freedom. In most countries, minimum wage has not been set at a level sufficient to reach a proper living standard. An alternative idea, namely that of a universal basic income that is distributed unconditionally, has been tested in Finland, Ontario, and Namibia, but has been challenged on the grounds that it is too costly, discourages employment, and leads to undesirable spending.[17]

Several other policies have been considered to battle economic inequality, such as the advancement of automation and digitalization that could enhance workers' productivity and, hence, earning. However, such initiatives often come at the expense of low-skilled labor and contribute to the digital divide in society while mostly serving the privileged capital owners. Another suggestion has been to adopt permissive policies that facilitate international migration and social mobility, which can promote economic equality across nations if not within nations, but such policies have been shown to maintain inequality rather than reduce it. Furthermore, international migration has not been well received by nationalistic and populistic movements. Such migration has become a source of political instability and conflict between neighboring countries, as evidenced by the rising tension between Poland and Belarus in November 2021 around the tragedy of Middle Eastern refugees that were held at their joint border. Still another measure involves the strengthening of labor unions and stricter labor market regulations.[18] However, between 1979 and 2019, the share of unionized workers dropped from 27 percent to 11.6 percent. As most governments have sought to maintain labor market flexibility, we have witnessed the weakening of such institutions, with many firms reducing employee compensation and benefits. De-unionization is estimated to account for up to 20 percent of the increasing inequality for women and 37 percent of the increasing inequality for men.[19]

Considering the increasing economic inequality, the 2020 World Social Report called for macroeconomic policies that promote equal access to opportunities while coping with prejudice and discrimination.[20] Indeed, two-thirds of Americans believe that it is the federal government's responsibility to reduce inequality. Moreover, 62 percent of Americans believe that it is also the responsibility of large corporations to fight inequality.[21] However, the United Nation's call is likely to remain unanswered given the interests of wealthy firms that do not gain from economic equality as well as the policy tradeoffs faced by governments. The desirable government policies have been known for decades, but governments have not changed their priorities. Those who can reverse the trend of greater economic inequality have no vested interest in pursuing such equality, and hence, the trend persists. Recognizing the conflicting interests of policymakers, some have called for grassroots collective action by the oppressed who are deprived of resources, urging them to rise up in their quest for justice and equality.[22] However, no practical prescription has been provided for such upheaval.

In the meanwhile, economic inequality has worsened, much in line with the "patrimonial capitalism" featured in the novels of 19th-century authors Jane Austen and Honoré de Balzac.[23] A recent survey by the Pew Research Center revealed that among low-income earners in the United States, 46 percent struggled to pay their bills, and 32 percent had difficulties paying their rent or mortgage, which has hardly been an issue among high-income earners.[24] The continuous increase in poverty and economic inequality fosters adverse social and economic consequences such as favoritism, corruption, and resource misallocation, and results in lower investments and greater financial and political instability. Attempts to deal with economic inequality have been partial, superficial, and insufficient. A more serious effort is needed to dismantle the motivations that drive economic inequality, of which greed is the most salient.

3.2   RESTRAINING PLATFORM OWNERS

Seven of the world's top ten firms based on market capitalization operate digital platforms.[25] The abuse of market power by these dominant Big Tech firms, including Amazon, Meta, Google, Apple, and Microsoft, has not escaped the eyes of regulators. The prolonged dominance of these firms has been costly to society, with the main remedy being policy making, antitrust laws, regulation, and enforcement by the judicial system. Regulation refers to the government's intervention by specifying legally enforceable rules and deliberately exercising public control over the behavior of private entities with the aim of restricting their business activities.[26] Such regulation complements antitrust laws that focus on restoring competition and maintaining competitive market output. For example, the exclusive dealings and preferential practices of platform owners such as Google and Meta fall under US antitrust laws such as the Sherman Act. However, antitrust enforcement has been limited, with the courts imposing a high burden of proof on plaintiffs. Some claim that antitrust suffers from an anti-enforcement bias, given its tendency to avoid false positives[27] and to restrict focus to static market outcomes rather than to the complex dynamics that support value creation.[28] This allows platform owners to become dominant before restrictive action is considered.[29] However, the core challenge is that traditional antitrust laws are difficult to apply in the case of multisided platforms that maintain no direct association between the prices charged to consumers and service costs. When it cannot be demonstrated that consumers suffer from excessive prices, current antitrust laws offer no justification for authorities to intervene despite the welfare losses inflicted on competitors, vendors, and employees.[30] Common proxies for market power such as market share and the industry concentration ratio may be inapplicable, while barriers to entry are often not a cause of concern.[31] Antitrust laws are rather costly to apply and have been slow to adapt to the complex and versatile economic system that features innovative business practices. Governments have acknowledged that their conventional antitrust laws and regulation are outdated and ill equipped to cope with dominant platform owners. Yet there are conflicting views about how authorities and regulators should react to these firms' dominance. For example, the court in the United Kingdom and the Paris Tribunal de Commerce reached opposing conclusions concerning Google's alleged foreclosing of competitors in its mapping business. Similarly, the court proceedings against Booking.com in France, Germany, Italy, and Sweden revealed substantial variation.[32]

The report filed by the US House Judiciary Committee on October 6, 2020, following its 16-month investigation of the Big Tech firms represents a turning point in the battle against the dominance of platform owners. This report outlined reforms that promote fair competition in platform ecosystems and reinforce antitrust laws. These reforms include proposals to (a) revise antitrust laws in order to restore antimonopoly goals through the use of structural separation, i.e., breaking up the lines of business of platform owners, (b) regulation that prevents discrimination and self-preferencing, and (c) requirements for interoperability (enabling computer systems or software to interface and work seamlessly) and sharing of commercial data, as well as (d) vigorous restriction of mergers and acquisitions that grant too much market power to the platform owners.[33] Such measures aim to prevent platform owners from abusing their power, while protecting emerging rivals and start-ups. The report's recommendations only provide overarching guidance to Congress, calling for future legislation, so that no immediate actions were foreseen upon its release. It remains to be seen how such recommendations are implemented by legislators and the courts. Nevertheless, shortly after the publication of the committee's report, the US Department of Justice filed a lawsuit against Google for its anticompetitive behavior, with similar legal procedures taking place against the Big Tech firms in other countries. I will proceed by discussing the prospects of the various measures that have been proposed, including divestitures, objection to acquisitions, restricting self-preferencing and expansion to new businesses, sharing business data with competitors and complementors, and restructuring platform ownership. My analysis will lead to the conclusion that these and other established antitrust measures are inadequate for coping with the dominance of platform owners.

The US House Judiciary Committee's proposed divestiture of the Big Tech firms may indeed weaken them while increasing competition, but if ill designed, it can undermine service quality and the network externalities that underlie these firms' value propositions. This can potentially harm complementors and consumers as well as employees of these firms. The question is whether a breakup would increase productivity, quality, and innovation while reducing prices, or rather merely make these firms smaller, inefficient, and unprofitable, while harming consumers as a result of negative network effects. The American history of forced structural breakups and spinoffs of businesses suggests that the Sherman Act for industry de-concentration has been effective in making dominant firms less attractive to consumers but has not dissipated market power. In digital markets featuring interconnected firms, economies of scale and network externalities do not necessarily lead to increased price and reduced service quality, so that breakups of such firms can generate undesirable consequences to society.[34]

The objection to acquisitions of related businesses by platform owners is likely to lead to outcomes such as discoordination and higher costs if the acquired businesses are already well integrated into the owner's organization. In some cases, such as revisiting Amazon's 2017 acquisition of Whole Foods, a breakup can have limited negative consequences to consumers. Even when the negative consequences turn out to be considerable, as in the case of acquisitions of start-ups by platform owners, prohibiting them is challenging under existing antitrust laws. This is because a start-up firm that offers a competing product imposes no threat to the dominant platform owner, whereas a start-up firm with a novel complementary or substitute solution may not show promise at an early stage or may not be considered a competitor at the time of acquisition based on traditional market definitions. For example, the Office of Fair Trading (OFT) in the United Kingdom determined in 2012 that "the evidence before the OFT does not show that Instagram would be particularly well placed to compete against Facebook in the short run." This is despite Mark Zuckerberg's stated earlier concern that, "In the time it has taken us to get our act together on this, Instagram has become a large and viable competitor to us on mobile photos, which will increasingly be the future of photos."[35]

Another form of regulation forbids vertical integration and thus prevents platform owners from offering their own products and services on the platform, or at least prevents them from self-preferencing their offering. However, platform owners such as Amazon may opt to drop the offering of the external vendor rather than exit its business, which is counterproductive. Yet another remedy for self-preference is the removal of anticompetitive defaults, such as allowing users to replace the Google search engine. But users may not be incentivized to do so. In some cases, such defaults minimize search costs without restricting competition.[36] Furthermore, bundling products does not violate antitrust laws if users are not coerced to take both products, so the courts have been conservative with such violations. Measures such as restricting expansion to new lines of business, as in Uber's expansion from passenger carrier service to food delivery or Amazon's expansion from books and media products to general retail, can be harmful to consumers and are unlikely to enhance competition. The idea of sharing commercial and user data with competitors in order to facilitate interoperability and level the playing field may be problematic if it conflicts with data privacy regulation, infringes on intellectual property rights of the platform owner, or facilitates free riding of its investments. These requirements can also disincentivize the platform owner's efforts to collect data, innovate, and improve the quality of service, even when it is unclear if the ported data can help emerging competitors to enhance their value propositions.

Another idea is to restructure the ownership of the platform, so that different units will be managed by separate entities. But separation of ownership and control does not prevent collusion and anticompetitive behavior, with the joint entity retaining its scale and dominance. An alternative is to transfer the management to a multiparty alliance or a consortium of different firms, but this complicates coordinated decision making.[37] Overall, antitrust laws are unlikely to be applied against platform owners whose anticompetitive behavior increases product availability while reducing prices, at least in the short term. Even if applied, these remedies can harm consumers and fail to foster competition.

As noted earlier, the unique characteristics and complexity of platform ecosystems make established legal and economic frameworks inadequate for analyzing and reacting to the market power of platform owners.[38] The traditional antitrust regulation, methodology, and analysis tools must be adjusted and expanded to fit the realm of digital platforms, which entail interdependencies across ecosystem members that are not vertically aligned as in traditional industries. In particular, the established regulation has adopted a narrow perspective that centers on consumer welfare, with the US Supreme Court focusing on damages relating to restricted output and price increases, rather than more broadly to restricted competition. However, such restriction is key for platform ecosystems, which often do not charge consumers for their services. Relaxing the restrictive terms of antitrust regulation is likely to bring many lawsuits to courts, which should in turn focus on fairness and anticompetitive actions. For example, in September 2021, the US federal court decided in the Apple vs. Epic Games case that Apple cannot force app developers to rely exclusively on its high-fee payment system, and instead must let users decide how to pay for their iPhone apps.[39] Similarly, in November 2020, the European Commission ruled that Amazon violated the law when using proprietary data of its third-party vendors to unfairly compete with them. In these cases, the economic benefits to complementors and consumers were clear. It will be interesting to see, however, how the judiciary system would cope with cases in which harm to consumers cannot be easily demonstrated, such as in the case of predatory pricing. Here, some harm can be inflicted on consumers, e.g., declining service quality and product availability, if the platform is marginalized or disintegrated.

Beyond considering the downsides of the alternative proposed measures, it is important to bear in mind that the Big Tech firms are unlikely to stand by in this battle.[40] They have already taken preemptive actions to accommodate some of the regulatory requirements in ways that better suit them, employed their army of lobbyists to restrict the scope and effects of regulation in-the-making, and found creative ways to benefit from the new regulation. This is best illustrated by Apple's change of its privacy policy in June 2020 following the General Data Protection Regulation (GDPR) requirements that prevented app developers from surveilling users on other apps without their consent. Apple used the new privacy policies as a competitive tool to severely cut Meta's income from targeted advertising on the iPhone platform, while increasing Apple's own advertising revenue share from 17 percent to 58 percent in 2021.[41] Apparently, Apple did not subject itself to the same restrictions imposed on its complementors. Additionally, Apple has used this recent regulation to justify its refusal to share useful commercial information with its complementary app developers.

Will the aggressive approach advanced by the US House Judiciary Committee achieve its objectives and level the playing field, ensure fair competition, and shift power from platform owners to complementors and consumers? Clearly, in some cases, such as in business breakups, consumers could be worse off if service quality and added value are eroded. Restricting and penalizing the platform owners do not necessarily guarantee that emerging competitors can step up and take market share. Moreover, the Big Tech firms may modify their business models and find innovative ways to bypass regulation, which is much slower in reacting to such business model innovation. For example, if self-preferencing is prohibited, platform owners may simply restrict product offerings, which would harm consumers.[42] It is also possible that platform owners would leverage extensive user data to feed sophisticated algorithms for the purpose of dynamic price discrimination or collusion without formal agreement and human interaction, thus evading regulation.[43] Even if the regulation is successful in weakening the dominant Big Tech firms, it is most likely that consumers would switch to other leading platform owners rather than support the emerging small competitors. The substitutes to the Big Tech firms are Chinese firms Baidu, Alibaba, Weibo, and Tencent, which already capture substantial global market share. As illustrated with the case of TikTok, which is owned by Chinese firm ByteDance and listed 1 billion users in 2021, it is probably not in the best interest of legislators in the United States to have consumers adopt Chinese substitutes. Start-ups in the United States have limited ability and incentives to contest the Big Tech firms considering the challenges of accumulating an installed base of users and in light of the winner-takes-all dynamics that would leave most of them lagging behind the emerging leader. It is quite challenging for policymakers to dismantle the power of the Big Tech firms without penalizing innovative firms.[44]

The proposed legislation in the EU following the Digital Markets Act[45] offers a paradigm shift, but can be considered lax compared to that advanced in the United States. It specifies when a platform owner can be considered a gatekeeper that limits competition and acts unfairly. It also details self-executing measures that such a gatekeeper must implement in order to meet obligations under the EU antitrust law, including procedures for independent audit and for initiating a market investigation that can result in fines and penalties in case of non-compliance. Still, it implies trust in the platform owner to regulate itself. This policy acknowledges the prevalent practice whereby platform owners dictate rules to various ecosystem members, and favor their own services and products due to their profit-maximizing objectives. Hence, the Digital Markets Act contends that dominant firms must not behave as pure profit-maximizers, but rather allow for proper functioning of the market while pursuing their objectives. Nevertheless, the proposed legislation is too vague and imprecise to be useful and is unclear about when the regulatory power of the platform owner violates antitrust laws. It is clearer about the requirement to avoid discrimination, exclusion, and impeding of free competition. But, as a recent review reveals, "it does not hold water in substance ... [and] employ[s] a pop culture cliché that with great power comes great responsibility ... It fails to pinpoint what is distinctive or particularly problematic about digital platforms."[46] This is because the claim that platform owners have extra obligations as regulators is not anchored in applicable antitrust laws, while the labeling "regulators" itself incorrectly implies that they are not subject to antitrust scrutiny by public regulators. It is unclear to what extent the special responsibility of the platform owners goes beyond uncompetitive behavior to concern the broader impact on society. In fact, some have argued that the regulation should not distinguish the digital domain from non-digital sectors, since "digital" is primarily a distribution channel rather than a way to delineate a market where competition takes place. It is, further, unclear whether the required responsibilities apply to platform owners that are not yet dominant. This is in part because of the lack of objective criteria and perceived arbitrariness in determining who is considered a gatekeeper and because of the implied threshold that distinguishes gatekeepers from other owners of digital platform ecosystems.[47]

More fundamentally, the legislation disregards the fact that ecosystem competition revolves around disruptive innovation rather than price setting, so current conditions cannot serve for predicting the future outcomes of competition.[48] Indeed, the Digital Markets Act takes a static approach to regulate a dynamic phenomenon, so the regulation "runs the risk of stifling innovation, harming consumers, and derailing the competitive process it aims to protect."[49] In particular, a concern has been raised that some obligations under this Act, e.g., the requirement for interoperability, may increase consumer cost while degrading quality. One advantage of the proposed EU legislation compared with the American proposal is that it allows for faster adaptation to changing business practices, as it shifts from ex post antitrust enforcement to ex ante regulatory compliance.[50] One major disadvantage is that it involves relatively weak enforcement that relies mostly on the internal code of conduct and voluntary compliance of platform owners. However, platform owners lack the incentive to self-regulate, with research showing that self-regulation can be effective only under the threat of sanctions from traditional regulation and law enforcement.[51] As demonstrated with the examples of Amazon, Meta, Google, and Apple, profit-maximizing motives tend to override such voluntary compliance, so there are no high hopes that the new regulation would restrain platform owners.

Other proposed remedies merely extend traditional antitrust laws and regulation, which may have worked well in traditional markets but are less effective in fostering competition in digital markets. Furthermore, while specifying penalties for violation, these measures do not offer incentives for the Big Tech firms to behave nicely, nor do they provide incentives for start-ups to take on the Big Tech firms. In fact, the proposed regulation can be considered economically harmful, may hinder innovation, and may penalize the most agile and disruptive firms.[52] Another concern relates to the complexity of the legislation, which delays swift reaction and is difficult to enforce given budgetary constraints of the authorities. This would favor simpler rules of conduct and relaxing the need to demonstrate harm caused to consumers on a case-by-case basis.[53]

Moreover, the work conditions of employees have not been part of this conversation, and to the extent that platform owners face divestitures and other challenges to their competitive advantage, their employees are unlikely to gain from that. Only in December 2021 did the European Commission publish a draft of its legislation calling on digital platform owners such as Uber and Deliveroo to abolish fake freelance work and grant their employees minimum wage and social benefits. The Commission acknowledged that digital platform owners "have used grey zones in our legislation [and] all possible ambiguities to develop their business models, resulting in a misclassification of millions of workers."[54] Nevertheless, platform owners can easily identify new ways to exploit legal loopholes as they refine their business models, because the profit-maximizing behavior of the platform owners has been taken for granted with no attempt to rectify it.

In conclusion, governments have failed to adjust and adapt their approaches for evaluating market distortions and their consequent damages to competition and consumers.[55] If regulation and antitrust laws are to restrain dominant platform owners, legislators and the courts must revisit and expand traditional market definitions, broaden the perspective on anticompetitive actions and their effects, e.g., with respect to acquisitions of innovative start-ups, and meanwhile develop remedies that leverage both regulation and antitrust action.[56] Unfortunately, platform ecosystems evolve much faster than the regulatory and legislative systems. The proposed reforms and revisions of the regulations and laws that focus on anticompetitive behavior may actually disadvantage consumers by increasing prices and reducing quality and innovation. However, given the complexity of the proposed regulation and corresponding laws and considering the budgetary constraints of the enforcement authorities, the conservative approach of the judiciary system is likely to prevail, with a limited increase in the number of cases deliberated in courts and their prolonged legal procedures. Under such conditions, the anticompetitive behavior of platform owners is unlikely to perish, and most stakeholders would continue to suffer the consequences.

3.3 REGULATING DATA PROTECTION AND PRIVACY

One area where regulation has made some strides in the defense against platform owners is data protection. Regulators have not been blind to the battle for data privacy and have begun to take a stand. The EU introduced the most rigorous policy with the GDPR.[57] The main purpose of the GDPR is to improve users' control over their personal data and furnish a supportive regulatory environment by specifying how firms should collect, store, protect, and process personal data. It underscores transparency and individuals' rights to access, modify, and delete their personal data as well as object to automated decisions. Based on this regulation, Meta and Google were sued in 2018 for their use of forced consent for data processing. According to enforcementtracker.com, by March 2022, more than 1,000 GDPR fines were issued with a cumulative amount of $1,575 million. Nevertheless, scrutiny would reveal that 65 percent of these fines were for violation of data access and gathering, with only 25 percent for improper protection policies, and 3 percent for improper usage.[58] It seems, then, that enforcement has focused on the measurable rather than on the most important violations. The fines per breached data record are negligible relative to the value that the violating firms gained from the violation, and thus have not deterred firms such as Google and Amazon. But the GDPR fines can be devastating to small to mid-size firms.[59] The administrative burden for meeting the regulatory requirements of the GDPR is overly demanding for small firms, and thus reinforces the competitive advantage of the Big Tech firms that have sufficient resources to meet these requirements. Furthermore, platform owners such as Google, Apple, and Meta have used the GDPR as an excuse to further restrict data access, which has harmed their complementors, and hence consumers.[60] For example, wearing the privacy protector hat, Google limited advertisers and developers' use of cookies, while Apple constrained app developers' ability to leverage user data generated by their apps under its new iOS 14.5 operating system. Paradoxically, restrictive privacy laws that aim to limit platform owners' ability to penetrate consumers' minds and misuse their data have only strengthened the grip of the Big Tech firms.

Although the GDPR seeks to regulate data protection and privacy, unlike the Digital Markets Act that imposes responsibilities on gatekeepers to restrict their market power and maintain efficient competition, it does not require the platform owners to follow special guidelines for restricting their use and abuse of users' data, which often serves as the basis for their market power. For instance, although the acquisition of WhatsApp by Meta received a green light from antitrust authorities on the grounds that it would not undermine competition in the advertising market, one could make the case that the consolidation of personal data with users' Facebook profiles could negatively impact user privacy. But the European Commission refused to consider the potential effect of this acquisition on privacy protection, because "[a]ny privacy related concerns flowing from the increased concentration of data within the control of Facebook as a result of the [t]ransaction do not fall within the scope of the EU competition law rules but within the scope of the EU data protection rules."[61] The WhatsApp acquisition was also cleared by the Federal Trade Commission in the United States. Two years after that acquisition, in 2016, Facebook updated its terms of service to allow it to link WhatsApp users' phone numbers to their Facebook profiles, and process that data. The main concern is that platforms owned by Meta, Amazon, Google, and Apple, among others, can control and manipulate the content available to users and thus shape public opinion and purchasing behavior. These platforms also engage in profiling of users and exercise control over freedom of speech in the digital media, although they are not subject to the editorial responsibilities of the printed press. The challenge with restraining this power is that unlike price and quality, data protection and privacy have not been considered by legislators and the courts as elements contributing to consumer welfare, and thus subject to antitrust regulation and enforcement. In the Facebook–WhatsApp case, it has been suggested that "the errors in the Commission's assessment can be explained by its failure to account for the economic role of privacy and the disclosure of personal data in its analysis of anticompetitive harm."[62] Indeed, current competition laws and data protection regulation can generate inconsistent outcomes, which calls for better alignment of these two branches of law.[63]

The rights to privacy and data protection are established by European human rights instruments such as the European Convention on Human Rights (ECHR) and the EU Charter of Fundamental Rights. However, these provide only normative foundations for legislative and regulatory measures, which have not been developed yet. The ECHR establishes that systematic collection and storing of publicly available personal data can interfere with the right to a private life irrespective of whether this data is sensitive. Although the convention does not elaborate on aggregation of personal data from various sources, some court rulings suggest that such data integration may reveal personal information that gives users the impression that they are under constant surveillance, leaving them vulnerable to influence and discrimination by platform owners.[64] Nevertheless, under this convention, it is not the obligation of private entities but the government's obligation to protect data and privacy. It makes sense to extend the application of this law and consequent responsibility to platform owners, but this has not been pursued yet. Hence, although the protection norms have been outlined, the EU data protection legislation requires further development and elaboration to support an effective response to violations. It has been suggested that firms that engage in big data accumulation and mining should be subject to designated regulatory measures for data protection and privacy as well as to more vigorous enforcement of data protection laws. Indeed, in April 2022, the EU introduced the Digital Services Act that targets the Big Tech platforms and imposes responsibilities for coping with false news and hate speech as well as providing regulators and independent researchers with access to platform data and algorithms, which could enhance transparency and accountability.[65] The implications of this latest legislation are yet to be seen.

Data protection and privacy laws in the United States lag behind the European legislation. Nevertheless, the House Judiciary Subcommittee has acknowledged that "[t]he best evidence of platform market power … is not prices charged but rather the degree to which platforms have

eroded consumer privacy without prompting a response from the market
… degrading user privacy can reasonably be considered equivalent to a
monopolist's decision to increase prices or reduce product quality."[66] This
report points out that users have no choice but to surrender personal
data given the central role that digital platforms play in the provision of
common services. It recognizes that consumers are typically unaware
of the extensive data collection and its use for eliciting behavior that is
misaligned with their preferences or best interest. Quite surprisingly,
then, although the 450-page report offers numerous recommendations,
none relates to securing data protection and privacy.

The hope was that the GDPR would compensate for this shortcoming of
the US legislation. This is because the GDPR is exterritorial and designed
to protect the data of European citizens regardless of the country in
which such data is accumulated and stored. The expectation has been
that the Big Tech firms would adjust their processes to meet the GDPR
requirements even when operating in the United States. However, in
addition to the limitations of the GDPR as noted above, the Big Tech
firms managed to use the GDPR to their advantage. According to
Paul-Olivier Dehaye, a privacy expert who helped uncover Facebook's
Cambridge Analytica scandal, "Big companies like Facebook are 10
steps ahead of everyone else, and 100 steps ahead of regulators."[67] The
Big Tech firms employed lobbyists to convince policymakers around the
world not to adopt GDPR-like laws. Furthermore, out of thousands of
privacy complaints, only a few have been deliberated in courts because
of the limited number of legal staff members with relevant expertise in
the judiciary agencies and disagreements about interpretations of the law.
Meanwhile, the Big Tech firms proceeded with almost no objection. For
example, Meta continued to deploy its facial recognition technology and
shared data between WhatsApp and the Facebook platform. Indeed, the
Big Tech firms began to ask users for consent, although regulators are not
convinced that users understand how their personal data is used once
giving consent. In turn, Google forced its publishers to verify user consent
if wishing to continue using its advertising services, which enabled
it to take over that data for its own use, claiming that these changes

were necessary under the GDPR. Jason Kint, chief executive of Digital Content Next, a trade body for publishers, commented: "It forced our members to give Google secondary use of their data. They're supposed to be transparent about what they're using the data for, but we don't really know."[68] While in the EU firms were not allowed to collect user data without explicit consent, the US legislation gave firms the right to collect such data without permission by default.

Nevertheless, one of the key challenges for legislators and enforcement authorities concerns not data collection but the use of personal data. As algorithms become more pervasive, sophisticated, and less transparent, they make it difficult to figure out when platform owners cause harm to users, e.g., by personalizing prices, discriminating users, manipulating choices, and preferencing options.[69] Algorithms empowered by artificial intelligence and machine learning reach decisions automatically via trial and error, so it is difficult to demonstrate intent to harm and establish liability, especially when several independent algorithms interact. Antitrust laws were formulated with human agents in mind, and entail explicit intent and evidence of human involvement, e.g., communication between conspiring parties. This makes it challenging for authorities to detect and react to anticompetitive behavior and to violations of data protection and privacy regulations.[70] In particular, current antitrust laws have yet to answer questions such as whether an algorithm can act in bad faith, whether an algorithm that acts as the user's agent has fiduciary duties toward that user, and who is responsible for the harm caused by an algorithm or algorithms involved in parallel conduct. In some cases, even the designer of the algorithm may be unaware of the implications of the algorithm's outcomes.[71]

Protective legislation and regulation have yet to be updated to cope with the economic and social challenges imposed by digital platforms, such as those concerning the protection of users' personal data, which has been exploited by platform owners.[72] The needed regulation relating to data protection and privacy calls for establishing dedicated government units with capabilities and expertise beyond those currently available to regulatory authorities. Interestingly, firms have already recognized that regulatory constraints are likely to impose a roadblock for the adoption of artificial intelligence technology.[73] Yet such regulation is still lagging behind recent technological developments. It is possible that regulators may need to specify constraints for algorithm developers beyond the typical constraints imposed on corporate conduct. This has been the case in China, where the Communist Party's leader Xi Jinping launched "Operation Cyber Sword" to regain control over China's Big Tech firms. The regulation forbids these firms from using algorithms that violate Chinese laws, requires firms to inform their users about algorithms, and enables their users to override their recommendations and remove tags that are analyzed by algorithms, while increasing transparency and accountability.[74] Consequently, Alibaba, Tencent, and JD.com, which heavily rely on these algorithms to make profit, announced that they will lay off about 15 percent of their employees.[75] Meanwhile, in the Western world, the Big Tech firms keep leading this waltz with the regulators.

Facebook's name change to Meta marks the next step in this dance of maneuvers, which creates new challenges for not only ensuring data protection and privacy but also for defending users' free choice. The metaverse—the next version of the Internet—is expected to provide a three-dimensional virtual environment that can potentially engage all senses while augmenting reality. If successfully launched, this virtual universe, already used in video gaming, may dominate all aspects of human interaction. In such an environment, the Big Tech firms can collect far more personal information using invasive sensors, and use more effective manipulations to deceive users, who would not be able to tell whether they are interacting with humans or profit-seeking machines. Meta has been working on patents for behavioral analysis of users based on physical and biometric data, including uncontrollable and awareness-free facial gestures, body movements, and brainwaves, which can soon make humans machine-readable. Another series of patents covers the monetization of the metaverse using aggressive advertising, service fees, and sponsorships based on such personal data.[76] Most alarming, however, is the possible leveraging of such profound physical and behavioral data by predatory algorithms that have been shown to apply manipulation and cause psychological harm for the sake of profit making.

Current legislation cannot cope with personal avatars and complex digital identities that encompass artificial intelligence, physical biometry, and refined emotional reactions. It is difficult to imagine preemptive or reactive legislation emerging in the coming decade to halt this sophisticated assault on data privacy and free choice. Regulation is also helpless in supporting efforts to monitor and control undesirable content and inappropriate behavior in real time, as such monitoring attempts would undermine privacy. Moreover, the metaverse's virtual economy will likely reinforce the hegemony of platform owners as well as reflect and even intensify economic inequality, because low-income users would lack the infrastructure and purchasing power needed to take part in virtual exchanges and upgrade their avatars.

With the revelation of the "Facebook Files" by whistle-blower Frances Haugen, it has become evident that some Big Tech firms mean harm. In the words of Roger McNamee, former advisor to Mark Zuckerberg:

> Facebook will not fix itself. All incentives direct the company to stay on its current course … our democracy and government are too broken to rein in any large company … CEOs like Zuckerberg claim they have a mandate to maximize shareholder value …, a single-minded focus on profits and shareholder value can be deployed to justify all manner of sins. Zuckerberg differs from other CEOs in the scope of harm his company can inflict and the absolute control he enjoys, but given the culture of business in America, I suspect far too many CEOs envy his power, and in his shoes would pursue the same strategy … At this point, any defense of continued self-regulation seems naïve … Internet platforms have launched an attack against democracy and self-determination.[77]

Indeed, the available remedies to protect society from the grip of platform owners and loss of privacy and free choice have fallen short of achieving these objectives.

3.4 ENHANCING SUSTAINABILITY

There have been extensive efforts to promote environmental sustainability in past years. Agenda 2030 of the United Nations and the adoption of the SDGs in 2015 demonstrate efforts to promote norms of sustainability and outline priorities. Although all SDGs are geared toward enhancing sustainability, some SDGs detail plans for responsible consumption and production (SDG 12), affordable clean energy (SDG 7), climate action (SDG 13), and protecting life on land (SDG 15) and in the sea (SDG 14), which are all related to the design of the economic system. In particular, SDG 12 calls for systemic alignment of production and consumption patterns following a normative vision for sustainability, with SDG 12.3 setting an ambitious target of cutting the per capita global food waste by retailers and consumers by 50 percent by 2030 compared to 2015. Responsible consumption helps conserve natural resources, reduce pollution, protect nature, and save extinct species. However, beyond a commitment for waste management, SDG 12 shows no commitment to reducing upstream resource consumption and distribution.[78] It also does not specify upper limits for consumption.[79] More importantly, SDG 12 may fail to restrict overconsumption because it counters the consumeristic culture fostered by firms' advertising campaigns and because it comes at the expense of consumers' short-term utility, i.e., their immediate benefits. Furthermore, there is an inherent contradiction between SDG 12, which is expected to reduce countries' GDP levels, and SDG 8, which calls for decent working conditions and continued economic growth in terms of increases in GDP. The reason for this contradiction is that it is challenging to identify alternatives to economic growth as a means for reducing poverty. Nevertheless, alternative approaches have been proposed for enhancing environmental sustainability and well-being at the expense of economic growth in search for a balance.[80] Such reformist approaches call for less centralized institutions or institutions that are decoupled from economic growth objectives, as well as for bottom-up grassroots initiatives and reorganization of the economy.[81] However, these calls have remained mostly unanswered.

Despite the importance of demand-side approaches for sustainability that concentrate on consumer behavior, public policy has not focused on reducing consumption but on enhancing the efficiency of production processes and making them environmentally friendly.[82] Policy recommendations have centered on agreeing on targets and measures for assessing environmental impact, collecting data, conducting research, and specifying scenarios and models for prediction. Practical recommendations include applying more environmentally friendly farming methods, such as irrigation control, crop rotations, and prudent use of fertilizers,[83] developing resource-efficient public procurement, encouraging firms to exploit resource efficiency potentials, increasing the recycling of materials, and using labels to inform consumers about the use of certain resources in products and about their durability, while striving to limit further growth in GDP in the long term.[84] This supply-side approach has not managed to reduce consumption of resources in most cases, however, because it focuses on enhancing efficiency rather than on ecological effectiveness. Even if an innovation can make a product more efficient to produce and operate, a rebound effect may generate a negative net effect on the environment. For example, an energy-saving LED may have many new uses for which light bulbs have not been previously used, or a fuel-saving engine may be installed in a heavy SUV. Specifically, between 1975 and 2013, the adjusted fuel economy in miles per gallon has improved by more than 80 percent, but average horsepower has increased by more than 60 percent, with the share of SUVs, vans, and pickup trucks increasing from 20 percent to 45 percent of the car market in the United States.[85] Hence, the technological improvement has in many cases led to increased consumption rather than to reduced use of natural resources.

Another supply-side approach involves developing and introducing products that use substitutes to natural resources. For instance, several biotech firms have developed and begun to offer synthetic cultured lab-grown meat to replace conventional biological meat. As previously noted, livestock farming requires extensive natural resources. In particular, it consumes 70 percent of the world's farmland, while polluting the land, air, and water sources, e.g., it accounts for 30 percent of the methane emissions. Nevertheless, some scrutiny would reveal that the production of cultured meat consumes extensive energy if derived from coal, oil, or natural gas, and that it can release more greenhouse gas emissions than livestock farming. This substitute requires transportation, water for growing protein sources such as soybeans, and waste management. Most likely, cultured meat will compete with plant-based meat substitutes, and some consumers who dislike unnatural food may reject it.[86] It may also create a rebound effect of increased meat consumption. Overall, these approaches cannot undo the overconsumption of natural resources. Another way to reduce emissions is to rely on renewable energy sources such as solar, wind, biomass, hydrothermal, and geothermal energy, which are more ecologically friendly than conventional energy sources, albeit not without limitations.[87]

Since the first United Nations Rio de Janeiro Earth Summit in 1992, the various measures set in the subsequent summits have failed to slow down the rise in consumption of natural resources and limit the degradation of nature. For example, by adopting low-till agriculture techniques, US farmers managed to reduce fuel consumption per ton of grain by 40 percent over a 30-year period.[88] Overall, 30 years of efficiency improvements led to 30 percent reduction in the volume of resources needed for producing one dollar of GDP. Nevertheless, during that period the overall consumption of resources has continued to grow,[89] with overconsumption reaching at least 56 percent above the planet's biocapacity by 2020. Whereas some policies, such as those relating to certified supply chains and protected areas, provide incentives to conserve nature, other economic policies offer incentives to degrade nature, e.g., subsidies related to the use of fossil fuels, fishing, and agriculture.[90]
By now, it has become clear that the eco-efficiency approach has fallen short of making a net positive environmental impact, in part because it has been tied to firms' profit making.[91] The overexploitation of natural resources, pollution, biodiversity loss, and climate change are driven by production policies and patterns of overconsumption, national public policies, international trade, migration, and urbanization, which are

difficult to overturn, although reducing food loss and waste presents an opportunity for restricting some of these undesirable consequences.

Shifting focus to demand-side approaches, advocates of environmental sustainability have often called for "slow consumption"[92] that extends product life cycles, keeps materials in circulation, conserves natural resources, and reduces waste. This can be achieved by reducing the consumption of products, reusing them, and recycling them. Recycling has received the most attention by policymakers, probably because consumers find it easier to adopt. However, recycling often entails substantial investments in collecting, dismantling, and reconstructing materials, including expensive processes of shipping, washing, chopping, and melting waste, which consume much energy and can generate pollution,[93] so the net effect of the $330 billion collection and recycling industry on natural resources may be questioned. Some refer to recycling as a myth because recycling estimates are based on collection rather than on recovery of materials. Even then, the global estimate is 20 percent recycling for materials such as plastic. Along the way, about 50 percent of the general waste finds its way to recycling bins, whereas automated sorting facilities cannot decompose mixed plastic packages, and the degraded quality of the recycled plastic makes it impossible to reuse. Furthermore, the recycling capacity of most nations does not meet the demand or is considered too costly, so much of the recycled waste is exported and finds its way to landfills, incineration plants, or the ocean. The waste management challenge has become more acute after the leading importers of waste, such as China and Malaysia, banned incoming recycled waste in recent years. Countries such as Germany that achieved relatively high recycling capacity have witnessed increasing consumption and generation of waste.[94]

The conclusion is that a meaningful reduction in consumption requires change in consumer behavior and lifestyle, in line with the idea of voluntary simplicity: "choosing to limit material consumption in order to free one's resources, primarily money and time, to seek satisfaction through non-material aspects of life."[95] Consumption can be reduced when consumers either avoid consumption of a product altogether (reject) or limit their consumption when avoidance is impossible (restrict). Finally, a product can be reused by restoring or repurposing it rather than disposing it (reclaim).[96] Patagonia is an example of a firm in the apparel industry that has promoted such consumer behavior. Its product lifecycle initiative encourages consumers to restrict consumption, repair damaged products, reuse them by exchanging or reselling them, and finally recycle them once they finished their lifecycle. Consumption can be further limited by means of collaborative consumption and sharing. In collaborative consumption, consumers coordinate the purchasing and allocation of the goods to minimize waste. In sharing, e.g., using car-pooling or ride-sharing services, consumers restrict their ownership by using other consumers' products or services.[97] Consumers can also engage in custodian behavior in which they salvage and safeguard products that would be otherwise discarded, e.g., wearing second-hand clothes.[98] Additionally, reuse of a product entails its repair and searching for new ways of using the product, adapting or repurposing it beyond its original intended use.[99] Finally, in addition to reducing consumption, consumers can boycott harmful products that overuse scarce resources. But boycotting requires effective communication and coordination, which are difficult to achieve.

Needless to say, other than some recycling programs, most of these initiatives are voluntary and unregulated. Another concern is that the change in consumer behavior has not always helped the environment, since, for example, the adoption of scooters and car sharing in cities has often substituted for walks, bike rides, and public transportation rather than reliance on private cars.[100] Indeed, a recent study reveals that shared scooters and bikes emit more carbon dioxide than the transport modes they have replaced.[101] From a policy standpoint, government policies have encouraged consumers to (a) avoid practices that are harmful to the environment, such as food waste, (b) shift to environmentally friendly practices, such as public transportation and cycling, and using low-carbon and recycled materials, and (c) improve their practices, e.g., replace processed food with fresh produce, rely on electric vehicles, etc.[102] Still, these behaviors have not become pervasive.

In recent years, several demand-side models have been proposed, acknowledging that consumers' demand, and hence consumption, is driven by socio-demographics, inequality, and habits[103] as well as by social norms and policies.[104] It has been suggested that policies and consequent behavior should focus on satisfying human needs and on meeting a decent standard of living rather than on inflating and fulfilling superfluous consumption.[105] Superfluous consumption includes the consumption of positional products, such as a Ferrari car, which are luxurious, expensive, and high-status. Such products have been linked to consumers' sense of happiness, but their consumption by the affluent also creates norms and aspirations among lower-income earners, and thus induces overconsumption.[106] Unlike superfluous consumption, necessary consumption that satisfies a real human need shows rapid diminishing returns with consumption.[107] Thus, by adopting a simpler, sufficiency-oriented lifestyle, it is possible to reduce consumption to levels that reside within planetary boundaries yet still satisfy the needs of society. In addition to switching to more energy-efficient solutions, this can be achieved by abstaining from excessively consuming products and services that damage the environment and waste natural resources, as well as by shifting from global to local supply chains.[108] The affluent consumers who are most responsible for overconsumption have not shown a tendency for voluntary change in lifestyle. Whereas affluent consumers are still expected to reduce consumption levels, there is also a need to ensure that the poor can reach a minimum standard of living by specifying low-bound limits for consumption.[109] Reducing resource consumption in affluent countries can help reach decent standards of living in poor countries as well as redistribute consumption within countries.[110]

Neither supply-side nor demand-side approaches for sustainability have been effective to date. An analysis of global trends over the past 50 years reveals a decrease in 14 out of 18 categories of nature's contributions to society's health, wealth, and well-being in areas such as regulation of pollution, climate change, and energy.[111] For the first time in the 15 years since its initiation, the 2020 World Economic Forum survey of economic and business risks has shown that the top five global risks are all environmental: climate change, biodiversity loss, extreme weather, natural disasters, and other human-made environmental disasters. These global risks may cause significant negative impact on several countries or industries within the next ten years.[112] Recent reports have called for "bold and well-defined goals and a credible set of actions to restore the abundance of nature to levels that enable both people and nature to thrive."[113] These reports note that the SDGs for 2030—including mitigating climate change; maintaining the quality of soil, water, and air; and furnishing a resilient basis for food, fuel, and fiber—are unlikely to be met if current trends persist. The reports acknowledge that traditional biodiversity conservation interventions such as protected areas remain important, but that what is needed are actions that can also cope with overconsumption and overexploitation of natural resources that drive the biodiversity loss.[114] They point out that "[u]ntil now, decades of words and warnings have not changed modern human society's business-as-usual trajectory," but "new modelling shows that with urgent action it is still possible to halt loss and reverse the trend of nature's decline."[115]

The United Nations Climate Change Conference convened in Glasgow in November 2021 amid a report revealing that even if all current targets for 2030 were reached, the world would witness a 2.4°C rise in temperatures by the end of the century.[116] This is beyond the stated target of 1.5°C in the 2015 Paris Agreement, and the updated target of 2°C in the 2021 Glasgow agreement (see Figures 3.1–3.3). Such global warming is expected to lead to the dissolution of glaciers, rise of sea level, extreme heat waves, and life-threatening rain, fires, and floods. The inability to agree on drastic measures was in part due to pressure from China and India, which account for 40 percent of the world's greenhouse gas emissions and which sought to retain their coal production. The presence of lobbyist groups did not help either. More than 500 fossil fuel lobbyists representing 100 firms from the oil and gas industry joined as delegates of 27 countries to the Glasgow conference, forming the largest delegation to the conference, and an observer commented: "The presence of hundreds of those being paid to push the toxic interests of polluting fossil fuel companies, will only increase the skepticism of climate activists who see these talks as more evidence of global leaders' dithering and delaying."[117] Furthermore, within three months of its launch during the conference, the UN's Green Investment

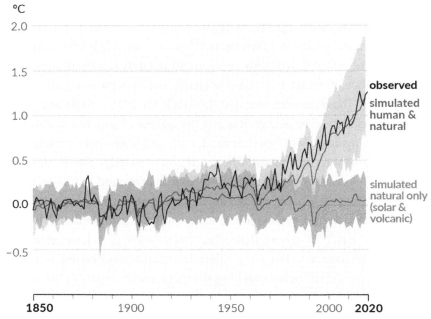

Figure 3.1   *Annual average change in global surface temperature.*

Source: Intergovernmental Panel on Climate Change[a]

a Intergovernmental Panel on Climate Change (2021), Climate change 2021—the physical science basis: summary for policymakers, Working Group I contribution to the Sixth Assessment Report of the Intergovernmental Panel on Climate Change, *IPCC AR6 WGI*, August 7, www.ipcc.ch/report/ar6/wg1/.

Fund was on the brink of failure because the major institutions and banks that had made financial commitments to the fund did not deliver on their promises.[118] Moreover, the conference's commitment to zero greenhouse gas emissions by 2050 is insufficient without a road map to reaching that target and given the lack of sanctions on countries that would not meet their commitments. The UN Secretary-General concluded that the Glasgow conference resolution is not enough to save the planet: "The approved texts are a compromise. They reflect the interests, the conditions, the contradictions and the state of political will in the world today."[119]

Prolonged climate change that influences food availability, including cold spells, droughts, and untimely rains, can facilitate migration, violence, and religious conflict, and eventually structurally modify the

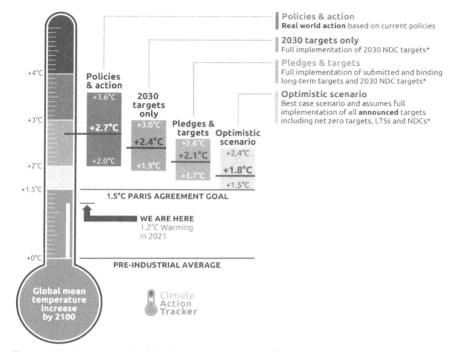

Figure 3.2 *Projections for global temperature increase by 2100.*

Source: Climate Action Tracker[a]

a Climate Action Tracker (2021), *The CAT thermometer*, November, https://climateactiontracker.org/global/cat-thermometer/. Copyright ©2021 by Climate Analytics and NewClimate Institute. All rights reserved.

society experiencing the crisis.[120] Human-induced climate change has damaged nature and undermined the physical and mental health of people throughout the world, disrupting economic and social conditions, and increasing food- and water-borne diseases, with more frequent and extreme events causing mortality and morbidity. The impacts have become more complex and difficult to cope with, thus calling for urgent action given the rapidly narrowing window of opportunity.[121] It has become clear that reversing the trends in overconsumption and overexploitation of natural resources entails the cooperation of policymakers, firms, and consumers. And while the former two have shown persistent efforts to develop and implement policies, it is now prime time for consumers to change their behavior, distinguish needs

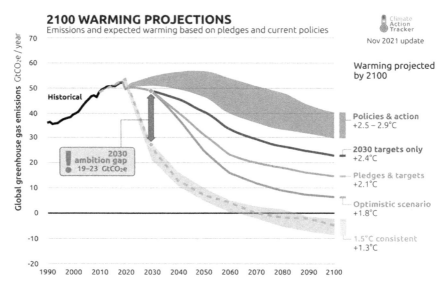

Figure 3.3   *Global greenhouse gas emission pathway estimates.*

Source: Climate Action Tracker[a]

a   Climate Action Tracker (2021), *2100 warming projections: emissions and expected warming based on pledges and current policies*, November, https://climateactiontrac ker.org/global/temperatures/. Copyright ©2021 by Climate Analytics and NewClimate Institute. All rights reserved.

from wants, and manage their exposure to advertisements that have fueled consumption.

The ultimate purpose is to secure well-being while engaging in equitable reduction of resource consumption, which is likely to be coupled with some reduction in GDP, i.e., degrowth.[122] However, this is unlikely to happen given the ramifications for the affluent and for the economies of the rich countries, which are likely to experience recession, job loss, collapse of the stock market, and bankruptcies. Hence, participants in the economic system, including capital owners, consumers, and employees, have mutual interest in maintaining capital accumulation, industrialization, economic growth, and increased consumption.[123] The reinforcing effects of superfluous consumption, barriers to sufficiency, and firms' advertising campaigns create feedback loops that leave demand-side solutions to overconsumption at the verge of the theoretical. For these reasons, most previously proposed solutions take economic growth for granted and seek remedies under this constraint. They relate happiness, well-being, and self-determination to economic expansion, cling to the virtues of capitalism, and suggest that the same force that has brought destruction to our planet can save us from its ramifications.[124] Such an approach can be misguided and naïve.

To transform the current economic system would require substantial reforms of public policy, starting with remedies such as investments in green industries and practices, strict eco-taxes, income caps, and guaranteed minimum income, and ending with calls for establishing a socio-ecological state system or a participatory democracy without state intervention in which collective ownership prevents capital accumulation.[125] However, even the most straightforward reforms, such as corrective taxation of resource consumption, are challenging to legislate, as they lack public support, whereas persuasion tactics aimed to convince consumers to voluntarily reduce consumption have had a limited effect.[126] More substantial reforms are unlikely to be implemented in capitalist societies, unless social movements take a stand at times of crisis, such as during the Covid-19 pandemic. Even then, it has long been acknowledged that "programs aimed solely at altering consumption attitudes or behaviors are likely to meet limited success. Instead, reducing resource consumption will require a fundamental shift away from self-interested, consumer-oriented values, … to limit consumption in the interest of environmental sustainability."[127] A cultural change and rejection of materialistic and consumeristic perspectives is required to battle overconsumption and its undesirable environmental ramifications. Consumers who adopt a sufficiency or voluntary simplicity lifestyle may regain work-life balance and experience enhancement to their well-being. However, unbundling perceived satisfaction from consumption patterns and culture is not an easy task.[128] Focusing campaigns on environmental benefits or changing particular consumer beliefs while ignoring the broader cultural aspects has been shown to have a limited impact.[129] Indeed, the reopening of the economy after temporary closures during the Covid-19 pandemic has been followed by increased consumption, which may have assisted economic growth but not the natural environment. Thus far, no practical solution has been proposed for revisiting the morality and ethics of consumption and for transforming consumers' value orientation. Changing social norms and gathering support for a major shift in consumer behavior is a worthy long-term endeavor but is unlikely to reverse the continuous trend of resource overconsumption and overexploitation in the near term. What, then, can be done? Pope Francis urged "all those who have political and economic responsibilities to act immediately with courage and farsightedness."[130] That is: not much, from a practical standpoint.

3.5   REVISITING GLOBALIZATION

Globalization has fostered economic growth and benefited multinational corporations, but has also facilitated economic inequality, concentration of market power, and overconsumption of resources, while undermining the national and cultural foundations of societies and communities. In light of the public backlash against globalization, several remedies have been proposed, but few were implemented, and none is likely to effectively undo the drawbacks of globalization.

One proposal has been for multinational corporations to incorporate the SDGs in their objectives, resource allocation, and investments in local subsidiaries, which can potentially generate positive externalities in host country communities and promote societal values other than profit generation.[131] But although multinational corporations have the means to impact the communities in which they operate, thus far, their contributions have been mostly limited to donations, educational projects, and volunteering. With few exceptions, these firms lack the incentives to incorporate the SDGs in their corporate agenda, unless this serves their profit maximization goal. One of the fallacies with this approach is that it considers multinational corporations to be not only part of the problem but also part of the solution. In essence, such an approach calls for changing the purpose of for-profit firms so that it underscores moral and ethical values while accommodating the expectations of stakeholders other than shareholders.[132] Proponents of stakeholder theory suggest that being attentive to various stakeholders and developing close relationships with them can support a firm's competitive advantage.[133] However, seeking deep corporate purpose beyond profit making is not free from tradeoffs, dilemmas, and pitfalls, which only a few firms can manage well.[134] There are not many honorable businesses that seek mutually beneficial transactions that benefit all parties involved.[135] Attempting to change the DNA of firms by promoting a pro-SDG organizational purpose that often conflicts with their shareholders' interests is likely to encounter resistance and would have little effect on the harms of globalization. For instance, amid deteriorating financial performance and after Unilever released the "Cook Clever, Waste Less" campaign for its Hellmann's brand, one of its main shareholders complained that "a company which feels that it has to define the purpose of Hellmann's mayonnaise has in our view clearly lost the plot" and that Unilever should be "focusing on the fundamentals of the business."[136]

The recent appeal to corporations is not the first attempt to involve firms in shaping the face of globalization. Back in 2002, Secretary-General Kofi Annan initiated the United Nations' Global Compact, bringing together UN agencies, nongovernmental organizations, and more than 12,000 firms, with the aim of establishing an equitable and inclusive global market following principles that advocate human rights, labor standards, and environmentally friendly practices.[137] Nevertheless, this did not prevent the unfolding drawbacks of globalization. Globalization has been effective in creating wealth, but the challenge has been to distribute this wealth fairly and to make the benefits of globalization evenly accessible, while accommodating local cultures and societal aspirations.

Another approach places the responsibility with governments and regulators, calling for policies that protect the environment and promote societal cohesion while imposing taxes on multinational corporations and restricting global capital movement and trade. Nevertheless, institutions such as the World Trade Organization, which promote institutional policies that facilitate international trade, have failed to protect environmental and societal values. Realizing this, the OECD has called for progressive taxation, corporate governance regulation, policies for competition and for social protection, labor market activation, scrutiny of financial markets, and development of physical, educational, and health systems, while battling tax avoidance, bribery, and corruption.[138] The main purpose of the OECD in promoting such international standards and agreements has been to strengthen the perceived legitimacy of globalization and making a more persuasive case for economic integration. Nonetheless, in devising such policies and standards, it could not reach a consensus given the diverse interests of member states. Even independently, many governments have been incapable of balancing economic forces and free trade with societal and environmental motives. For example, national policies such as protectionism have been bypassed by multinational corporations that flexibly relocated their activities across various countries.[139] In fact, it is globalization that has weakened governments by precluding intervention and implementation of independent macroeconomic policies. Low-income countries with weak and undiversified production and those lacking well-functioning institutions have remained most vulnerable.[140]

Another drawback of globalization concerns the global integration and complexity of the international financial system and the interdependent yet fragile global supply chain. This intricate networked infrastructure can promptly dissipate a local crisis at a global scale. No remedies have been offered to this drawback beyond developing firms' risk management practices. It has been suggested that governments and firms should analyze the implications of systemic risks, explore various scenarios with respect to institutions and firms' abilities to contain their expected impacts, and redesign governance systems to better cope with the risks of globalization. However, no specific suggestions for revision have been offered.[141] Clearly, greater transparency and accountability of financial institutions and firms' practices can help foresee emerging crises and perhaps allow for managing them more effectively. But the most honest conclusion, as pointed out in a recent OECD report, is that "we urgently need to fix globalization, but we don't fully know how to do so."[142] It has been suggested that instead of attempting to repair globalization, policymakers should seek to rebuild it in a way that secures an equal distribution of benefits, preserves public goods such as natural resources, and protects the interests of citizens and employees.[143] The open question, then, is how to rebuild a system without destroying it first.

3.6 PUTTING THE SOLUTIONS IN PERSPECTIVE

Several approaches have been taken to remedy the drawbacks of the modern economic system, yet they have met with limited success. In some cases, solutions have been proposed, but not implemented. In others, the implemented solutions turned out to be ineffective, had marginal impact, or generated unexpected negative consequences for stakeholders. Each solution was designed to solve a specific problem, so some solutions conflict with others, as in the case of those relating to antitrust laws versus protection of data privacy, responsible consumption of resources versus decent employment conditions and economic growth, and labor market regulation versus flexibility. The global nature of the economy calls for coordinated action, but countries have pursued their divergent interests, which often led to a compromise or shifted the problem from one nation to another without solving it. The primary means for attempting to solve these problems involve regulation, legislation, and enforcement via the judiciary system. This approach has been taken when proposing taxation and welfare schemes to reduce economic inequality, when promoting antitrust regulation to restrain platform owners, when legislating data privacy laws to protect consumers, when offering resolutions that shield the environment and enhance its sustainability, or when signing multilateral trade treaties that seek to benefit from globalization. Common to these instances is the fact that the proposed approach has been too slow and ineffective in responding to the concerns that elicited it. It may take years to respond to an emerging undesirable corporate behavior, such as that relating to platform owners' leveraging of their market power. Then it is likely to take years to advance proposals, reach international consensus, and craft the needed regulation or legislation, which often suffers from loopholes. Finally, even if the necessary resources and personnel are allocated, it takes time to prosecute and enforce specific violations. Furthermore, the courts are often deliberating on offenses that are easy to trace rather than those that cause most harm. In turn, firms can engage in business model innovation and swiftly adjust their business practices to preempt, bypass, or overcome the set defenses. Even when remedies are applied, as in the case of restraining platform owners, such remedies do not necessarily benefit consumers and competitors, and in some cases leave them worse off.

Whereas some solutions require government intervention, others call for changes to firms' policies or in consumer behavior. However, governments often face policy tradeoffs, whereas firms' profit-making agenda conflicts with the required measures. Expecting firms to regulate themselves is simply naïve and, in any case, ineffective. The expected change from consumers has remained voluntary and conflicts with their self-interested behavior. Furthermore, no overarching solution has been proposed to engage the various stakeholders to address the myriad interdependent problems that have transpired in the economic system. By now, the window of opportunity for incremental or isolated solutions to specific problems has closed. This does not mean that traditional approaches for remedying these problems should cease, only that more effective alternatives should be considered.

Previously attempted solutions aimed to fix the current economic system rather than to offer an alternative to it. None of the solutions manages to solve the underlying cause of the problems that this system has fostered. Interestingly, there is a common cause to all these problems, which has to do with the greed motive and firms' profit maximization objectives. As illustrated, even when firms seek to accommodate societal values such as equality and environmental sustainability, their profit maximization goal diverts or overrides these efforts. History has shown that firms will not adopt altruistic or prosocial behavior if it is not aligned with their wealth creation mission. Greed is not a unique characteristic of firms, however. Consumers also seek to maximize their utility, while governments are interested in accumulating geopolitical power by increasing national growth and wealth. Greed has been regarded as an inherent human trait. Perhaps because of that, policymakers have considered it a force majeure and have not attempted to offer solutions that remedy it. Although greed is not limited to firms, it is firms, and especially platform owners, that have emerged as the dominant force in ecosystems, and hence have been most entrepreneurial in capitalizing on opportunities. It seems that society has been serving firms rather than having firms and institutions serve society. Organization theory suggests that firms have come about to enhance the scale and efficiency of production, and thus contribute to value creation and to the prosperity of society. But we ended up with an economic system that creates wealth for a few at the expense of many—a system that concentrates power and wealth, yet exploits society and its communities, destroys the planet, and places us at a risk of annihilation.

Advocates of globalization, open economy, aggressive capitalism, and consumerism claim that the consequences of known alternatives, such as communism and state-owned enterprises, are worse, and they are probably right. However, even to them, it has become clear that the cosmetic surgery and patching up of the existing economic system are insufficient remedies. It has become clear that incremental changes to the economic system are unlikely to resolve its known deficiencies. An effective solution would bring a radical change in conventional economic thinking, challenge long-held assumptions, relax mental and physical constraints, and offer a design for a new economic system that places societal values at the core. But what should be the nature of such a system, what would be its underlying logic, and how can it overcome the greed-driven tendency of humankind? How can it be implemented? Until now, these questions have remained unanswered.

NOTES

1 Montiel, I., Cuervo-Cazurra, A., Park, J., Antolın-Lopez, R., & Husted, B.W. (2021), "Implementing the United Nations' Sustainable Development Goals in international business," *Journal of International Business Studies*, 52, pp. 999–1030.

2 United Nations (2015), "Transforming our world: the 2030 Agenda for Sustainable Development," https://sustainabledevelopment.un.org/post2015/transformingourworld.

3 Global Reporting Initiative, United Nations Global Compact, & World Business Council for Sustainable Development (2015), *SDG Compass: the guide for business action on the SDGs*, https://sdgcompass.org/wp-content/uploads/2015/12/019104_SDG_Compass_Guide_2015.pdf.

4 B Lab & United Nations Global Compact (2020), *SDG action manager*, www.unglobalcompact.org/take-action/sdg-action-manager, accessed November 4, 2021.

5 Montiel, I., Cuervo-Cazurra, A., Park, J., Antolın-Lopez, R., & Husted, B.W. (2021), "Implementing the United Nations' Sustainable Development Goals in international business," *Journal of International Business Studies*, 52, pp. 999–1030.

6 Easterly, W. (2015), "The SDGs should stand for senseless, dreamy, garbled," *Foreign Policy*, https://foreignpolicy.com/2015/09/28/the-sdgs-are-utopian-and-worthless-mdgs-developmentrise-of-the-rest/; Nilsson, M., Chisholm, E., Griggs, D., Howden-Chapman, P., McCollum, D., Messerli, P., Neumann, B., Stevance, A.S., Visbeck, M., & Stafford-Smith, M. (2018), "Mapping interactions between the sustainable development goals: lessons learned and ways forward," *Sustainability Science*, 13(6), pp. 1489–1503.

7 Piketty, T. (2014), *Capital in the twenty-first century*, Harvard University Press.

8 Clausing, K., Saez, E., & Zucman, G. (2020), "Ending corporate tax avoidance and tax competition: a plan to collect the tax deficit of multinationals," Independent Commission for the Reform of International Reform, September 24, www.icrict.com/you-should-also-read/2020/9/24/ending-corporate-tax-avoidance-and-tax-competition-a-plan-to-collect-the-tax-deficit-of-multinationals1.

9 Dabla-Norris, E., Kochhar, K., Suphaphiphat, N., Ricka, F., & Tsounta, E. (2015), *Causes and consequences of income inequality: a global perspective*, International Monetary Fund, June.

10 Gneiting, U., Lusiani, N., & Tamir, I. (2020), *Power, profits and the pandemic: from corporate extraction for the few to an economy that works for all*, OXFAM Briefing Paper, http://hdl.handle.net/10546/621044.

11 Gilens, M., & Page, B.I. (2014), "Testing theories of American politics: elites, interest groups, and average citizens," *Perspectives on Politics*, 12(3), pp. 564–581.

12 International Federation of Accountants & Association of Chartered Certified Accountants (2019), G20 public trust in tax, surveying public trust in G20 tax systems, January.

13 Rappeport, A., & Alderman, L. (2021), "Global deal to end tax havens moves ahead as nations back 15% rate," *New York Times*, October 8, www.nytimes.com/2021/10/08/business/oecd-global-minimum-tax.html.

14 E.g., Gibson, C.B. (in press), "Investing in communities: forging new ground in corporate community co-development through relational and psychological pathways," *Academy of Management Journal*.

15 United Nations (2020), *World social report 2020: inequality in a rapidly changing world*, Department of Economic and Social Affairs.

16 Lawson, M., Chan, M.-K., Rhodes, F., Butt, A.P., Marriott, A., Ehmke, E., Jacobs, D., Seghers, J., Atienza, J., & Gowland, R. (2019), "Public good or private wealth?," *OXFAM Briefing Paper*, https://oxfamilibrary.openrepository.com/bitstream/handle/10546/620599/bp-public-good-or-private-wealth-210119-summ-en.pdf.

17 United Nations (2020), *World social report 2020: inequality in a rapidly changing world*, Department of Economic and Social Affairs.

18 Economic Policy Institute (2021), *Unions help reduce disparities and strengthen our democracy*, April 23, https://files.epi.org/uploads/226030.pdf.

19 Shierholz, H. (2019), "Working people have been thwarted in their efforts to bargain for better wages by attacks on unions," Economic Policy Institute, August 27, www.epi.org/publication/labor-day-2019-collective-bargaining/.

20 United Nations (2020), *World social report 2020: inequality in a rapidly changing world*, Department of Economic and Social Affairs.

21 Horowitz, J., Igielnik, R., & Arditi, T. (2020), *Most Americans say there is too much economic inequality in the U.S., but fewer than half call it a top priority*, Pew Research Center, January 9, www.pewresearch.org/social-trends/wp-content/uploads/sites/3/2020/01/PSDT_01.09.20_economic-inequailty_FULL.pdf.

22 Phillips, B. (2020), *How to fight inequality (and why that fight needs you)*, Polity Press.

23 Piketty, T. (2014), *Capital in the twenty-first century*, Harvard University Press.

24 Parker, K., Minkin, R., & Bennet, J. (2020), *Economic fallout from Covid-19 continues to hit lower-income Americans the hardest*, Pew Research Center, September 24, www.pewresearch.org/social-trends/2020/09/24/economic-fallout-from-covid-19-continues-to-hit-lower-income-americans-the-hardest/.

25 United Nations Conference on Trade and Development (UNCTAD) (2021), "Competition law, policy and regulation in the digital era," Trade and Development Commission, United Nations, 19th Session, Item 5, Geneva, 7–9 July.

26 Baldwin, R., Cave, M., & Lodge, M. (2011), *Understanding regulation: theory, strategy, and practice*, 2nd edn., Oxford University Press.

27 Hovenkamp, H. (2021), "Antitrust and platform monopoly," *Yale Law Journal*, 130(8), pp. 1952–2050.

28 Petit, N., & Teece, D. (2021), "Innovating big tech firms and competition policy: favoring dynamic over static competition," *Industrial and Corporate Change*, 30(5), pp. 1168–1198.

29 Coyle, D. (2018), "Practical competition policy implications of digital platforms," *Antitrust Law Journal*, pp. 835–860.

30 Biggar, D., & Heimler, A. (2021), "Antitrust policy towards digital platforms and the economic foundation of competition law," *Industrial and Corporate Change*, 30(5), pp. 1230–1258.

31 Jenny, F. (2021), "Changing the way we think: competition, platforms and ecosystems," *Journal of Antitrust Enforcement*, 9, pp. 1–18.

32 Coyle, D. (2018), "Practical competition policy implications of digital platforms," *Antitrust Law Journal*, pp. 835–860.

33 Nadler, J., & Cicilline, D.N. (2020), Investigation of competition in digital markets—majority staff report and recommendations, Subcommittee on Antitrust, Commercial and Administrative Law of the Committee on the Judiciary, US House of Representatives, United States.

34 Hovenkamp, H. (2021), "Antitrust and platform monopoly," *Yale Law Journal*, 130(8), pp. 1952–2050.

35 Jenny, F. (2021), "Changing the way we think: competition, platforms and ecosystems," *Journal of Antitrust Enforcement*, 9, pp. 1–18, p. 11.

36 Portuese, A. (2021), *The Digital Markets Act: European precautionary antitrust*, Information Technology & Innovation Foundation, May 2021.

37 Hovenkamp, H. (2021), "Antitrust and platform monopoly," *Yale Law Journal*, 130(8), pp. 1952–2050.

38 Moss, D.L., Gundlach, G.T., & Krotz, T.T. (2021), *Market power and digital business ecosystems: assessing the impact of economic and business complexity on competition and remedies*, American Antitrust Institute, June, http://dx.doi.org/10.2139/ssrn.3864470.

39 Chayka, K. (2021), "How Epic Games made a dent in Apple's app store domination," *New Yorker*, September 17, www.newyorker.com/culture/infinite-scroll/how-epic-games-made-a-dent-in-apples-app-store-domination.

40 Sokol, D.D., & Van Alstyne, M. (2021), "The rising risk of platform regulation," *MIT Sloan Management Review*, 62(2), pp. 6A–10A.

41 McGee, P. (2021), "Apple's privacy changes create windfall for its own advertising business," *Financial Times*, October 16, www.ft.com/content/074b881f-a931-4986-888e-2ac53e286b9d.

42 Portuese, A. (2021), *The Digital Markets Act: European precautionary antitrust*, Information Technology & Innovation Foundation, May.

43 Coyle, D. (2018), "Practical competition policy implications of digital platforms," *Antitrust Law Journal*, pp. 835–860.

44 Lamoreaux, N. (2019), "The problem of bigness: from Standard Oil to Google," *Journal of Economic Perspectives*, 33(3), pp. 94–117.

45 Crémer, J., de Montjoye, Y.-A., & Schweitzer, H. (2019), *Competition policy for the digital era*, European Commission, April 2019; European Commission (2020), *Proposal for a regulation of the European Parliament and of the Council on contestable and fair markets in the digital sector (Digital Markets Act)*, December 15, https://eur-lex.europa.eu/legal-content/EN/TXT/HTML/?uri=CELEX:52020PC0842&rid=8.

46 Dunne, N. (2021), "Platforms as regulators," *Journal of Antitrust Enforcement*, 9, pp. 244–269, pp. 251, 260, 268.

47 Portuese, A. (2021), *The Digital Markets Act: European precautionary antitrust*, Information Technology & Innovation Foundation, May.

48 Jenny, F. (2021), "Changing the way we think: competition, platforms and ecosystems," *Journal of Antitrust Enforcement*, 9, pp. 1–18.

49 Portuese, A. (2021), *The Digital Markets Act: European precautionary antitrust*, Information Technology & Innovation Foundation, May, p. 4.

50 Coyle, D. (2018), "Practical competition policy implications of digital platforms," *Antitrust Law Journal*, pp. 835–860; Portuese, A. (2021), *The Digital Markets Act: European precautionary antitrust*, Information Technology & Innovation Foundation, May.

51 Cusumano, M., Gawer, A., & Yoffie, D. (2021), "Can self-regulation save digital platforms?," *Industrial and Corporate Change*, 30(5), pp. 1259–1285.

52 Portuese, A. (2021), *The Digital Markets Act: European precautionary antitrust*, Information Technology & Innovation Foundation, May.

53 Schweitzer, H., & Welker, R. (2019), "Competition policy for the digital era," *CPI Antitrust Chronicle*, December, pp. 2–10.

54 Rankin, J. (2021), "Gig economy workers to get employee rights under EU proposals," *The Guardian*, December 9, www.theguardian.com/business/ 2021/dec/09/gig-economy-workers-to-get-employee-rights-under-eu-proposals.

55 Coyle, D. (2018), "Practical competition policy implications of digital platforms," *Antitrust Law Journal*, pp. 835–860.

56 Moss, D.L., Gundlach, G.T., & Krotz, T.T. (2021), *Market power and digital business ecosystems: assessing the impact of economic and business complexity on competition and remedies*, American Antitrust Institute, June, http:// dx.doi.org/10.2139/ssrn.3864470.

57 GDPR (2016), General Data Protection Regulation 2016/679, *Official Journal of the European Union*, L119/1, May 4, https://eur-lex.europa.eu/legal-cont ent/EN/TXT/PDF/?uri=CELEX:32016R0679.

58 CMS (2021), *GDPR enforcement tracker report*, 2nd edn., May, https://cms. law/en/media/local/cms-hs/files/publications/publications/gdpr-enforcem ent-tracker-report-2021-executive-summary.

59 Haraminac, D. (2021), "GDPR and the increasing cost of cybersecurity," *Value Examiner*, July–August, pp. 19–23.

60 Damien, G., Theano, K., & Dimitrios, K. (2021), "GDPR myopia: how a well-intended regulation ended up favouring large online platforms—the case of ad tech," *European Competition Journal*, 17(1), pp. 47–92.

61 Jenny, F. (2021), "Changing the way we think: competition, platforms and ecosystems," *Journal of Antitrust Enforcement*, 9, pp. 1–18.

62 Deutscher, E. (2019), "How to measure privacy-related consumer harm in merger analysis? A critical reassessment of the EU Commission's merger control in data-driven markets," Chapter 6 in Lundqvist, B., & Gal, M. (eds.), *Competition law for the digital economy*, Elgar Publishing, pp. 173–211.

63 Kira, B., Sinha, V., & Srinivasan, S. (2021), "Regulating digital platforms: bridging the gap between competition policy and data protection," *Industrial and Corporate Change*, 30(5), pp. 1337–1360.

64 Lynskey, O. (2019), "Grappling with 'data power': normative nudges from data protection and privacy," *Theoretical Inquiries in Law*, 20(1), pp. 189–220.

65 European Commission (2022), *The Digital Services Act package*, April 23, https://digital-strategy.ec.europa.eu/en/policies/digital-services-act-package.

66 Nadler, J., & Cicilline, D.N. (2020), Investigation of competition in digital markets—majority staff report and recommendations, Subcommittee on

Antitrust, Commercial and Administrative Law of the Committee on the Judiciary, US House of Representatives, United States, pp. 51–52.

67 Scott, M., Cerulus, L., & Overly, S. (2019), "How Silicon Valley gamed Europe's privacy rules," *Politico*, May 22, www.politico.eu/article/europe-data-protection-gdpr-general-data-protection-regulation-facebook-google/.

68 Scott, M., Cerulus, L., & Overly, S. (2019), "How Silicon Valley gamed Europe's privacy rules," *Politico*, May 22, www.politico.eu/article/europe-data-protection-gdpr-general-data-protection-regulation-facebook-google/.

69 Competition and Markets Authority (2021), *Algorithms: how they can reduce competition and harm consumers*, Research and analysis final report, January 19, www.gov.uk/government/publications/algorithms-how-they-can-reduce-competition-and-harm-consumers/algorithms-how-they-can-reduce-comp etition-and-harm-consumers.

70 Abrardi, L., Cambini, C., & Rondi, L. (2021), "Artificial intelligence, firms and consumer behavior: a survey," *Journal of Economic Surveys*, pp. 1–23.

71 Gal, M.S., & Elkin-Koren, N. (2017), "Algorithmic consumers," *Harvard Journal of Law & Technology*, 30(2), pp. 309–353.

72 Jacobides, M.G., & Lianos, I. (2021), "Ecosystems and competition law in theory and practice," *Industrial and Corporate Change*, 30(5), pp. 1199–1229.

73 Protiviti (2019), *Competing in the cognitive age: how companies will transform their businesses and drive value through advanced AI*, www.protiviti.com/sites/default/files/united_states/insights/ai-ml-global-study-protiviti.pdf.

74 Kharpal, A. (2022), "China's next regulatory target—algorithms, the secret of many tech giants' success," CNBC, January 7, www.cnbc.com/2022/01/07/china-to-regulate-tech-giants-algorithms-in-unprecedented-move.html.

75 Zhu, J., Yang, Y., & Tian, Y.L. (2022), "Reeling from China's crackdown, Alibaba and Tencent readying big job cuts-sources," Reuters, March 16, www.reuters.com/technology/reeling-chinas-crackdown-alibaba-tencent-readying-big-job-cuts-sources-2022-03-16/.

76 Murphy, H. (2022), "Facebook patents reveal how it intends to cash in on metaverse," *Financial Times*, January 18, www.ft.com/content/76d40aac-034e-4e0b-95eb-c5d34146f647.

77 McNamee, R. (2021), "Facebook will not fix itself," *Time*, October 7, https://time.com/6104863/facebook-regulation-roger-mcnamee/.

78 Bengtsson, M., Alfredsson, E., Cohen, M., Lorek, S., & Schroeder, P. (2018), "Transforming systems of consumption and production for achieving the sustainable development goals: moving beyond efficiency," *Sustainability Science*, 13, pp. 1533–1547.

79 Vladimirova, K. (2020), "Justice concerns in SDG 12: the problem of missing consumption limits," in McNeill, L. (ed.), *Transitioning to responsible consumption and production*, Transitioning to Sustainability Series 12, MDPI, pp. 187–224.

80 E.g., Jackson, T. (2021), *Post growth—life after capitalism*, Polity Press.

81 E.g., Wiedmann, T., Lenzen, M., Keyßer, L.T., & Steinberger, J.K. (2020), "Scientists' warning on affluence," *Nature Communications*, 11, p. 3107, https://doi.org/10.1038/s41467-020-16941-y.

82 Brosius, N., Fernandez, K.V., & Cherrier, H. (2013), "Reacquiring consumer waste: treasure in our trash?," *Journal of Public Policy & Marketing*, 32(Fall), pp. 286–301.

83 United Nations Food and Agriculture Organization (2015), *Status of the world's soil resources*, www.fao.org/3/i5199e/I5199E.pdf.

84 Giljum, S., Hinterberger, F., Bruckner, M., Burger, E., Frühmann, J., Lutter, S., Pirgmaier, E., Polzin, C., Waxwender, H., Kernegger, L., & Warhurst, M. (2009), *Overconsumption? Our use of the world's natural resources*, Sustainable Europe Research Institute, September 9, https://cdn.friendsoftheearth.uk/sites/default/files/downloads/overconsumption.pdf?_ga=2.196529449.48826011.1633979826-654500657.1633979826.

85 Plumer, B. (2013), "Cars in the U.S. are more fuel-efficient than ever. Here's how it happened," *The Washington Post*, December 13, www.washingtonpost.com/news/wonk/wp/2013/12/13/cars-in-the-u-s-are-more-fuel-efficient-than-ever-heres-how-it-happened/.

86 Chriki, S., & Hocquette, J.-F. (2020), "The myth of cultured meat: a review," *Frontiers in Nutrition*, 7, pp. 1–9.

87 Sayed, E.T., Wilberforce, T., Elsaid, K., Rabaia, M.K.H., Abdelkareem, M.A., Chae, K.J., & Olabi, A.G. (2021), "A critical review on environmental impacts of renewable energy systems and mitigation strategies: wind, hydro, biomass and geothermal," *Science of the Total Environment*, 766, p. 144505.

88 Brown, L.R. (2006), *Plan B 2.0: rescuing a planet under stress and a civilization in trouble*, W.W. Norton.

89 Giljum, S., Hinterberger, F., Bruckner, M., Burger, E., Frühmann, J., Lutter, S., Pirgmaier, E., Polzin, C., Waxwender, H., Kernegger, L., & Warhurst, M. (2009), *Overconsumption? Our use of the world's natural resources*, Sustainable Europe Research Institute, September 9, https://cdn.friendsoftheearth.uk/sites/default/files/downloads/overconsumption.pdf?_ga=2.196529449.48826011.1633979826-654500657.1633979826.

90 Almond, R.E.A., Grooten, M., & Petersen, T. (eds.) (2020), *Living planet report 2020—bending the curve of biodiversity loss*, WWF.

91 Geyer, R. (2021), *The business of less: the role of companies and households on a planet in peril*, Routledge.

92 Cooper, T. (2005), "Slower consumption reflections on product life spans and the 'throwaway society,'" *Journal of Industrial Ecology*, 9(1/2), pp. 51–67.

93 Barr, S., Gilg, A.W., & Ford, N.J. (2001), "Differences between household waste reduction, reuse and recycling behavior: a study of reported behaviors, intentions and explanatory variables," *Environmental & Waste Management*, 4(2), pp. 69–82.

94 Franklin-Wallis, O. (2019), " 'Plastic recycling is a myth': what really happens to your rubbish?," *The Guardian*, August 17, www.theguardian.com/envi ronment/2019/aug/17/plastic-recycling-myth-what-really-happens-your-rubbish; Wecker, K. (2018), "Plastic waste and the recycling myth," DW.com, October 12, www.dw.com/en/plastic-waste-and-the-recycling-myth/a-45746 469.

95 Huneke, M.E. (2005), "The face of the un-consumer: an empirical examination of the practice of voluntary simplicity in the United States," *Psychology & Marketing*, 22(7), pp. 527–550, p. 528.

96 Lee, M., Roux, D., Cherrier, H., & Cova, B. (2011), "Anticonsumption and consumer resistance: concepts, concerns, conflicts and convergence," *European Journal of Marketing*, 45(11/12), pp. 1680–1687.

97 Belk, R. (2014), "You are what you can access: sharing and collaborative consumption online," *Journal of Business Research*, 67(8), pp. 1595–1600.

98 Cherrier, H. (2010), "Custodian behavior: a material expression of anti-consumerism," *Consumption, Markets and Culture*, 13(3), pp. 259–272.

99 Scott, K.A., & Weaver, T.S. (2018), "The intersection of sustainable consumption and anticonsumption: repurposing to extend product life spans," *Journal of Public Policy & Marketing*, 37(2), pp. 291–305.

100 E.g., Sustrans (2021), "Our position on e-scooters," October 25, www.sustr ans.org.uk/our-blog/policy-positions/all/all/our-position-on-e-scooters; Van Hout, N. (2021), "Electric scooters: owning vs sharing," *Swifty Scooters*, February 22, https://swiftyscooters.com/blogs/journal/electric-scooter-own ing-vs-sharing.

101 Reck, D.J., Martin, H., & Axhausen, K.W. (2022), "Mode choice, substitution patterns and environmental impacts of shared and personal micro-mobility," *Transportation Research Part D*, 102, pp. 1–18.

102 Creutzig, F., Roy, J., Lamb, W.F., Azevedo, I.M.L., Bruine de Bruin, W., Dalkmann, H., Edelenbosch, O.Y., Geels, F.W., Grubler, A., Hepburn, C., Hertwich, E.G., Khosla, R., Mattauch, L., Minx, J.C., Ramakrishnan, A., Rao, N.D., Steinberger, J.K., Tavoni, M., Ürge-Vorsatz, D., & Weber, E.U. (2018), "Towards demand-side solutions for mitigating climate change," *Nature Climate Change*, 8, pp. 260–271.

103 Shove, E. (2010), "Beyond the ABC: climate change policy and theories of social change," *Environment and Planning A: Economy and Space*, 42, pp. 1273–1285.

104 Nyborg, K., Anderies, J.M., Dannenberg, A., Lindahl, T., Schill, C., Schlüter, M., Adger, W.N., Arrow, K.J., Barrett, S., Carpenter, S., Chapin, S.F., Crépin, A.-S., Daily, G., Ehrlich, P., Folke, C., Jager, W., Kautsky, N., Levin, S.A., Jacob, O., Stephen, M., Marten, P., Brian, S., Elke, W., Weber, U., Wilen, J., Xepapadeas, A., & de Zeeuw, A. (2016), "Social norms as solutions," *Science*, 354, pp. 42–43.

105 Rao, N.D., & Min, J. (2018), "Decent living standards: material prerequisites for human wellbeing," *Social Indicators Research*, 138, pp. 225–244.

106 Wiedmann, T., Lenzen, M., Keyßer, L.T., & Steinberger, J.K. (2020), "Scientists' warning on affluence," *Nature Communications*, 11, p. 3107, https://doi.org/10.1038/s41467-020-16941-y.

107 O'Neill, D.W., Fanning, A.L., Lamb, W.F., & Steinberger, J.K. (2018), "A good life for all within planetary boundaries," *Nature Sustainability*, 1, pp. 88–95.

108 Alexander, S. (2015), *Sufficiency economy: enough, for everyone, forever*, Simplicity Institute; O'Neill, D.W., Fanning, A.L., Lamb, W.F., & Steinberger, J.K. (2018), "A good life for all within planetary boundaries," *Nature Sustainability*, 1, pp. 88–95; Wiedmann, T., Lenzen, M., Keyßer, L.T., & Steinberger, J.K. (2020), "Scientists' warning on affluence," *Nature Communications*, 11, p. 3107, https://doi.org/10.1038/s41467-020-16941-y.

109 Di Giulio, A., & Fuchs, D. (2014), "Sustainable consumption corridors: concept, objections, and responses," *GAIA Ecological Perspectives for Science and Society*, 23, pp. 184–192; Spangenberg, J.H. (2014), "Institutional change for strong sustainable consumption: sustainable consumption and the degrowth economy," *Sustainability: Science, Practice, & Policy*, 10, pp. 62–77; Vladimirova, K. (2020), "Justice concerns in SDG 12: the problem of missing consumption limits," in McNeill, L. (ed.), *Transitioning to responsible consumption and production*, Transitioning to Sustainability Series 12, MDPI, pp. 187–224.

110 Lockyer, J. (2017), "Community, commons, and degrowth at Dancing Rabbit Ecovillage," *Journal of Political Ecology*, 24, pp. 519–542; Rao, N.D., Min, J., & Mastrucci, A. (2019), "Energy requirements for decent living in India, Brazil and South Africa," *Nature Energy*, 4, pp. 1025–1032; Trainer, T. (2019), "Remaking settlements for sustainability: the simpler way," *Journal of Political Ecology*, 26(1), pp. 202–223.

111 Díaz, S., Settele, J., Brondízio, E.S., Ngo, H.T., Agard, J., et al. (2019), "Pervasive human-driven decline of life on Earth points to the need for transformative change," *Science*, 366, p. eaax3100.

112 Almond, R.E.A., Grooten, M., & Petersen, T. (eds.) (2020), *Living planet report 2020—bending the curve of biodiversity loss*, WWF.

113 Mace, G.M., Barrett, M., Burgess, N.D., Cornell, S.E., Freeman, R., Grooten, M., & Purvis, A. (2018), "Aiming higher to bend the curve of biodiversity loss," *Nature Sustainability*, 1, pp. 448–451.

114 Grooten, M., & Almond, R.E.A. (eds.) (2018), *Living planet report*, WWF.

115 Almond, R.E.A., Grooten, M., & Petersen, T. (eds.) (2020), *Living planet report 2020—bending the curve of biodiversity loss*, WWF, pp. 8, 14.

116 Climate Action Tracker (2021), Warming projections global update, November, https://climateactiontracker.org/documents/997/CAT_2021-11-09_Briefing_Global-Update_Glasgow2030CredibilityGap.pdf.

117 Global Witness (2021), Hundreds of fossil fuel lobbyists flooding COP26 climate talks, November 8, www.globalwitness.org/en/press-releases/hundreds-fossil-fuel-lobbyists-flooding-cop26-climate-talks.

118 Talman, K., & Temple-West, P. (2022), "Climate ETF on brink of failure after UN summit launch," *Financial Times*, February 18, www.ft.com/content/84196790-2030-44d7-988c-b6e3408f9b4b.

119 United Nations (2021), Glasgow compromise not enough to save planet, Secretary-General says, urging continued fight against climate crisis as world steps into "emergency mode," November 13, www.un.org/press/en/2021/sgsm21022.doc.htm.

120 Ulus, T., & Ellenbaum, R. (2021), "How long and how strong must a climatic anomaly be in order to evoke a social transformation? Historical and contemporaneous case studies," *Humanities and Social Science Communications*, 8(252), pp. 1–12.

121 Intergovernmental Panel on Climate Change (2022), Climate change 2022—impact, adaptation and vulnerability, Working Group II contribution to the Sixth Assessment Report of the Intergovernmental Panel on Climate

Change, *IPCC AR6 WGI*, April 12, www.ipcc.ch/report/sixth-assessment-rep ort-working-group-ii/.

122 Hickel, J. (2020), *Less is more: how degrowth will save the world*, Penguin Random House; Wiedmann, T., Lenzen, M., Keyßer, L.T., & Steinberger, J.K. (2020), "Scientists' warning on affluence," *Nature Communications*, 11, p. 3107, https://doi.org/10.1038/s41467-020-16941-y.

123 Wiedmann, T., Lenzen, M., Keyßer, L.T., & Steinberger, J.K. (2020), "Scientists' warning on affluence," *Nature Communications*, 11, p. 3107, https://doi.org/10.1038/s41467-020-16941-y.

124 Terzi, A. (2022), *Growth for good: reshaping capitalism to save humanity from climate catastrophe*, Harvard University Press.

125 Alexander, S., & Rutherford, J. (2014), *The deep green alternative: debating strategies of transition*, Simplicity Institute; Alexander, S., & Gleeson, B. (2019), *Degrowth in the suburbs: a radical urban imaginary*, Springer; Jackson, T. (2017), *Prosperity without growth: foundations for the economy of tomorrow*, Earthscan.

126 Brown, P.M., & Cameron, L.D. (2000), "What can be done to reduce overconsumption?," *Ecological Economics*, 32, pp. 27–41.

127 Brown, P.M., & Cameron, L.D. (2000), "What can be done to reduce overconsumption?," *Ecological Economics*, 32, pp. 27–41.

128 Waters, J. (2021), "Overconsumption and the environment: should we all stop shopping?," *The Guardian*, May 30, www.theguardian.com/lifeandst yle/2021/may/30/should-we-all-stop-shopping-how-to-end-overconsumpt ion.

129 Stern, P.C., Dietz, T., & Guagnano, G.A. (1995), "The new ecological paradigm in social-psychological context," *Environment and Behavior*, 27, pp. 723–743.

130 *The Herald* (2021), "Pope urges world leaders to act with courage following Cop26 deal," November 14, www.heraldscotland.com/news/national/19716 054.pope-urges-world-leaders-act-courage-following-cop26-deal/.

131 Montiel, I., Cuervo-Cazurra, A., Park, J., Antolın-Lopez, R., & Husted, B.W. (2021), "Implementing the United Nations' Sustainable Development Goals in international business," *Journal of International Business Studies*, 52, pp. 999–1030.

132 Edmans, A. (2020), *Grow the pie: how great companies deliver both purpose and profit*, Cambridge University Press; George, G., Haas, M.R., McGahan, A.M., Schillebeeckx, S.J.D., & Tracey, P. (in press), "Purpose in the for-profit

firm: a review and framework for management research," *Journal of Management*.

133 Harrison, J.S., Bosse, D.A., & Phillips, R.A. (2010), "Managing for stakeholders, stakeholder utility functions, and competitive advantage," *Strategic Management Journal*, 31, pp. 58–74; Jones, T.M., Harrison, J.S., & Felps, W. (2018), "How applying instrumental stakeholder theory can provide sustainable competitive advantage," *Academy of Management Review*, 43, pp. 371–391.

134 Gulati, R. (2022), *Deep purpose: the heart and soul of high-performance companies*, Penguin Business.

135 Otteson, J.R. (2019), *Honorable business: a framework for business in a just and humane society*, Oxford University Press.

136 Evans, J., & Agnew, H. (2022), "Mayonnaise with 'purpose' rebuke shows discontent Unilever is facing," *Financial Times*, January 12, www.ft.com/content/8feb8f98-c6d9-4288-9ce8-9e68be621a60.

137 United Nations (2002), *Global compact*, www.unglobalcompact.org/, accessed November 4, 2021.

138 OECD (2017), *Fixing globalisation: time to make it work for all*, April, https://read.oecd-ilibrary.org/economics/fixing-globalisation-time-to-make-it-work-for-all_9789264275096-en#page2.

139 Gray, J. (1998), *False dawn: the delusions of global capitalism*, Granta Books.

140 Murshed, S.M. (2002), "Perspectives on two phases of globalization," in Murshed, S.M. (ed.), *Globalization, marginalization and development*, Routledge, pp. 1–19.

141 Goldin, I. (2012), "Preparing for the pitfalls of interconnectivity," *IESE Insight* 12, pp. 21–28.

142 OECD (2017), *Fixing globalisation: time to make it work for all*, April, https://read.oecd-ilibrary.org/economics/fixing-globalisation-time-to-make-it-work-for-all_9789264275096-en#page2, p. 4.

143 Pisani-Ferry, J. (2020), "Globalisation needs rebuilding, not just repair," Bruegel, October 29, www.bruegel.org/2020/10/globalisation-needs-rebuilding-not-just-repair/.

CHAPTER FOUR

Laying the foundations for the cooperative economy

DOI: 10.4324/9781003336679-4

The failed efforts to remedy the economic system and mitigate its undesirable consequences for society paint a dire picture of the prospects of promoting economic equality, escaping the grip of dominant platform owners, regaining privacy and private choice, reducing the consumption and overuse of natural resources, and overcoming the caveats of globalization. It all comes down to combating greed and profit maximization. But how can we win in a battle against human nature?

Let me proceed with some optimism. First, the fact that all problems have a common root cause assists in finding a solution. Second, greed and profit maximization are not universally inherent to human nature and are rather reinforced by the design of the current economic system, which can potentially be modified. Therefore, it is possible to design an economic system that is more aligned with societal values and relaxes the constraint imposed by the greed motive. Nevertheless, such design requires more than an incremental modification of the current economic system. Rather, it entails a radical change to its foundation, which is why I call for designing a new economic system, what can be referred to as the cooperative economy.

I proceed by challenging the assumption that individuals are self-interested, driven by greed, and seek to maximize utility. I build my argument in two steps: first identifying pay-it-forward behavior in which recipients of acts of kindness act kindly to others, and then discussing a more general case of prosocial behavior that requires no trigger, i.e., being a recipient of such acts. Pay-it-forward and prosocial behaviors are rather rare in the current economic system but can be reinforced in the cooperative economy. I conclude by outlining the fundamental design principles for the proposed cooperative economy that should be instituted based on prosocial behavior.

4.1 PAYING IT FORWARD VERSUS GREED

The field of strategic management has emerged by challenging some of the core assumptions in economic theory, such as the assumption of perfect competition that, once relaxed, can leave room for firms' efforts to capitalize on market imperfections and gain competitive advantage.[1] Nevertheless, one assumption that has not been seriously challenged concerns the motivations of consumers and vendors. When I was pursuing my undergraduate studies in economics, like many students I followed Hal Varian's seminal textbook on microeconomics.[2] This book clarifies that consumers seek to maximize their utility while vendors seek to maximize their profit. The question is: what does utility mean? Although utility was originally associated with happiness, modern economics has simplified and hence distorted this notion, which came to mean derived value or benefit that can be quantified by the price consumers are willing to pay for a product or service. As for vendors that produce products and provide services, the assumption is clear: "the owners would be interested in maximizing the profits of their firm."[3] The assumptions concerning the maximization of utility and profit suggest that consumer and corporate behaviors are guided by the efforts of self-interested individuals to maximize their personal economic gains. Each participant in this economic system seeks to maximize its own value rather than optimize the collective value of the participants involved in the economic exchange.[4] In fact, followers of transaction cost economics[5] go one step further to assume that individuals behave opportunistically, that is, they pursue self-interest with guile. The implication is that vendors and consumers would use opportunities to increase their utility or profit even if this comes at the expense of others and involves unethical behavior. Indeed, the history of corporate misconduct as well as many of the examples I discussed earlier attest to this reality. For example, an instance of such opportunistic behavior is Meta's algorithms that maximize advertising income while promoting social divide and extreme views that knowingly harm users. Other examples are Amazon's mistreatment of its warehouse employees or its use of the proprietary business information of its marketplace vendors to offer competing products and outmaneuver them. This seems to be a common behavior in the modern economy. Indeed, when vendors realize that competitive advantage is within reach, their opportunistic behavior is expected, and they may even behave immorally. Similarly, consumers who strive to survive can also behave in such a manner.

Proponents of the assumption of self-interested behavior in economics trace it back to *The Wealth of Nations*, which Adam Smith first published in 1776. However, Adam Smith did not make such a strong assumption concerning human selfishness and egoism. In *The Theory of Moral Sentiments*, which he wrote more than a decade earlier, Smith[6] acknowledges that individuals not only look after themselves but also have a natural tendency for empathy towards others. He argues that when individuals show concern for others, they enjoy a sense of perceived approval from society. Smith concludes that a truly virtuous individual is characterized by moral behavior, i.e., reveals prudence, justice, beneficence, and self-command. More recently, Ghoshal and Moran[7] have taken aim at transaction cost economics, noting that the assumption of opportunistic behavior can be a self-fulfilling prophecy. They distinguish *opportunism*, aka greed—an attitude that represents an individual's propensity to behave opportunistically—from *opportunistic behavior*—the observed manifestation of the behavior resulting from such propensity. Accordingly, we can infer that opportunistic behavior is not a universal human trait. It is typical only of greedy individuals. The mistake that economic models make is not in assuming that individuals and firms pursue self-interest and behave opportunistically, but in assuming that *all* individuals and firms potentially do. The other shortcoming is in adopting a narrow perspective that centers on profits and economic utility, while not realizing that once their physical needs are secured, what individuals truly seek is happiness, which can be achieved in various other ways.

We cannot blame economists for these faults, as we ourselves often forget or do not realize that what matters in life is the pursuit of happiness beyond the mere satisfaction of material needs. Although the economics discipline has offered many useful insights, I will share some research evidence that casts doubt about its core assumption. But before I do, let me first offer an intuitive experiment. Find a homeless person or a beggar in your neighborhood or town, and to the extent that you believe that this individual is truly in need, give them five dollars or the equivalent in your local currency. After you have done so, proceed and meet a colleague or a friend and ask them to give you the same amount of money. According to standard economic models, in the first transaction you lost and in the second one you gained, so that you should certainly feel happier with the second transaction than with the first one. But which transaction actually made you feel happier? (You can reply on the cooperativeeconomy.net webpage.) For most people, giving to others is a more fulfilling experience than receiving from others. As the 14th Dalai Lama noted, "If you contribute to other people's happiness, you will find the true goal, the true meaning of life." I will get back to this experiment, but let me first attend to more rigorous research findings.

If the rationale outlined in economics textbooks is indeed characteristic of corporate behavior or more broadly of human nature, we would not expect to observe cooperative behavior whereby vendors assist their competitors or individuals help strangers without expecting reciprocity. Nevertheless, such instances have been documented. For example, in the craft beer industry in the United States, small craft beer producers formed a cohesive community, with established breweries helping new entrants to the industry category with sourcing raw materials and obtaining certifications, by sharing best practices, and by collaborating in marketing and distribution. The owners of the small breweries adopted a paying-it-forward mentality, recalling that they also had received support when entering the business and so felt compelled to help others.[8] Paying-it-forward behavior was also documented in Silicon Valley, where the culture has been to help start-up firms solve technical problems even when they may become potential competitors of the helping firm.[9] At the individual level, it has been shown that in the workplace, after receiving help from a co-worker, an employee is more likely to help another employee without expecting a reward.[10] Similarly, grateful recipients

of help are more likely to give money to needy strangers.[11] The greater
the help received, the greater the help provided to others.[12] Yet paying it
forward is evidenced even in the smallest gestures, such as holding the
door for those arriving next after someone has held the door for you.[13]
In literature, a notable example is Jean Valjean, a former convict in Victor
Hugo's novel *Les Misérables*. Valjean takes shelter with Bishop Myriel but
steals his silverware. After Valjean is captured by the police, the bishop
testifies that he willingly gave the silverware to Valjean and mentions that
Valjean forgot to take two silver candlesticks. Valjean is released, and the
bishop informs Valjean that God spared his life, and that he should use
the silverware to become an honest man. Valjean's gratitude leads to his
transformation into a man who seeks to help others and benefit society.

In all these instances, we witness generalized exchange or indirect
reciprocity whereby a sense of gratitude and group norms guide a
beneficiary to reciprocate not with the benefactor who provided
the benefit, but with other third parties in the community.[14] Stated
differently: individuals who receive voluntary support from someone,
are likely to provide support to someone else. The underlying logic is
that individuals demonstrate kindness to strangers to the extent that
these individuals have been themselves the beneficiaries of such acts
of kindness involving someone else's intentional, voluntary, and costly
efforts. A feeling of gratitude prompts these individuals to repay by being
generous not only to their benefactors but also to third parties in their
community.[15] This facilitates a cascade of kindness in the community.

Why do we observe little of this cooperative behavior in the modern
economy? Well, the paying-it-forward principle is self-reinforcing,
but so is opportunistic behavior. As much as an individual is likely to
repay a favor by showing generosity, victims of opportunistic behavior
are likely to behave selfishly and exploit others after experiencing
such mistreatment themselves.[16] The more individuals observe others
cheating and behaving opportunistically in their community, the more
they perceive opportunistic behavior as acceptable and the more they
tend to become dishonest and behave opportunistically themselves.[17]
The modern economy facilitates moral disengagement by diffusing and

displacing responsibility.[18] In other words, even for individuals that hold moral standards, after they observe or experience opportunistic behavior by others in this system, the belief that everyone behaves opportunistically decouples their moral standards from their actions, so they do not feel distress when behaving opportunistically. Even if an individual departs from that convention and attempts to be generous to others, such cooperation fails to evolve and transpire in the community if no proximate others in that community are willing to reciprocate.[19] Hence, past experience affects the emerging nature of generalized exchange. To the extent that opportunistic behavior is frequent and prevalent in the economic system, it is likely to be self-reinforced and disseminated in that system, which is exactly what we observe in the modern economy.

Regardless of the nature of the reinforced behavior, reciprocity is not an automated reaction to others' acts of kindness or opportunism, but a matter of individuals' perception. In particular, indirect reciprocity emerges only if the preceding acts of kindness were intentional and not driven by a strategic motivation such as building one's reputation.[20] That is, paying-it-forward behavior is more likely when the beneficiary concludes that the benefactor had a genuine intent to act kindly.

Can acts of kindness occur in the modern economic system? It has been shown that social norms of fairness and reciprocity can elicit generosity even in economic systems that otherwise promote self-interested materialistic consumerism.[21] Social norms are "rules and standards that are understood by members of a group, and that guide and/or constrain social behaviors without the force of laws."[22] Therefore, clear norms of reciprocity can counter self-interested behavior in an economic system.[23] When social norms are ambiguous, generalized exchange depends on the perception or belief concerning the behavior of others in the community, but individuals often misperceive such behavior.[24] Interestingly, when concrete information is unavailable, individuals tend to overestimate the generosity of others, and hence are willing to pay more for products or services as well as engage in paying-it-forward behavior, which suggests that individuals are influenced by social motives as much as by self-interest.[25] By observing others' behavior, individuals can learn about prevalent social norms of fairness and reciprocity and are inclined to follow such norms even if they conflict with their personal judgment.[26] Nevertheless, paying it forward is more prevalent in cohesive communities in which individuals maintain social interaction;[27] otherwise, this behavior is likely to transpire only in small groups[28] and be transient.[29] Furthermore, a sense of gratitude was found to be stronger than norms of reciprocity in driving paying-it-forward behavior.[30] Still, the fact that we observe mostly opportunistic behavior in the modern economic system suggests that norms of fairness, kindness, and reciprocity as well as a sense of gratitude in economic exchange are quite rare and insufficient to counter opportunistic behavior in this economic system.

4.2 THE EMERGENCE OF PROSOCIAL BEHAVIOR

Is being a recipient of acts of kindness necessary for individuals to show kindness to strangers? It has been shown that even when they are not direct recipients of acts of kindness, observers of a generous behavior by an individual are inspired to behave generously toward strangers, with this cascade of altruistic behavior spreading from one actor to another to yet another recipient in a community.[31] Taking this one step further, many studies have examined the notion of prosocial behavior, whereby individuals help and promote the welfare of others.[32] Prosocial behavior does not require the actor to be a recipient of benefits from others. There is debate about whether prosocial behavior requires only the intent to help another or rather also necessitates an actual outcome of welfare promotion.[33] Altruism is considered a specific type of prosocial behavior "which is not performed with the expectation of receiving external rewards or avoiding externally produced aversive stimuli or punishments."[34] Examples of altruism include helping a stranger with a flat tire, helping an old neighbor carry their shopping bags, or, as customary in Southern Italy, entering a bar and ordering a "caffè sospeso," whereby a generous customer receives one coffee but pays for two, so another unknown customer who visits the bar and cannot afford to pay for coffee can enjoy it for free.

Another example of altruistic prosocial behavior is Grandma Shula's Cake Project, in Israel. Roey Haviv regularly visited his grandmother in between Covid-19 closures, and one day she asked him to visit other elderly residents who had no family and were lonely. Roey asked the municipality for the contacts of such individuals, his wife baked cakes, and his kids prepared drawings. When Roey realized that his family could only visit ten elderly people per weekend, other families joined the project. Sometimes the elderly would wait for the kids with presents. Eventually, the project was formalized with the municipal school system, which organized baking workshops and encouraged school pupils to volunteer for the project.[35] Such acts of solidarity became common during the pandemic.

Hence, when prosocial behavior is motivated by the pure intent to improve the other's welfare as opposed to receiving some recognition or reward for the behavior, it is considered altruistic. In that sense, altruistic behavior is beneficial to the recipient and costly with respect to the resources invested by the prosocial actor. Another approach associates prosocial behavior with behavior that is viewed positively by the individual's community or society,[36] thus requiring normative approval rather than promotion of welfare per se. This includes contributing to the public good, e.g., reducing the consumption of natural resources and protecting the environment, as in the case of volunteers undertaking beach cleanups or contributing to countryside wildlife and conservation by improving habitats and clearing invasive varieties to allow native species to thrive.

Although most studies demonstrate that individuals' contributions to the public good exceed those that can be explained by self-interest, in addition to such prosocial behavior, these studies document opportunistic behavior.[37] Such opportunistic behavior involves greedy individuals behaving selfishly in self-interest to receive favors without contributing back to the community. Examples include false advertising, hidden costs and unfulfilled promises in the hospitality industry, a mechanic who leverages asymmetric information to overcharge for unnecessary repairs, or a real estate agent who hides known flaws in a property to inflate his or her commission. Such opportunistic behavior can be seen as the flip side of prosocial behavior: whereas prosocial behavior increases others' welfare at one's own expense, opportunistic behavior increases one's own welfare at the expense of others. Overall, researchers report variation in the tendency for prosocial behavior, in departure from the assumption of universal self-interested behavior.[38]

Once we realize that prosocial behavior and opportunistic behavior rest on two ends of the same continuum, the question is: what drives prosocial behavior as opposed to opportunistic behavior? Researchers have identified differences in individuals' preferences, so that some are more inclined to exhibit prosocial behavior than others. A sizable proportion of individuals are willing to forgo some payoffs to benefit others. For example, researchers report variation in tendencies to exhibit prosocial behavior, with 18.7 percent revealing low tendency, 52.8 percent revealing medium tendency, and 29.6 percent revealing high tendency for prosocial behavior, with these tendencies remaining stable from childhood to adolescence.[39] In another example, Fischbacher and Gächter[40] reported that 55 percent of individuals in their experiment were willing to contribute as long as others contributed, 23 percent were free riders who never contributed, and 12 percent increased their contribution with the contributions of others up to a point before reducing it. This illustrates the fact that prosocial behavior can be conditional on the perceived contributions of others. Hence, as illustrated here, although individuals tend to overestimate the contributions of others, as they observe a decline in such contributions, they are likely to adjust their perceptions and reduce their own contributions. This suggests that prosocial behavior is fragile and challenging to maintain. To maintain prosocial behavior, individuals need to avoid contributing to free riders, or exclude free riders that behave opportunistically from the group.[41]

But who is likely to exhibit free riding? More importantly, who is more prone to engage in prosocial behavior? Researchers have identified personality traits that can help predict prosocial behavior. One of these traits is agreeableness, i.e., the individual's orientation toward interpersonal relationships. This trait is indicative of the motivation to cooperate under resource constraints[42] and has been linked to the tendency to help others.[43] However, this trait has been found to predict prosocial behavior in some studies but not in others.[44] More conclusive findings were obtained for the honesty-humility trait, which is part of the HEXACO personality model that also includes emotionality, extraversion, agreeableness, conscientiousness, and openness to experience.[45] This model distinguishes agreeableness—which captures the extent to which an individual is patient, tolerant, lenient, and forgiving, as opposed to ill-tempered, stubborn, confrontational, and vindictive—from honesty-humility—which refers to the extent to which an individual is sincere, not greedy, modest, and fair, as opposed to selfish, pretentious, manipulative, and arrogant. Unlike agreeableness, which is reactive to the behavior of others who may exploit the individual, and thus can be linked to nonretaliation, honesty-humility reveals an active tendency to be fair and genuine when interacting with others, and thus cooperate and avoid exploiting them for personal gain, even when noncooperative behavior can pay off. Individuals who score high on honesty-humility tend to project their inclination to others, and thus form positive social expectations and trust others. Accordingly, this trait can be a better predictor of prosocial behavior than agreeableness. Of the various facets of honesty-humility, fairness and to an extent greed avoidance were found to be positively related to actual prosocial behavior as opposed to self-interested behavior.[46] Accordingly, whereas greed drives opportunistic behavior, it is fairness that facilitates prosocial behavior in the economic system.

Therefore, while in aggregate, individuals do not follow self-interest as predicted by most economic models, some do selfishly pursue utility maximization, while others are prosocial. Thus, individuals characterized by honesty and fairness are expected to exhibit prosocial behavior.

However, the association between honesty and prosocial behavior is contingent on one's sense of certainty. Individuals that feel uncertainty tend to increase group identification[47] and turn to materialism.[48] This makes them less inclined to reflect their trustworthiness on others and form positive social expectations about unknown others, which then undermines the effect of honesty on prosocial behavior.[49] Overall, honest individuals are not unconditionally prosocial. Rather, they are willing to cooperate as long as they perceive others in their community as cooperative.[50]

In addition to personality traits, prosocial behavior is shaped by cultural and institutional factors. For instance, it has been demonstrated that individuals tend to be less intrinsically honest in countries that have experienced rule violations such as corruption, tax evasion, or political fraud. Indeed, in countries in which fraudulent tactics such as rigging elections, nepotism, and embezzlement have been endemic, parents nurture positive attitudes toward corruption and dishonesty as a means to make progress and succeed in life.[51] This suggests that culture and institutions can influence individuals' honesty and hence their tendency to exhibit prosocial behavior. Moreover, although kinship motivates costly cooperation in close clans,[52] impersonal prosocial behavior is more prevalent in countries in which kin-based institutions (organizational forms based on family ties, such as clans, lineages, and kindreds) are less prevalent, so individuals are less socially embedded and committed to their immediate clan, and instead of complying with kinship norms of conformity, obedience, and loyalty, they exhibit impersonal fairness and cooperation with strangers. This is the case in many Western industrialized countries, which are typically affluent, democratic, and have an educated population. Indeed, impersonal prosocial behavior captured by generalized trust and fairness as well as with indicators such as voluntary blood donations has been more prevalent in Western countries that feature less intensive kinship. In these countries, we observe small nuclear households, weak family ties, less conformity, and more individualism.[53] It is important to clarify that in countries characterized by strong interpersonal embeddedness, prosocial behavior may still be prevalent, but it is more likely to be restricted to members of the family or clan rather than directed to strangers. In that case, it takes the form of in-group favoritism, whereby group members seek to advance the welfare of the group at the expense of outgroup members. An example includes hiring an employee or admitting to a university degree program an individual from the same country or town at the expense of a more capable candidate originating from elsewhere. In fact, when a group is in conflict with external groups and is under threat from them, this reinforces cohesion and cooperation within that group,[54] and prompts prosocial behavior toward group members. Within groups, the presence of a dominant prestigious leader whose behavioral cues are followed can reinforce prosocial behavior to the extent that such behavior is promoted by that leader.[55]

Given that in large-scale groups and impersonal societies it is difficult to monitor the prosocial behavior of others, it is puzzling that prosocial behavior has been prevalent in such societies. A possible explanation relates to the role of institutions in administering punishment and establishing reputation for prosocial behavior. Punishing those who do not cooperate or fail to contribute to the public good can eliminate such undesirable behavior.[56] It is even possible to elicit guilt and hence facilitate prosocial behavior among those who violated social norms by informing them about the negative consequences of their undesirable behavior.[57] In turn, sharing information about the relative standing of individuals in the community with respect to their prosocial behavior can reinforce it, as long as dissemination of such information is efficient. For example, in a community in Fiji, members were expected to follow social norms such as contributing to community projects and sharing food. When a member repeatedly failed to follow the norms, that member's family was subject to sanctions by other members, e.g., their crop was looted and their field was torched.[58] Hence, norms of fairness, cooperation, and reciprocity in a community are followed by some individuals who recognize the legitimacy of normative expectations, while others follow them because of rewards and punishment that mitigate self-interest.[59] Nevertheless, reputation, reciprocation, and retribution can reinforce any normative behavior in a community, leaving open the question of why prosocial behavior has become ingrained in the community's culture in the first place.[60]

One explanation for the prevalence of prosocial behavior in large societies has to do with dissemination of prosocial religious beliefs.[61] According to some of those religions, God, as a personified social agent, monitors human behavior and rewards morality or punishes for the mistreatment of others, either in this life or in the afterlife. For example, a primary religious rule in Judaism is "Love your neighbor as yourself" or "Do unto others as you would have them do unto you." The Kabbalah elaborates that an individual can expect to receive from the universe what he or she gives to others and that giving should be covert, with the right intention, unconditional, and with no expectation of reciprocity. Much like Judaism, Christianity and Islam advocate generosity, compassion, sharing, donating, and helping others. In Hinduism and Buddhism, there is no powerful God that punishes or forgives sins. Instead, the universal notion of karma suggests that actions toward others in this life can determine an individual's destiny in the next incarnations. This idea resonates with those who believe that reward and punishment are automatically granted based on the universal laws of creation. Overall, along with the evolution of societal institutions and community norms that exert cultural influence on prosocial behavior, in difficult-to-monitor conditions such as large-scale societies, religious beliefs can reinforce prosocial behavior by consideration of the superior surveillance and sanction by God[62] or by virtue of universal natural laws that establish cause-effect. Hence, genuine religious devotion facilitates cooperation and trust among the religious group's members.[63] Accordingly, several studies have shown that religious beliefs can predict prosocial behavior, and that priming religious motives and spirituality increases prosocial behavior.[64] Although these studies mostly document prosocial behavior within the religious group, such behavior can also be directed to strangers. In particular, believers in karmic religions such as Buddhism have shown greater prosocial behavior within their religious group, while those believing in the afterlife have expressed a tendency for prosocial behavior toward strangers.[65] In sum, religious beliefs influence expectations about the implications of prosocial behavior, and thus facilitate such behavior in society. Finally, prosocial behavior can be facilitated using normative framing. When individuals have moral concerns and seek to act appropriately, they are more likely to engage in pro-environmental behavior, especially when such behavior is also aligned with self-interest.[66] The tendency to exhibit prosocial behavior following normative framing and judgment by the community has been also demonstrated in lab experiments.[67] In contrast, moral disengagement amplifies unethical behavior and reduces prosocial behavior.[68]

But does prosociality pay off? Research on prosocial behavior reveals that it is emotionally beneficial to be prosocial.[69] Prosocial behavior such as donating money to others or volunteering one's time to help others has been shown to increase happiness, with this effect persisting in various cultures and across diverse socio-economic contexts.[70] Prosocial behavior also facilitates a subjective sense of well-being, including greater positive affect (tendency to experience positive emotions and adopt a positive perspective in coping with challenges) and greater life satisfaction, especially when individuals have freedom to choose whether and how to help, feel connected to those they help, and can observe how their help makes a difference.[71] For instance, it has been demonstrated that public service employees who had the opportunity to connect with those who benefited from their prosocial behavior were more motivated and more successful in soliciting donations.[72] Similarly, autonomous motivation relates to positive feelings and greater tendency to help others at the workplace.[73] There is also evidence that individuals who receive help may gain material resources but cannot enhance their sense of self like those who help others.[74] Overall, then, prosocial behavior does pay off, and the emotional benefits of prosocial behavior can reinforce it despite the costs incurred by prosocial individuals.

In conclusion, I started with the observation that the illnesses of the modern economic system are rooted in greed that motivates opportunistic behavior, which tends to be reinforced in that system.

Nevertheless, firms and individuals are not universally and inherently greedy. There are differences in their tendencies to pursue self-interest at the expense of others, with a sizable proportion of individuals exhibiting prosocial behavior that benefits others in their community while generating a sense of happiness. Conscious individuals seek happiness rather than utility or profit. This may explain why in the simple five dollars experiment, you felt better when giving to the needy as opposed to receiving favors from acquaintances. Such prosocial behavior is associated with a sense of fairness and is self-reinforced when observing others who exhibit prosocial behavior in the community or perceiving them as prosocial. Prosocial behavior is also more prevalent in cohesive societies where institutions, norms, culture, and religious beliefs advocate such behavior.

In all economic systems, the pursuit of happiness can take two forms: opportunistic behavior, i.e., self-interested profit maximization, which increases one's welfare at the expense of others, or prosocial behavior, which increases others' welfare at one's own economic expense but also generates emotional benefits to the prosocial actor. The question is whether the design of the economic system rewards opportunistic behavior and penalizes prosocial behavior, or rather the opposite. The incentives in the modern economic system advocate opportunistic behavior and drive out prosocial behavior, so that the balance tilts toward the former. However, to the extent that the economic system would motivate prosocial behavior and exclude greedy individuals, it is possible to overpower opportunistic behavior. It is worth noting that individuals vary in their prosociality tendencies, and even the same individual may exhibit different levels of prosocial behavior in different contexts and under alternative conditions. Nevertheless, what matters for the cooperative economy is the type of prosocial behavior that transpires in economic exchange and whether prosocial behavior dominates opportunistic behavior at the system level. Prosocial behavior enables individuals to cooperate in the fair distribution of value, and thus serves as the essential building block of the cooperative economy.

4.3 GUIDING PRINCIPLES FOR DESIGNING THE COOPERATIVE ECONOMY

The cooperative economy is an ethical, community-driven exchange system that relies on collective action to promote societal values while accounting for resource constraints. Societies may underscore distinct values, including some conflicting values, so it is essential to define which societal values are to be pursued. The cooperative economy advocates a balanced set of societal values that includes equality, well-being, social responsibility, sustainability, fairness, equal opportunities, and personal freedoms such as the right to private property, freedom of occupation, freedom of opinion, and the right to privacy. By dismantling the elements that reinforce opportunistic behavior, the design of the cooperative economy removes the main obstacle to pursuing these societal values. Provided here are several guiding principles that can subdue the greed motive and mitigate opportunistic behavior while promoting prosocial behavior. Notably, the purpose is not to facilitate a broad shift in behavior from opportunistic to prosocial, but to maintain the dominance of prosocial behavior in the context of economic exchange. It is possible that a given individual would behave opportunistically outside of the system in ways that are foreign to the specific application of such behavior in the system. It is sufficient that participants in economic exchange exhibit prosocial behavior that allows for the proper functioning of the system and are perceived as prosocial by other participants. Although the cooperative economy may generate positive externalities that promote prosocial behavior in various contexts beyond its boundaries, this is not its stated purpose. Furthermore, the cooperative economy can be instituted using a platform ecosystem, much like in the modern economic system, as long as the platform owner (referred to here as the platform operator) is prosocial and subjected to restrictions that limit its opportunistic behavior. The principles outlined below are designed to enhance economic equality and shift power from the platform operator to users, while protecting users' interests, restricting the overuse and abuse of natural resources, and restraining the harms of globalization. These principles include the following: community focus, semi-open system, subsidizing the needy, consumption per need, free choice, reasonable vendor earning, fair competition, quality assurance, individual differences, respectful employment, sustainability, leveraging technology, rebalanced ownership, transparency, and symbiosis (see Box 4.1 for short explanations).

Many of these principles extend the notion of social responsibility, which has thus far centered on CSR, to encompass the social responsibilities of all stakeholders, namely the platform operator, consumers, vendors, and employees. CSR refers to firms' internal initiatives aimed at promoting positive social change by such means as enhancing production methods to reduce undesirable environmental impact, investing in the infrastructure of local communities, and engaging in philanthropy.[75] Researchers have focused on firms' responsibilities, paying less attention to the responsibilities of other stakeholders in striving for the same aims. Some researchers have acknowledged that the firm and its stakeholders are mutually committed and engage in interdependent activities in the process of value creation.[76] Such value goes beyond that accumulated by shareholders or other stakeholders to mean social welfare in the broader sense.[77] Nevertheless, the discussion has been limited to stakeholders' commitments to the firm[78] rather than to their broader responsibilities for society. The cooperative economy calls for social responsibility from all stakeholders. This includes platform social responsibility (PSR), vendor social responsibility (VSR), consumer social responsibility (CNSR), and employee social responsibility (ESR). The responsibilities of each stakeholder group vary. For instance, vendors should commit to incorporating environmental-friendly production processes and restricting their profits, whereas consumers should commit to limiting their consumption. Having each stakeholder group fulfill its responsibilities ensures that social welfare is served and joint value is created and then fairly distributed. The social responsibilities of stakeholders in the cooperative economy are embodied in the design principles that I discuss next.

BOX 4.1 PRINCIPLES OF THE COOPERATIVE ECONOMY

1. **Community focus**—The economy is organized as a constellation of self-sufficient and cohesive local communities to maintain proximity and market efficiency while facilitating prosocial behavior

2. **Semi-open system**—To maintain its integrity, the system welcomes any vendor or consumer who follows the system's rules, while excluding those exhibiting opportunistic behavior

3. **Subsidizing the needy**—High-income consumers subsidize low-income consumers via differential pricing that relies on mutual responsibility and balances purchasing power

4. **Consumption per need**—The system serves needs rather than desires, restricts excessive consumption, prohibits advertising, facilitates donations, and reduces waste, thus limiting overconsumption

5. **Free choice**—Participants follow individual preferences in consumption and occupation, while restricting external influences

6. **Reasonable vendor earning**—Profit is capped, with excess profit redistributed to consumers

7. **Fair competition**—The platform operator cannot compete with vendors, while market access is guaranteed to new vendors, thus fostering entrepreneurship

8. **Quality assurance**—There are strict requirements for quality standards and sustainability objectives, with consumers providing quality assessments for screening and prioritizing vendors

9. **Individual differences**—Consumers are profiled to exclude the greedy; discriminating based on income; otherwise respecting diversity and promoting professional aspirations and individual choice, while ensuring mutual support

10. **Respectful employment**—The system reduces pay differences in the workplace, ensures benefits packages to employees,

and creates a respectful work environment that enhances job satisfaction

11. **Sustainability**—The system prioritizes and excludes vendors based on their sustainability index, imposes consumption limits, and reuses resources by facilitating exchange of goods among consumers

12. **Leveraging technology**—Technology is used to serve societal values, promote prosocial behavior, and secure the interests of stakeholders, rather than benefit the platform operator at the stakeholders' expense

13. **Rebalanced ownership**—Non-tradable platform shares are distributed at equal proportions to active consumers, vendors, and employees, but not to other shareholders

14. **Transparency**—The platform builds trust via transparency, including inspection of algorithms

15. **Symbiosis**—The cooperative economy operates alongside the current economic system, which continues to serve non-members

Community focus. Unlike the global scope of our current economic system with its caveats, to elicit prosocial behavior the cooperative economy must be organized around local communities. These communities are social units that are each characterized by a confined geographical area and shared identity, norms, and values, which support physical interaction among consumers as well as between consumers and vendors. Nevertheless, communities that exhibit cohesion on some dimensions may be diverse on others, and while the social context shapes economic exchange, it is the embeddedness in interpersonal and interorganizational network relations that complements social norms and values in driving behavior.[79] This communality structure is expected to facilitate in-group prosocial behavior, but the question is: what should be the boundaries of the community? On the one hand, the community should be large enough to strive for self-sufficiency and to support a minimum volume of transactions that makes the market efficient. On the other hand, the community should not be so large that it hinders physical interaction and creates a sense of alienation that undermines cohesiveness. Hence, at the outset, it is advisable to rely on established communities in small towns, with each functioning as a cohesive social unit. Eventually, for practical reasons, a community can be specified for a large metropolitan area, such as the cities of London, Paris, and New York, or for a region such as the 26 sovereign cantons of Switzerland, the 20 regions of Italy, and the 50 states of the United States. International trade, i.e., imports and exports across countries, as well as commerce between regions within a country is possible, but geographical proximity should be prioritized. Furthermore, it is mostly vendors that would source raw materials and ingredients rather than consumers who would purchase foreign products and services through the system. The community focus limits exposure to some deficiencies of globalization, such as fragility of the supply chain and excessive transportation, while promoting prosocial behavior. A remaining question is how a community-focused grassroots initiative can mitigate grand challenges on a global scale. In that regard, recent research has revealed the power of connected communities whose efforts scale up to effectively cope with societal grand challenges.[80] Because it will be implemented as a digital platform system, scaling up the cooperative community can be rather straightforward.

Semi-open system. The economic system should be open to any consumer or vendor who adheres to its rules. This is an application of the more general principle of clearly defined boundaries for common-pool resources, whereby external unentitled parties are excluded from the system.[81] Nevertheless, for practical reasons, given the expected extensive number of users, the system cannot be collectively self-governed by its users, and thus it should be governed by clear operating principles. The expectation is that admitted consumers should be adults who are able to contribute to society. However, free riders, those who are driven by greed, and those violating system rules should be excluded from the cooperative economy and resort instead to the current economic system. Given that both opportunistic behavior and prosocial behavior are contagious, it is important to exclude greedy consumers who may exploit the system and take advantage of prosocial consumers. For prosocial behavior to dominate in the cooperative economy, it is insufficient to reward prosocial behavior and punish opportunistic behavior. Ensuring sufficient interaction among prosocial participants in economic exchange requires selection.[82] Unfortunately, we cannot afford to have this selection occur naturally over generations.[83] Hence, as part of their social responsibility, admitted consumers commit to comply with system rules, such as providing correct information and avoiding arbitrage opportunities. Given the challenge of identifying greedy consumers upfront, measures should be taken to verify the information provided by consumers and scrutinize their behavior for violations of system rules. Violations should be penalized, with greedy consumers excluded to retain the integrity of the economic system that is instituted on community norms of prosocial behavior. The evaluation of vendors is more straightforward given that the system is designed to eliminate potential exploitation of consumers by vendors. Some verification of the information provided by vendors may be necessary to ensure that their product and service offerings meet quality standards and that they repay excess profit. In sum, exclusion and penalties can help deter opportunistic participants and reinforce prosocial behavior. Nevertheless, screening and control should be kept to the minimum necessary to sustain the system because unnecessary and excessive sanctions can reinforce rather than deter sophisticated opportunistic behavior.[84] Screening, monitoring, and penalties for opportunistic behavior in the cooperative economy can be minimal in highly cohesive religious or spiritual communities whose social norms are aligned with the system's rules.

Subsidizing the needy. A distinctive feature of the cooperative economy is the subsidizing of low-income consumers by high-income earners. This principle promotes economic equality, not by altering salaries and earnings but by price discrimination. The notion of price discrimination is already practiced by vendors in the current economic system, but is set based on a collective criterion rather than on personal income. In particular, geographical location has served for proxying for income level. For example, in 2021, the price of a Big Mac burger in US dollars was 24.7 percent higher in Switzerland than in the United States. It was 11.5 percent higher in Norway, 15.9 percent lower in Britain, 22.8 percent lower in Brazil, 39.2 percent lower in Poland, and 54.9 percent lower in India.[85] Whereas this pricing may reflect the varying cost of raw materials and production, it also indicates the extent to which a country is rich versus poor. Even within countries, the same product may be sold at different prices. For instance, in Israel, a can of cola is likely to be more expensive in Tel Aviv (the most expensive city in the world, according to CNN[86]) than in Haifa, and even cheaper in peripheral villages or poor towns. Although these price differences are approximately associated with the average purchasing power of consumers in these different communities, they do not account for interpersonal differences in available income within these communities. In the cooperative economy, depending on their available income and household size, some consumers would be expected to pay more than others for the same products and services, with the differential price determined by the subsidizing process. The higher the income, the higher the requested price, but the price ratio should be lower than the income ratio to avoid free riding by low-income consumers. Progressive taxation of income transfers funds from the individual to the government, which may then decide to allocate some of the accumulated funds to support the poor. In contrast, the subsidizing process in the cooperative economy transfers funds directly among consumers, and thus creates a sense of giving as opposed to losing. In the current economic system, taxation is imposed rather than voluntary, and there is no guarantee that the funds would reach those whom the taxpayer wishes to benefit. Because taxation provides discretion to politicians rather than to the paying individual, it fails to create the sense of happiness that accompanies prosocial behavior. The key question is: why would some consumers in the cooperative economy be willing to pay more for a product or service that they can purchase for less in external markets? The answer has to do with the essence of prosocial behavior, whereby giving to the needy creates a sense of happiness and well-being that supersedes the satisfaction felt when maximizing economic utility. The act of kindness can be prompted by altruism, spiritual beliefs, or other motivations. Donating consumers also realize that they may become a beneficiary of the system one day if they lose their job or experience reduction in income. This notion of mutual responsibility and community support has been demonstrated in various contexts, such as in several immigrant and minority communities in the United States.[87] Nevertheless, to avoid a sense of shame among those who receive subsidies, the subsidization process should be designed in a way that, regardless of the income level, each consumer is perceived as donating to consumers at lower income levels than one's own. At the lowest income level, consumers will be expected to reciprocate through donations in kind, even symbolically, based on their capacity. This can facilitate a sense of happiness, as all consumers can be perceived as givers rather than merely receivers of benefits. Finally, the willingness of high-income consumers to support low-income consumers is expected as long as the high-income consumers perceive the subsidized consumers to be members of the same community. Recent research reveals that privileged individuals often consider equality as necessarily harmful because it restricts their access to resources, but this misperception of equality disappears when equality is pursued within the group as opposed to across groups.[88]

Consumption per need. Mahatma Gandhi famously said, "There is enough for everyone's need, but not for everyone's greed." Unlike the current economic system in which overconsumption is fueled by desires and wishes, the cooperative economy would facilitate consumption to satisfy consumers' actual needs rather than their wishes. This principle is central to consumers' social responsibility and serves for restricting overconsumption of natural resources. The challenge is to define such needs, as consumers differ in preferences and expectations. An effort should be made to specify what is considered excessive consumption per household, so that consumers limit their consumption beyond such a threshold. Indeed, consumers could purchase products and services in markets outside the cooperative economy, but placing consumption limits in the cooperative economy restricts opportunities for arbitrage with external markets. The hope is that consumers who choose to join the cooperative economy would be mindful about overconsumption. In any case, the system should also provide opportunities to donate products and services that would be otherwise wasted. Finally, to avoid the promotion of desires that inflate consumption, the economic system would avoid any form of advertising, although vendors could advertise outside the system, e.g., on their own websites.

Free choice. The cooperative economy promotes free choice in the sense that the system restricts the influence of vendors on individuals' preferences. For consumers, this can be achieved by forbidding advertisements and avoiding exposure to information about other products and services purchased by like-minded consumers. There should be no attempt to profile consumers and analyze consumption patterns with the aim of predicting and influencing their choices. Consumers should be able to independently collect information about products and services, but such information would not be forced upon them through the system. One exception is the provision of quality ratings of products, services, and vendors, as assessed by consumers, which could also serve in ensuring that vendors meet quality standards.

Another application of the free choice principle concerns employment and occupational choice. By increasing the purchasing power of low-income consumers, the system's subsidizing process can enable individuals to escape the rat race of earnings, reduce their workload, and achieve a better work-life balance. A concern may be raised that by doing so, the system would encourage underemployment and facilitate productivity loss. I would argue the opposite by suggesting that the system would enable individuals to pursue their professional aspirations, and thus enhance productivity. Consider job satisfaction in the United States. In 2021, only 65 percent of employees reported that they were satisfied with their job.[89] This is in line with an earlier report revealing that in 2015, 37 percent of employees were very satisfied, whereas 51 percent reported that they were only somewhat satisfied, with the rest being unsatisfied.[90] More alarming is the finding that only 20 percent of employees are passionate about their job. Thus, to the extent that employees can abandon their unsatisfying positions and find greater job satisfaction in pursuing other career paths, their productivity and contributions to society and firm performance can increase.[91] For example, with the proposed system, an artist, a poet, or a musician may be able to devote time to their craft as opposed to taking underpaid jobs as a warehouse employee, cashier, or waiter. A remaining question is: who would take these unsatisfying blue-collar jobs? To the extent that there is an insufficient number of employees who are willing to take on these positions, some of these jobs can be replaced with business process redesign, robots, or other technological substitutes. For example, throughout the world, some restaurants have been using robot waiters to make up for shortage in human waiters while enhancing efficiency and making the job of the remaining human waiters easier. A case in point is the Tea Terrace in London, an early adopter of this technology.[92] As another example, in April 2022 Dyson revealed its development of an autonomous robot capable of carrying out household chores such as moving dishes and vacuuming out seat cushions.[93] In sum, being a productive member of the community is part of employees' social responsibility, but regardless, the principle of free choice of occupation can increase happiness without jeopardizing productivity.

Reasonable vendor earning. Unlike the current economic system in which firms seek to maximize profits and shareholder value at the expense of consumers and other stakeholders, in the cooperative economy, earnings should be capped to ensure that the platform operator and vendors gain reasonable earnings, but not more than that. This principle is part of their social responsibility and is meant to ensure redistribution of value back to consumers. The question is: what earning is considered reasonable? One possibility is to estimate reasonable profitability based on industry average. Another is to decide on a threshold level that would be applicable to all industries. In any case, such a limit should be lower than the current maximal profitability in industries, yet still sufficient to attract vendors. Another question is: how can this rule be enforced? It is possible to specify in the commercial contact between the platform operator and the vendors that excess profit should be redistributed to consumers. The application of this rule can eliminate the motivation of vendors to exploit consumers.

Fair competition. The current economic system allows for unfair business practices, or at least is ineffective in preventing the use of such practices in competition. In the cooperative economy, practices such as self-preferencing would be avoided by having the platform operator take on the social responsibility to not operate in its vendors' businesses and engage only in activities that are necessary to maintain the platform. Accordingly, the platform operator should not operate warehouses or provide delivery and fulfillment services; these services should be provided by independent vendors. This principle eliminates the conflict of interests that is inherent to the current economic system. Fair competition also involves providing entrepreneurs with opportunities. In the current economic system, it is difficult for start-up firms to enter the market and cope with dominant vendors. To encourage competition and foster entrepreneurship, the proposed economic system can guarantee equal opportunities to vendors, regardless of whether they are established firms or entrepreneurial ventures. This can also be achieved by securing minimum sales for new entrants that need to build their reputation in the market. The principle could also encourage individuals to start a new business, knowing that their market access is ensured, at least at the outset.

Quality assurance. In the cooperative economy, more attention should be paid to quality assurance to ensure that products and services meet quality standards. As part of their social responsibility, vendors can be subject to stricter requirements to meet technical standards and environmental sustainability objectives as well as to some verification of the information provided by them. This process could result in the exclusion of products, services, and vendors that fail to meet the standards. Further emphasis would be placed on developing and reporting reliable quality assessments based on consumers' evaluations of the products and services. These quality assessments should serve for facilitating consumer choice, screening, and prioritizing vendors, as well as excluding those that do not meet minimum quality standards.

Individual differences. Platform owners and vendors can profile consumers in the current economic system in order to personalize product and service offerings and influence consumer behavior. The platform operator in the cooperative economy would avoid such practices but profile individuals to discern those who are prosocial from the opportunistic. Moreover, acknowledging that individuals differ with respect to their needs, skills, behaviors, and aspirations, the economic system would strive to be receptive to diversity. It should avoid discrimination, except for adjusting prices per available income and tracing and excluding greedy consumers. Recognizing individual differences also serves in promoting flexibility in career choices. The system would enable individuals to pursue their professional aspirations by more easily gaining their desirable jobs, receiving professional training, or starting a business, without risking substantial loss in purchasing power. It is important to clarify that recognizing individual differences does not call for individualism. To the contrary: if managed well, collaboration among different individuals in a community can be synergetic.[94] By underscoring the affiliation of individuals as members of their community, the proposed system would manage to overcome some of the caveats of globalization and support collective action and mutual responsibility. Hence, whereas individual differences are celebrated, egoism is not.

Respectful employment. The current economic system has facilitated income disparity and undermined employees' work conditions and social welfare. The cooperative economy would seek to remedy this by reducing salary differences among a firm's employees and by guaranteeing a basic package of benefits, e.g., medical insurance and vacation days. The redistribution of income can be achieved by maintaining a low ratio of high-to-low salaries in a firm. Restricting salary differences should be easier to pursue once prices are adjusted based on income levels. Earning more means paying more for products and services, so there is less incentive to earn a higher salary. However, differential pay is not completely discouraged, as some level of differential pay can provide incentives to invest effort, be entrepreneurial, and excel in competition for professional promotion. Hence, to an extent, income differences do support career development and compensate for managerial positions that entail greater responsibility. Yet there is no justification for a CEO to earn a hundred times the average salary of the rank and file. Furthermore, the proposed system would battle the loss of employee rights in the gig economy. Employees would be respected as organizational members rather than viewed as contracted service providers. The overall purpose is to secure a minimum standard of living and offer a respectful work environment without jeopardizing productivity. As noted earlier, job satisfaction, which is expected to be enhanced with this remedy, is positively related to productivity. How can this system succeed where many labor unions have failed? Employers are more likely to buy in when desirable employment conditions are related to a broader ideology that benefits society rather than a particular stakeholder group such as employees, and when the social responsibility of all stakeholders is called for while underscoring the privileges that come with it.

Sustainability. The overconsumption and abuse of natural resources in the current economic system is a major challenge. To cope with this, the cooperative economy would consider environmental and social sustainability concerns in all decision points. As part of their social responsibility, vendors would be measured per sustainability indices and report their scores on that metric, with the risk of being excluded if they do not meet minimum sustainability standards. The system would also offer opportunities for reducing waste and reusing resources by facilitating donations and exchange of products and services among consumers. Finally, in line with consumers' social responsibility, an integral element of the system would involve caps on the consumption of products and services to limit overconsumption of resources.

Leveraging technology. Technologies such as digital platforms, electronic commerce, artificial intelligence, machine learning, and sophisticated algorithms have been used extensively in the current economic system. They have served to maximize profits, profile consumers, and influence consumers' choices, thus harming consumers and vendors. The fault is not in the technology but in its use. The cooperative economy would make use of the same technologies but for the opposite purpose, that is, to secure the interests of consumers, employees, and other stakeholders while restricting the power of the platform operator. The efficiency of the Internet infrastructure would serve for setting up a platform that supports electronic commerce and other forms of exchange. The corresponding network externalities would promote prosocial behavior rather than establish monopolies. Sophisticated algorithms would be used to reduce economic inequality and determine price levels in a dynamic equilibrium rather than for profiling consumers and setting maximum prices. Artificial intelligence could be used to screen those who behave opportunistically rather than, as platforms currently do, to promote overconsumption. Finally, machine learning could be employed to identify the optimal parameters for the newly proposed system. One technology that would be avoided is the metaverse, which distances individuals by offering them an alternate virtual reality that disguises identity. Prosocial behavior entails a sense of a real community rather than a fake one. Thus, the system would promote physical interaction among consumers and vendors, which is essential for establishing trust and revealing courtesy. These behaviors are marginalized in virtual exchanges typical of the current economic system.

Rebalanced ownership. The current economic system serves the interests of shareholders at the expense of all other stakeholders, namely consumers, vendors, and employees. This is due to the system's dependence on financial markets, investors, and debt, which have facilitated economic inequality.[95] To rebalance power and serve the interests of society, the cooperative economy would reverse this. The platform operator in the cooperative economy would retain authority but would adopt a cooperative structure that eliminates independent shareholders while enabling other stakeholders such as vendors and consumers to take a more active role in the organization of economic activities.[96] To avoid influence by shareholders, when funding the platform, traditional sources of funding such as venture capital and the stock market would be avoided. Instead, alternative sources such as grants, donations, and crowdfunding would be used to finance the setup of the platform's operations without distributing shares. The platform's shares could be subsequently distributed at equal proportions and at no cost to active consumers, vendors, and employees. Although such shares could not be traded, they would give a sense of ownership to those actively involved in the daily operations of the cooperative economy. More importantly, making consumers, vendors, and employees the shareholders of the platform eliminates the potential conflict of interests between shareholders and other stakeholders. This enables the platform to strive for cooperative advantage, which is achieved through collaboration and which benefits all stakeholders, as opposed to competitive advantage, which comes at the expense of these stakeholders.[97] Although shareholders may retain their ownership stakes in vendors, their indirect influence on the platform operator will be restricted, because each vendor has an equal stake in the platform regardless of its capital.

Transparency. Lack of transparency has been a source of competitive advantage for platform owners in the current economic system. In the cooperative economy, which calls for prosocial behavior, trust and transparency are critical. Here there is a need for regulation that would not only strive to constrain undesirable business practices but also require platform operators to submit their algorithms for inspection, with the aim of preventing practices that can cause harm to users. The European Commission's proposal for an Artificial Intelligence Act[98] is a step in the right direction, but the cooperative economy would call for higher standards of transparency, requiring platform operators to completely expose their algorithms for inspection by state authorities. This would not only guarantee that no harm is done, but also build confidence in the system, which is essential for its scaling up.

Symbiosis. This last principle does not concern the cooperative economy per se, but the inter-relationship between the cooperative economy and the current economic system. In that regard, it is important to clarify that the cooperative economy would not fully replace the modern economic system, but coexist with it side by side, especially during its launch phase. This is because as long as there are greedy consumers and firms that are excluded from the cooperative economy, the existing economic system can host them. Whereas greed and self-interest are the oil that feeds the machine in the current economic system, prosocial behavior is the corresponding oil that makes the cooperative economy work, and it should subdue opportunistic behavior to avoid negative network externalities. Because greedy individuals are meant to be excluded from the cooperative economy, they must have an alternative economic system in which they can operate and continue their pursuit of economic gains. Preserving the current economic system at a sufficient scale, at least while greed remains a characteristic of a sizable proportion of the population, can allow the cooperative economy to thrive. In the current economic system, greed and opportunistic behavior overpower prosocial behavior. Once the cooperative economy emerges, it will provide a setting in which prosocial behavior can overcome opportunistic behavior. Under the assumption that the majority of the population is conditionally prosocial, the expectation is that eventually, the cooperative economy will encompass a substantial proportion of the economic activity in the world. Furthermore, the prosocial behavior that it fosters would diffuse beyond its boundaries to the current system.

4.4 NEITHER CAPITALISM NOR COMMUNISM

One possible concern that may arise is that the cooperative economy seems to have an anti-capitalistic flavor and may even remind some of communism, which has failed miserably as an economic system. For that reason, I clarify how the cooperative economy differs from communism and where it departs from capitalism. Capitalism refers to a profit-driven economic system that relies mostly on privately owned and controlled means of production and waged labor, with trade managed through an open market. Hence, the core features of capitalism include private ownership of assets and independent decisions of consumers and vendors that transact via the market without the state's intervention in resource allocation.[99] In contrast, communism strives for social equality by eliminating the profit motive and relying on public ownership of assets, with the ruling party or state dictating the terms of production and trade, and a social system coordinating the allocation of benefits based on needs.[100]

The cooperative economy can be contrasted with both economic regimes. The cooperative economy is an ethical market exchange system organized around communities in which prosocial behavior supports a balanced distribution of benefits. The cooperative economy relies on market exchange, much like in capitalism, except that the market is organized around local communities and is not global as in our current economic system. Still, the market exchange is free, unlike communism in which the terms of exchange, such as the types and quantities of goods produced as well as their prices, are set by the state. In contrast to communism, in which the regime is often totalitarian, the governance of the system is democratic in the cooperative economy, much like in capitalism. Nevertheless, scrutiny would reveal that individuals cannot vote for changing the fundamental principles of the cooperative economy, only elect those who oversee it, which is perhaps more democratic than in capitalism where managers are elected by executive boards that represent only the shareholders' interests. However, unlike capitalism, which creates economic classes based on the distribution of wealth, the cooperative economy has egalitarian aspirations as in communism. The reputation of individuals is measured not by their income, but rather by their prosocial behavior or donations. This also differs from communism, where individuals are measured based on their allegiance to the regime, which is the primary concern of the system. Much like in capitalism, the cooperative economy promotes individual freedoms. In fact, it seeks to offer more freedoms compared to modern capitalism in which employees are overworked and consumers are overpowered by algorithm-empowered firms. Moreover, in the cooperative economy the individual is perceived as a member of the community rather than as an isolated decision maker.

In the cooperative economy, the human motive is prosocial, i.e., individuals seek happiness by being kind to each other. This can be contrasted with capitalism, where the assumption is that of Homo economicus, i.e., self-interested individuals that seek opportunities for profit making and are thus driven by greed. This can be also contrasted with communism, in which the state's control eliminates self-interest,

Table 4.1 Comparison of capitalism, communism, and the cooperative economy.

	Capitalism	Communism	Cooperative Economy
Orientation	A profit-driven, privately owned market system	State-controlled distributive social system	Community-set prosocial exchange system
Market	Free global competition	State-controlled	Free local competition
Governance	Democratic	Totalitarian	Democratic
Social system	Economic classes	Egalitarian	Egalitarian
Primary concern	Individual freedoms	Regime	Individual within a community
Human motive	Self-interest, greed	Control	Prosocial behavior, fairness
Concentration of power	Corporations	State	Stakeholders
Government intervention	Reduced	Extensive	Limited
Price system	Competitive	Fixed	Income-based
Wealth accumulation	Individual effort	Distributed per need	Balanced
Incentives	Salary and profit	No profit, state recognition	Restricted salary and profit, happiness
Assets and property	Privately held	State-owned	Privately held
Employment	Free labor market	Assigned by state	Free choice
Business development	Individual entrepreneurship	State-owned	Empowered individual entrepreneurship

although it is rare to find control without corruption. Another important distinction concerns the concentration of power. Communism concentrates power in the hands of the state or ruling party, whereas in modern capitalism, it is multinational corporations or the owners of platform ecosystems that dominate all other stakeholders. The cooperative economy seeks to shift power back to such stakeholders, namely consumers, employees, and small vendors. Interestingly, with respect to government intervention, the cooperative economy goes beyond capitalism, which reduces the government's intervention in the market. By redistributing income among consumers and restraining economic inequality, the cooperative economy can limit the government's role in managing taxation and transfers. A key distinction concerns pricing. Whereas in a communist system, prices are dictated by the state, in a capitalistic system they are set by the intersection of demand and supply. Free competition exists only in theory, however, since in some markets that are dominated by platform owners, there is not much room for free competition. The cooperative economy departs from these conventions by encouraging competition and by setting baseline prices based on competitive forces, but then differentiating prices based on consumers' available income. Another distinction concerns the incentives of individuals and the prospects for accumulating wealth. In capitalism, individuals invest efforts to earn salaries and make profit; however, wealth is accumulated mostly by the owners of capital rather than by employees. Communism prohibits the accumulation of profit and wealth, with benefits distributed per need. Employees are expected to make efforts as per their abilities for the glory of the state, but this has been a weak incentive. In comparison, the cooperative economy allows for profits and accumulation of wealth, but strives for equality, and thus restricts profits and salaries with the aim of balancing the distribution of value among participants in economic exchange. Its underlying assumption is that finding happiness rather than profit making is the primary incentive of individuals in the economic system.

Moreover, much like capitalism and unlike communism, which retains assets and property under state ownership, the cooperative economy supports the private ownership of assets and property. Unlike alternative approaches,[101] it does not call for the confiscation of assets or change in property rights as a means for redistributing value. In striking contrast to communism, in which the state dictates employees' professional training and job assignments, the cooperative economy seeks complete freedom of one's career choices, assuming that after the earning constraint is relaxed, individual diversity would naturally lead to a variety of professions. This is even more pronounced than in capitalism, where individuals have such freedom in theory, but in practice they need to compromise on their preferences in the labor market in order to secure their standard of living. Finally, much like in capitalism and unlike in communism, the cooperative economy leaves room for individual entrepreneurship, and may foster more such entrepreneurship by providing opportunities as well as a cushion that protects entrepreneurs in the case of failure. In sum, the cooperative economy is unlike communism, although it adopts some of its favorable foundations. It is also unlike capitalism, although it retains some of its positive elements (for a summary, see Table 4.1). It is neither compassionate capitalism nor entrepreneurial communism, but a unique system in its own right. Whereas the failure of communism is well documented,[102] so are the caveats of capitalism,[103] which became visible during the financial crisis of 2008[104] as well as during the Covid-19 pandemic. Whether the cooperative economy would thrive remains to be seen.

4.5 COMPARISON TO OTHER ALTERNATIVE ECONOMIC MODELS

In addition to comparing the cooperative economy to communism and capitalism, it is worthwhile to compare it to other relevant alternatives. It is by no means possible within the scope of this book to conduct a thorough analysis of all previous attempts to establish cooperative economic models and identify the reasons for their limited success.

This is a worthwhile topic for a separate study. Here I point to some notable examples of such models and briefly explain how the cooperative economy departs from them. One such alternative is the Israeli kibbutz, which has adopted a socialist economic organization that adheres to principles of collective ownership of property, equality, democratic decision making, and voluntarism. Much like in the cooperative economy, the community plays a central role in this system. With a few nuances, in both systems the principle of "from each according to his ability, to each according to his need" applies, suggesting that all those who can work are expected to contribute, while those who cannot, benefit from the mutual responsibility.[105] However, unlike the kibbutz, the cooperative economy allows for private ownership of assets. Whereas the notion of equality in the kibbutz goes beyond the economic realm to consider also political and social stands, the cooperative economy strives for an egalitarian society from an economic standpoint, while acknowledging personal differences. It is the synergy that arises from the harmony of unique individual contributions and voices that creates value in the cooperative economy. Furthermore, it is not a majority vote that determines admission to the system and social affairs, as in the kibbutz, but alignment with the stated behavioral rules and norms in the cooperative economy. Interestingly, the kibbutz has gone through reforms that transferred the ownership of some assets such as homes to its members. The kibbutz has also begun to charge members for utilities, while allowing them to keep more of their income, with some kibbutzim allowing members to earn differential wages depending on their profession. This revised system narrows wage differences but does not eliminate them, which is more in line with the cooperative economy. About 76 percent of kibbutzim have offered differential wages to their members,[106] with this proportion increasing over the years. Finally, whereas the kibbutz offers a communal way of life that encompasses labor, education, childcare, and social affairs, among many other aspects of life, the cooperative economy limits its concern to economic transactions, otherwise leaving the community context intact. The kibbutz is only one of many types of communes and utopian communities aspiring to equality, among other societal values, but encountered practical challenges.[107]

Another notable case is the country of Bhutan, with its 775,000 inhabitants. Following the philosophy of Buddhism, which underscores calmness, contentment, and compassion and which promotes spirituality and meditation, in 1972, Bhutan's then king, Jigme Singye Wangchuck, determined that "Gross national happiness is more important than gross domestic product." His successor, King Jigme Khesar Namgyel Wangchuck, has institutionalized the Gross National Happiness (GNH) index, which provides a compass toward a just, harmonious, and sustainable society. The index is based on a 3-hour detailed survey covering aspects relating to health, psychological well-being, time use, living standards, community viability, good governance, education, ecological diversity, and cultural diversity. Citizens of Bhutan enjoy free education and healthcare as well as subsidized electricity that is available to all. The recent survey's results reveal that 8.42 percent of the respondents were deeply happy, 34.97 percent were extensively happy, 47.87 percent were narrowly happy, and 8.75 percent were unhappy.[108] Moreover, Bhutan was ranked only 97 out of 156 countries in the United Nation's 2018 World Happiness Report. Nevertheless, with 72.5 percent of the country covered by forest, Bhutan is the world's only carbon-negative country. It also achieved the best governance score in the group of least developed countries. Its poverty was reduced from 36 percent to 10 percent between 2007 and 2019, while its GDP increased by 217 percent from $1.168 billion to $2.531 billion during that period.[109] Bhutan features a cohesive community with a shared belief system that prioritizes societal values over material gains despite its economic growth. Although its national policy does not center on economic exchange within the community, in many ways its economy demonstrates that the underlying logic of the cooperative economy can work. Nevertheless, Bhutan has a monarchy rather than a system based on mutual responsibility whereby fortunate consumers subsidize those in need. In its survey, the only indicator of prosocial behavior is donation of money and volunteering, based on which only 43 percent of the survey respondents report sufficiency. This indicator ranks 29 out of 33 indicators of happiness in Bhutan's survey,[110] leaving room for improvement.

It is also interesting to consider the Amish church, which is known for its simple rural lifestyle, manual labor, self-sufficiency, humility, and submission to God's will. Whereas the strong sense of community and simple lifestyle that defies materialistic and consumeristic approaches is something that the cooperative economy can aspire to, the remaining elements and the motivations are quite distinct. Amish community units are rather small compared to those proposed for the cooperative economy, and while self-sufficiency is advocated in both, the Amish tradition presents a more extreme version of it. Still, this church demonstrates an alternative lifestyle that prioritizes societal values over self-interested pursuit of monetary rewards.

Straddling capitalism and communism is democratic socialism. Adler[111] suggested it as a remedy to some illnesses of capitalism, such as economic turmoil, workplace disempowerment, unresponsive government, environmental degradation, social disintegration, and international rivalry. His more recent application focuses on climate change.[112] He advocates the pooling of national resources and granting democratic control over firms and the entire economy. But in addition to raising the question of how private ownership would be transferred to the public, this remedy seems insufficient. In fact, a reduced version of this idea that gives more voice to stakeholders has been practiced in some European countries such as Germany, with its social market system, without achieving the desirable objective of remedying the illnesses of capitalism. By itself, establishing a new regime or changing the corporate mission cannot amend the flaws of our current economic system.

Also of relevance are cooperative associations that are managed by their stakeholders throughout the world. The top 100 cooperatives employ around three million employees, mostly in Europe, including more than 850,000 employees in Germany and more than 600,000 employees in France, which accounts for 25 percent of the turnover of the top 100 cooperatives.[113] One of the largest cooperatives, Mondragon in Spain, is an international project encompassing 141 production plants in 37 countries with more than 80,000 employees and sales in 150 countries. It strives to accomplish its business mission while promoting a sustainable society, fair distribution of wealth, and grassroots democratic management. Mondragon is open to anyone who accepts its principles, and it relies on democratic voting for its elected governance and major decisions. Capital ownership does not provide voting rights, and profits are allocated to members based on their respective contributions. Mondragon offers wage solidarity to maintain internal equality while keeping an external benchmark. Its various units cooperate to enhance solidarity and efficiency, while committing to support the development of local communities. It also invests in education to promote the ideas of democracy and cooperation. In 2018, this cooperative had a turnover of $14.43 billion.[114] Unlike in the proposed cooperative economy, Mondragon's activities are embedded in the global economy and are guided by its members' interests rather than by an overarching ideology at the system level. It focuses on supply-side rather than on demand-side initiatives but demonstrates how it is possible to prioritize the voice of internal stakeholders over that of independent shareholders.

The cooperative economy is also distinct from platform cooperatives, such as Fairbnb.coop, Fairmondo, and the Green Taxi Cooperative. These stakeholder-oriented platforms are jointly owned by workers or consumers of the service and rely on democratic decision making by these stakeholders. They share profits and promote the interests of their membership. Hence, while they distribute value more fairly and restrict the platform owner's control, they do not necessarily promote societal values or seek to offer an alternative to the global economy. Their ownership structure differs from that of the cooperative economy, whose agenda cannot be well served using collective or distributed decision making. Although these platforms often follow the community principle in organizing exchange within delineated geographical or niche markets, their activities cannot appreciably evolve beyond these boundaries. Furthermore, none of these alternative platforms relies on prosocial behavior as the driving force. Therefore, these examples cannot be considered failed attempts to implement the cooperative economy because they lack the aspiration to provide an alternative to the global economy and miss the essential engine of prosocial behavior.

Cooperative arrangements may reveal nuanced differences that are worth considering.[115] There are several accounts of cooperatives that managed for a while to fight poverty and redistribute value while relying on democratic governance in certain communities.[116] Nevertheless, these cooperatives seek to serve their members rather than communities and society at large. They tend to remain contained within a particular sector and follow traditional practices of economic exchange rather than promote prosocial behavior. Some cooperatives that began with the idea of solidarity and making products more affordable to the working class have actually ended up as for-profit corporations. They rely on democratic control rather than on set principles, and their redistribution of value is based on membership rather than on ability or need. But such cooperatives can more easily adopt the principles of the cooperative economy when joining as vendors. Overall, none of the various models that I discussed here offers an alternative to the modern economy or aims to solve societal grand challenges at a global scale, so it would be unfair to infer that they have failed to achieve their purpose. This also means that even if the cooperative economy is fully implemented in a couple of isolated communities, it cannot claim to have succeeded in achieving its mission.

In conclusion, the cooperative economy offers an alternative economic system that seeks to serve society rather than have society serve the system, which is the case with the current economic system that is instituted on the greed motive. I have demonstrated that self-interested pursuit of profit is not a universal behavior and that individuals differ in the extent to which they exhibit opportunistic behavior versus prosocial behavior. Furthermore, receiving acts of kindness prompts a paying-it-forward behavior, which is a private case of prosocial behavior. Prosocial behavior can be reinforced in an economic system as long as opportunistic behavior that sets negative externalities such as free riding and exploitation is avoided. Thus, the cooperative economy should seek to provide an appropriate setting for the emergence of prosocial behavior. This entails a sense of community and mutual responsibility. Here, I outlined the guiding principles for the cooperative economy that determine who can take part in economic exchange, how payoffs are to be distributed, how stakeholders can enjoy greater ownership, choice, and flexibility, and what constraints are imposed on profits and salaries. I also discussed standards relating to such aspects as employment, quality, and sustainability, and alluded to principles that provide the foundation for the proposed solution. Nevertheless, there is a non-trivial distance between setting principles and bringing the cooperative economy from theory to practice. Beyond the claim that an economic system can replace opportunistic behavior with prosocial behavior, a remaining challenge is to demonstrate the inner workings of such a system and provide a clear set of directions for its implementation. If you are less interested in the practicality of the idea, you can skip Chapter 5.

NOTES

1 Grant, R.M. (2021), *Contemporary strategy analysis*, 11th edn., Wiley & Sons.
2 Varian, H.R. (1987), *Intermediate microeconomics: a modern approach*, W.W. Norton.
3 Varian, H.R. (2010), *Intermediate microeconomics: a modern approach*, 8th edn., W.W. Norton, p. 347.
4 Donaldson, T., & Walsh, J.P. (2015), "Toward a theory of business," *Research in Organizational Behavior*, 35, pp. 181–207.
5 Williamson, O.E. (1985), *The economic institutions of capitalism*, Free Press.
6 Smith, A. (1982), *The theory of moral sentiments*, Liberty Fund.
7 Ghoshal, S., & Moran, P. (1996). "Bad for practice: a critique of transaction cost theory," *Academy of Management Review*, 21(1), pp. 13–47.
8 Mathias, B.D., Huyghe, A., Frid, C.J., & Galloway, T.L. (2018), "An identity perspective on coopetition in the craft beer industry," *Strategic Management Journal*, 39(12), pp. 3086–3115.
9 Ready, K. (2012), "Paying it forward: Silicon Valley's open secret to success," *Forbes*, August 23, www.forbes.com/sites/kevinready/2012/08/23/paying-it-forward-silicon-valleys-open-secret-to-success/#19303c532ec3.
10 Deckop, J.R., Cirka, C.C., & Andersson, L.M. (2003), "Doing unto others: the reciprocity of helping behavior," *Journal of Business Ethics*, 47(2), pp. 101–113.

11 DeSteno, D., Barlett, M.Y., Baumann, J., Williams, L.A., & Dickens, A. (2010), "Gratitude as moral sentiment: emotion-guided cooperation in economic exchange," *Emotion*, 10(2), pp. 289–293.

12 Baker, W.E., & Bulkley, N. (2014), "Paying it forward vs. rewarding reputation: mechanisms of generalized reciprocity," *Organization Science*, 25(5), pp. 1493–1510.

13 Santamaria, J.P., & Rosenbaum, D.A. (2011), "Etiquette and effort: holding doors for others," *Psychological Science*, 22, pp. 584–588.

14 Flynn, F.J. (2005), "Identity orientations and forms of social exchange in organizations," *Academy of Management Review*, 30(4), pp. 737–750.

15 McCullough, M.E., Kimeldorf, M.B., & Cohen, A.D. (2008), "An adaptation for altruism? The social causes, social effects, and social evolution of gratitude," *Current Directions in Psychological Science*, 17(4), pp. 281–285.

16 Gray, K., Ward, A.F., & Norton, M.I. (2014), "Paying it forward: generalized reciprocity and the limits of generosity," *Journal of Experimental Psychology: General*, 143(1), pp. 247–254.

17 Ariely, D. (2012), *The honest truth about dishonesty: how we lie to everyone— especially ourselves*, HarperCollins.

18 Bandura, A. (1990), "Selective activation and disengagement of moral control," *Journal of Social Issues*, 46, pp. 27–46; Moore, C. (2015), "Moral disengagement," *Current Opinion in Psychology*, 6, pp. 199–204.

19 Axelrod, R. (1984), *The evolution of cooperation*, Basic Books.

20 Stanca, L., Bruni, L., & Mantovani, M. (2011), "The effect of motivations on social indirect reciprocity: an experimental analysis," *Applied Economics Letters*, 18, pp. 1709–1711; Sun, Z., Ye, C., He, Z., & Yu, W. (2020), "Behavioral intention promotes generalized reciprocity: evidence from the director game," *Frontiers in Psychology*, 11, p. 772.

21 E.g., Falk, A., & Fischbacher, U. (2006), "A theory of reciprocity," *Games and Economic Behavior*, 54, pp. 293–315.

22 Cialdini, R.B., & Trost, M.R. (1998), "Social influence: social norms, conformity, and compliance," in Gilbert, D.T., Fiske, S.T., & Lindzey, G. (eds.), *The handbook of social psychology*, McGraw-Hill, pp. 151–192, p. 152.

23 Fehr, E., & Schurtenberger, I. (2018), "Normative foundations of human cooperation," *Nature Human Behavior*, 2(7), pp. 458–468.

24 E.g., Frederick, S. (2012), "Overestimating others' willingness to pay," *Journal of Consumer Research*, 39, pp. 1–21.

25 Jung, M.H., Nelson, L.D., Gneezy, A., & Gneezy, U. (2014), "Paying more when paying for others," *Journal of Personality and Social Psychology*, 107(3), pp. 414–431.

26 Prentice, D.A., & Miller, D.T. (1993), "Pluralistic ignorance and alcohol use on campus: some consequences of misperceiving the social norm," *Journal of Personality and Social Psychology*, 64, pp. 243–256.

27 Chiang, Y.-S., & Takahashi, N. (2011), "Network homophily and the evolution of the pay-it-forward reciprocity," *PLoS ONE*, 6(12), p. e29188.

28 Boyd, R., & Richerson, P. (1989), "The evolution of indirect reciprocity," *Social Networks*, 11, pp. 213–236.

29 Horita, Y., Takezawa, M., Kinjo, T., Nakawake, Y., & Masuda, N. (2016), "Transient nature of cooperation by pay-it-forward reciprocity," *Scientific Reports*, 6, p. 19471.

30 Bartlett, M.Y., & DeSteno, D. (2006), "Gratitude and prosocial behavior: helping when it costs you," *Psychological Science*, 17(4), pp. 319–325.

31 Fowler, J.H., & Christakis, N.A. (2010), "Cooperative behavior cascades in human social networks," *Proceedings of the National Academy of Science*, 107(12), pp. 5334–5338.

32 Schroeder, D.A., & Graziano, W.G. (2015), "The field of prosocial behavior," in Schroeder, D.A., & Graziano, W.G. (eds.), *Oxford handbook of prosocial behavior*, Oxford University Press, pp. 3–35; Staub, E. (1978), *Positive social behavior and morality*, Academic Press.

33 Batson, C.D., & Powell, A.A. (2003), "Altruism and prosocial behavior," in Millon, T., Lerner, M.J., & Weiner, I.B. (eds.), *Handbook of psychology*, John Wiley & Sons, pp. 463–484.

34 Eisenberg, N., & Miller, P. (1987), "The relation of empathy to prosocial and related behaviors," *Psychology Bulletin*, 101, pp. 91–119, p. 92.

35 Ynet (2022), "So that no one feels alone: the cake project of Grandma Shula," February 16, www.ynet.co.il/activism/article/skumtypy9.

36 Dovidio, J.F. (1984), "Helping behavior and altruism: an empirical and conceptual overview," in Berkowitz, L. (ed.), *Advances in experimental social psychology*, Academic Press, pp. 361–427.

37 Fischbacher, U., & Gächter, S. (2010), "Social preferences, beliefs, and the dynamics of free riding in public goods experiments," *American Economic Review*, 100(1), pp. 541–556.

38 Lönnqvist, J.-E., Verkasalo, M., & Walkowitz, G. (2011), "It pays to pay: Big Five personality influences on co-operative behavior in an incentivized and

hypothetical prisoner's dilemma game," *Personality and Individual Differences,* 50, pp. 300–304.

39 Flynn, E., Ehrenreich, S.E., Beron, K.J., & Underwood, M.K. (2015), "Prosocial behavior: long-term trajectories and psychosocial outcomes," *Review of Social Development,* 24(3), pp. 462–482.

40 Fischbacher, U., & Gächter, S. (2010), "Social preferences, beliefs, and the dynamics of free riding in public goods experiments," *American Economic Review,* 100(1), pp. 541–556.

41 Okada, I. (2020), "A review of theoretical studies on indirect reciprocity," *Games,* 11(27), pp. 1–17.

42 Denissen, J.J.A., & Penke, L. (2008), "Motivational individual reaction norms underlying the five-factor model of personality: first steps towards a theory-based conceptual framework," *Journal of Research in Personality,* 42, pp. 1285–1302.

43 Graziano, W.G., Habashi, M.M., Sheese, B.E., & Tobin, R.M. (2007), "Agreeableness, empathy, and helping: a person × situation perspective," *Journal of Personality and Social Psychology,* 93, pp. 583–599.

44 Hilbig, B.E., Glöckner, A., & Zettler, I. (2014), "Personality and prosocial behavior: linking basic traits and social value orientations," *Journal of Personality and Social Psychology,* 107(3), pp. 529–539.

45 Ashton, M.C., & Lee, K. (2007), "Empirical, theoretical, and practical advantages of the HEXACO model of personality structure," *Personality and Social Psychology Review,* 11, pp. 150–166.

46 Hilbig, B.E., Glöckner, A., & Zettler, I. (2014), "Personality and prosocial behavior: linking basic traits and social value orientations," *Journal of Personality and Social Psychology,* 107(3), pp. 529–539.

47 Hogg, M.A. (2007), "Uncertainty–identity theory," *Advances in Experimental Social Psychology,* 39, pp. 69–126.

48 Chang, L., & Arkin, R.M. (2002), "Materialism as an attempt to cope with uncertainty," *Psychology & Marketing,* 19(5), pp. 389–406.

49 Pfattheicher, S., & Böhm, R. (2018), "Honesty-humility under threat: self-uncertainty destroys trust among the nice guys," *Journal of Personality and Social Psychology,* 114(1), pp. 179–194.

50 Fischbacher, U., Gächter, S., & Fehr, E. (2001), "Are people conditionally cooperative? Evidence from a public goods experiment," *Economics Letters,* 71, pp. 397–404.

51 Gächter, S., & Schulz, J.F. (2016), "Intrinsic honesty and the prevalence of rule violations across societies," *Nature,* 531(7595), pp. 496–499.

52 Curry, O.S., Mullins, D.A., & Whitehouse, H. (2019), "Is it good to cooperate? Testing the theory of morality as cooperation in 60 societies," *Current Anthropology*, 60(1), pp. 47–69.

53 Schulz, J.F., Bahrami-Rad, D., Beauchamp, J.P., & Henrich, J. (2019), "The Church, intensive kinship, and global psychological variation," *Science*, 366(6466), p. 7.

54 Hugh-Jones, D., & Zultan, R. (2013), "Reputation and cooperation in defense," *Journal of Conflict Resolution*, 57(2), pp. 327–355; Theelen, M.M., & Bohm, R. (2021), "The conflict-cooperation effect persists under intragroup payoff asymmetry," *Group Processes & Intergroup Relations*, 4(5), pp. 815–835.

55 Henrich, J., Chudek, M., & Boyd, R. (2015), "The Big Man Mechanism: how prestige fosters cooperation and creates prosocial leaders," *Philosophical Transactions of the Royal Society B. Biological Sciences*, 370, p. 20150013.

56 E.g., O'Gorman, R., Henrich, J., & Van Vugt, M. (2009), "Constraining free riding in public goods games: designated solitary punishers can sustain human cooperation," *Proceedings of the Royal Society B, Biological Science*, 276(1655), pp. 323–329.

57 Ilies, R., Peng, A.C., Savani, K., & Dimoatkis, N. (2013), "Guilty and helpful: an emotion-based reparatory model of voluntary work behavior," *Journal of Applied Psychology*, 98(6), pp. 1015–1059.

58 Henrich, J., & Henrich, N. (2014), "Fairness without punishment: behavioral experiments in the Yasawa Island, Fiji," in Ensminger, J., & Henrich, J. (eds.), *Experimenting with social norms: fairness and punishment in cross-cultural perspective*, Russell Sage Foundation, pp. 171–218.

59 Bicchiery, C. (2002), *The grammar of society: the nature and dynamics of social norms*, Cambridge University Press.

60 Boyd, R., & Richerson, P. (2009), "Culture and the evolution of human cooperation," *Philosophical Transactions of the Royal Society B. Biological Science*, 364, pp. 3281–3288.

61 Henrich, J., Ensimger, J., McElreath, R., Barr, A., Barrett, C., Bolyanatz, A., Cardenas, J., Gurven, M., Gwako, E., Henrich, N., Lesorogol, C., Marlowe, F., Tracer, D., & Ziker, J. (2010), "Markets, religion, community size, and the evolution of fairness and punishment," *Science*, 327, pp. 1480–1484.

62 Bering, J. (2011), *The belief instinct: the psychology of souls, destiny, and the meaning of life*, W.W. Norton.

63 Norenzayan, A., Shariff, A.F., Gervais, W.M., Willard, A., McNamara, R., Slingerland, E., & Henrich, J. (2016), "The cultural evolution of prosocial religions," *Behavioral and Brain Sciences*, 39, pp. 1–19.

64 Batara, J.B.L., Franco, P.S., Quiachon, M.A.M., & Sembrero, D.R.M. (2016), "Effects of religious priming concepts on prosocial behavior towards ingroup and outgroup," *European Journal of Psychology*, 12(4), pp. 635–644; Preston, J.L., & Ritter, R.S. (2013), "Different effects of religion and God on prosociality with the ingroup and outgroup," *Personality and Social Psychology Bulletin*, 39(11), pp. 1471–1483; Tsang, J.-A., Al-Kire, R.L., & Ratchford, J.L. (2021), "Prosociality and religion," *Current Opinion in Psychology*, 40, pp. 67–72; Stamatoulakis, K.K. (2013), "Religiosity and prosociality," *Procedia—Social and Behavioral Sciences*, 82, pp. 830–834.

65 Willarda, A.K., Baimelb, A., Turpinc, H., Jongd, J., & Whitehouse, H. (2020), "Rewarding the good and punishing the bad: the role of karma and afterlife beliefs in shaping moral norms," *Evolution and Human Behavior*, 41, pp. 385–396.

66 Lindenberg, S., & Steg, L. (2007), "Normative, gain and hedonic goal frames guiding environmental behavior," *Journal of Social Issues*, 63(1), pp. 117–137.

67 E.g., House, B.R., Kanngiesser, P., Barrett, H.C., Broesch, T., Cebioglu, S., et al. (2020), "Universal norm psychology leads to societal diversity in prosocial behaviour and development," *Nature and Human Behaviour*, 4(1), pp. 36–44.

68 Moore, C. (2015), "Moral disengagement," *Current Opinion in Psychology*, 6, pp. 199–204.

69 E.g., Aknin, L.B., Van de Vondervoort, J.W., & Hamlin, J.K. (2018), "Positive feelings reward and promote prosocial behavior," *Current Opinion in Psychology*, 20, pp. 55–59; Dunn, E.W., Aknin, L.B., & Norton, M.I. (2008), "Spending money on others promotes happiness," *Science*, 319, pp. 1687–1688; Lin, K.J., Savani, K., & Ilies, R. (2019), "Doing good, feeling good? The roles of helping motivation and citizenship pressure," *Journal of Applied Psychology*, 104(8), pp. 1020–1035.

70 E.g., Aknin, L.B., Barrington-Leigh, C.P., Dunn, E.W., Helliwell, J.F., Burns, J., Biswas-Diener, R., Kemeza, I., Nyende, P., and Norton, M.I. (2013), "Prosocial spending and well-being: cross-cultural evidence for a psychological universal," *Journal of Personality and Social Psychology*, 104, pp. 635–652; Aknin, L.B., Broesch, T., Hamlin, J.K., & Van De Vondervoort, J.W. (2015), "Prosocial behavior leads to happiness in a small-scale rural society," *Journal of Experimental Psychology*, 144, pp. 788–795; Dunn, E.W., Aknin, L.B., & Norton, M.I. (2008), "Spending money on others promotes happiness," *Science*, 319, pp. 1687–1688; Helliwell, J.F., Wang, S., Huang, H., &

Norton, M. (2022), *World happiness report 2022*, chapter 2, pp. 15–52, https://happiness-report.s3.amazonaws.com/2022/WHR+22_Ch2.pdf; Khanna, V., Sharma, E., Chauhan, S., & Pragyendu (2017), "Effects of prosocial behavior on happiness and well-being," *International Journal of Indian Psychology*, 4(2), pp. 76–86.

71 Aknin, L.B., Whillans, A.V., Norton, M.I., & Dunn, E.W. (2019), "Happiness and prosocial behavior: an evaluation of the evidence," chapter 4 in Helliwell, J.F., Layard, R., & Sachs, J.D. (eds.), *World happiness report*, Sustainable Development Solutions Network, pp. 67–86.

72 Grant, A.M. (2008), "Employees without a cause: the motivational effects of prosocial impact in public service," *International Public Management Journal*, 11(1), pp. 48–66.

73 Lin, K.J., Savani, K., & Ilies, R. (2019), "Doing good, feeling good? The roles of helping motivation and citizenship pressure," *Journal of Applied Psychology*, 104(8), pp. 1020–1035.

74 Uy, M.A., Lin, J.J., & Ilies, R. (2017), "Is it better to give or receive? The role of help in buffering the depleting effects of surface acting," *Academy of Management Journal*, 60(4), pp. 1442–1461.

75 Aguilera, R.V., Rupp, D.E., Williams, C.A., & Ganapathi, J. (2007), "Putting the S back in corporate social responsibility: a multilevel theory of social change in organizations," *Academy of Management Review*, 32(3), pp. 836–863.

76 Bacq, S., & Aguilera, R.V. (2022), "Stakeholder governance for responsible innovation: a theory of value creation, appropriation, and distribution," *Journal of Management Studies*, 59, pp. 29–60; Klein, P.G., Mahoney, J.T., McGahan, A.M., & Pitelis, C.N. (2019), "Organizational governance adaptation: who is in, who is out, and who gets what," *Academy of Management Review*, 44(1), pp. 6–27; McGahan, A.M. (2021), "Integrating insights from the resource-based view of the firm into the new stakeholder theory," *Journal of Management*, 47(7), pp. 1734–1756.

77 Bridoux, F., & Stoelhorst, J.W. (2016), "Stakeholder relationships and social welfare: a behavioral theory of contributions to joint value creation," *Academy of Management Review*, 41(2), pp. 229–251.

78 E.g., Parmar, B.L., Wicks, A.C., & Freeman, E.R. (2022), "Stakeholder management & the value of human-centred corporate objectives," *Journal of Management Studies*, 59(2), pp. 569–582.

79 Granovetter, M. (2005), "The impact of social structure on economic outcomes," *Journal of Economic Perspectives*, 19(1), pp. 33–50.

80 Chatterjee, A., Ghosh, A., & Leca, B. (in press), "Double weaving: a bottom-up process of connecting locations and scales to mitigate grand challenges," *Academy of Management Journal*.

81 Ostrom, E. (1990). *Governing the commons: the evolution of institutions for collective action*, Cambridge University Press.

82 Boyd, R., & Richerson, P. (2009), "Culture and the evolution of human cooperation," *Philosophical Transactions of the Royal Society B. Biological Science*, 364, pp. 3281–3288.

83 Bowles, S., & Gintis, H. (2011), *A cooperative species: human reciprocity and its evolution*, Princeton University Press.

84 Ghoshal, S., & Moran, P. (1996). "Bad for practice: a critique of transaction cost theory," *Academy of Management Review*, 21(1), pp. 13–47.

85 *The Economist* (2021), "Burgernomics: the Big Mac index," July 21, www.economist.com/big-mac-index.

86 O'Hare, M. (2021), "These are the world's most expensive cities in 2021," CNN Travel, December 1, https://edition.cnn.com/travel/article/world-most-expensive-cities-2021/index.html.

87 Putnam, R.D. (2000), *Bowling alone: the collapse and revival of American community*, Simon & Schuster.

88 Brown, N.D., Jacoby-Senghor, D.S., & Raymundo, I. (2022), "If you rise, I fall: equality is prevented by the misperception that it harms advantaged groups," *Science Advances: Psychological Science*, 8, pp. 1–18.

89 Apollo Technical (2021), "11 surprising job satisfaction statistics (2021)," April 21, www.apollotechnical.com/job-satisfaction-statistics/.

90 Society for Human Resource Management (2016), "Employee job satisfaction and engagement: revitalizing a changing workforce," April 18, www.shrm.org/hr-today/trends-and-forecasting/research-and-surveys/pages/job-satisfaction-and-engagement-report-revitalizing-changing-workforce.aspx.

91 Bakotic, D. (2016), "Relationship between job satisfaction and organisational performance," *Economic Research*, 29(1), pp. 118–130; Oswald, A.J., Proto, E., & Sgroi, D. (2015), "Happiness and productivity," *Journal of Labor Economics*, 33(4), pp. 789–822.

92 Kang, A. (2020), "The restaurant of the future? London tea room chain to reopen with robots," *Forbes*, May 23, www.forbes.com/sites/annakang/2020/05/23/the-restaurant-of-the-future-london-tea-room-chain-to-reopen-with-robots/.

93 Dent, S. (2022), "Dyson's been secretly working on robots that do household chores," *Engadget*, May 25, https://engadget.netblogpro.com/dysons-been-secretly-working-on-robots-that-do-household-chores-113548530.html?src=rss.

94 E.g., van Knippenberg, D., Nishii, L.H., & Dwertmann, D.J.G. (2020), "Synergy from diversity: managing team diversity to enhance performance," *Behavioral Science & Policy*, 6(1), pp. 75–92.

95 Davis, G., & Kim, S. (2015), "Financialization of the economy," *Annual Review of Sociology*, 41, pp. 203–221.

96 Schneiberg, M. (2011), "Toward an organizationally diverse American capitalism? Cooperative, mutual, and local, state-owned enterprise," *Seattle University Law Review*, 34, pp. 1409–1434.

97 Child, J., Durand, R., & Lavie, D. (2021), "Competitive and cooperative strategy, part 4," in Hitt, M.A., Lyles, M., & Duhaime, I.M. (eds.), *Strategic management: state of the field and its future*, Oxford University Press, pp. 223–242; Parmar, B.L., Wicks, A.C., & Freeman, E.R. (2022), "Stakeholder management & the value of human-centred corporate objectives," *Journal of Management Studies*, 59(2), pp. 569–582.

98 European Commission (2021), *Proposal for a regulation of the European Parliament and of the Council laying down harmonised rules on artificial intelligence (Artificial Intelligence Act) and amending certain Union legislative acts*, April 21, 2021/0106 (COD), Brussels.

99 Klein, P.G., Holmes, R.M., Foss, N., Terjesen, S., & Pepe, J. (2022), "Capitalism, cronyism, and management scholarship: a call for clarity," *Academy of Management Perspectives*, 36(1).

100 Zimbalist, A., & Sherman, H.J. (1984), *Comparing economic systems: a political-economic approach*, Academic Press.

101 Adler, P. (2019), *The 99 percent economy: how democratic socialism can overcome the crises of capitalism*, Oxford University Press.

102 Clark, J., & Wildavsky, A. (1990), "Why communism collapses: the moral and material failures of command economies are intertwined," *Journal of Public Policy*, 10(4), pp. 361–390.

103 Henderson, R.B. (2020), *Reimagining capitalism in a world on fire*, Harvard Business Press.

104 Posner, R. (2009), *A failure of capitalism: the crisis of '08 and the descent into depression*, Harvard University Press.

105 Cheng, E., & Sun, Y. (2015), "Israeli kibbutz: a successful example of collective economy," *World Review of Political Economy*, 6(2), pp. 160–175, p. 163.

106 Leviatan, U. (2013), "Values and organizational commitment," *International Critical Thought*, 3(3), pp. 315–331.

107 Kanter, R.M. (1972), *Commitment and community: communes and utopias in sociological perspective*, Harvard University Press.

108 Ura, K., Alkire, S., Zangmo, T., and Wangdi, K. (2015), *Provisional findings of 2015 Gross National Happiness Survey*, Centre for Bhutan Studies & GNH Research, www.grossnationalhappiness.com/SurveyFindings/Provisional Findingsof2015GNHSurvey.pdf.

109 Sharma, L.L., & Adhikari, R. (2021), "What Bhutan got right about happiness—and what other countries can learn," World Economic Forum, October 25, www.weforum.org/agenda/2021/10/lessons-from-bhutan-econo mic-development/.

110 Ura, K., Alkire, S., Zangmo, T., and Wangdi, K. (2015), *Provisional findings of 2015 Gross National Happiness Survey*, Centre for Bhutan Studies & GNH Research, www.grossnationalhappiness.com/SurveyFindings/Provisional Findingsof2015GNHSurvey.pdf.

111 Adler, P. (2019), *The 99 percent economy: how democratic socialism can overcome the crises of capitalism*, Oxford University Press.

112 Adler, P. (2022), "Capitalism, socialism, and the climate crisis," *Organization Theory*, 3, pp. 1–16.

113 Voniea, A. (2022), "French co-ops represent 25% of the global turnover of top 100 co-ops," *Coop News*, April 14, www.thenews.coop/161786/topic/econ omy/french-co-ops-represent-25-of-the-global-turnover-of-the-top-100-co-ops/.

114 World Cooperative Monitor (2021), *Exploring the cooperative economy: report 2020*, February 4, https://monitor.coop/sites/default/files/publication-files/wcm2020-1727093359.pdf.

115 Roelants, B., Eum, H., Esim, S., Novkovic, S., & Katajamäki, W. (2019), *Cooperatives and the world of work*, Routledge.

116 Williams, R. (2007), *The cooperative movement: globalization from below*, Routledge.

CHAPTER FIVE

A practical guide for the cooperative economy

DOI: 10.4324/9781003336679-5

Although the fundamental principles provide insights into how the cooperative economy differs from the current economic system, here I discuss practical considerations to guide the establishment of the cooperative economy. My purpose is not to describe the final design of the system but to offer concrete ideas for its preliminary design while highlighting aspects that require further development and experimentation. It is a starting point for a debate that can be settled only after testing alternative practices and demonstrating a proof of concept. Nevertheless, it is important to introduce this road map for implementation in order to show that the cooperative economy can be materialized. I welcome a conversation with informed readers who wish to contribute to the refinement of the ideas presented here. This chapter informs those who seek to establish the cooperative economy, as well as policymakers, vendors, and consumers who wonder about the practicality of the idea and the prospects of taking part in the cooperative economy.

The cooperative economy should be organized as a set of three digital platforms that correspondingly support electronic commerce, barter, and donations by its participants (for brevity, I often refer to them jointly as "the platform"). This platform can be managed by a designated platform operator—an entrepreneurial entity—established specifically for this aim. The platform operator can be incorporated as the Cooperative Economy Foundation, to distinguish it from firms or corporations. The primary form of exchange will be a two-sided market in which the platform brings together vendors and consumers who trade various products and services in exchange for payments. Secondary exchanges will be set up for the bartering of products and services among consumers and vendors without payment, and for the donation of products and services to needy consumers free of charge (see Box 5.1).

BOX 5.1   PLATFORMS OF THE COOPERATIVE ECONOMY

The Cooperative Economy—An ethical market exchange system organized around communities in which prosocial behavior supports a balanced distribution of benefits; includes two-sided market, barter, and donation platforms

1. *Two-sided market platform*—A platform that enables vendors to sell products and services to consumers for payment, with prices set based on consumers' income levels
2. *Barter platform*—A platform that matches consumers for direct exchange of products and services without monetary payment based on consumers' respective income levels
3. *Donation platform*—A platform that enables vendors and consumers to donate products and services to consumers who meet certain requirements free of charge

---

The cooperative economy platform differs from sharing economy platforms. There is no consensus about what the sharing economy is, but most refer to a digital platform that supports peer-to-peer sharing of underutilized goods through an intermediary, without any change of ownership.[1] Examples include Airbnb and Uber, among other platforms. Unlike these platforms, all three cooperative economy platforms involve the transfer of ownership of exchanged products without sharing, while services are provided by qualified vendors. Furthermore, the vendor or owner of the goods does not receive any monetary payment in the barter and donation platforms. Most importantly, the sharing economy benefits mostly the platform owner at the expense of employees, vendors, and consumers, thus preventing a fair distribution of value. In that regard, the cooperative economy seeks to offer an alternative to sharing economy platforms.

With respect to the scope of the cooperative economy, it can be implemented worldwide as a constellation of communities, with each operating a separate market system. The platform can be used for all types of products and services but will be restrictive in that consumers and vendors are admitted based on their estimated prosocial behavior, with other consumers continuing to rely on the current economic system. Hence, the cooperative economy can exist alongside the current economic system—not replacing but supplementing it. In this chapter, I elaborate on the processes for admitting consumers and vendors to the system, the subsidization process for setting prices for products and services, and the roles of purchase limits and quality ratings for products, deliveries, vendors, and sustainability. I then elaborate on the privileges and social responsibilities of consumers and vendors in the cooperative economy, the social responsibilities of the platform operator, and the management of its operations. I conclude with practical suggestions for fundraising, marketing, and implementation of the system.

5.1   ADMISSION TO THE SYSTEM

Because it is a semi-open system, it is essential to define who can be admitted as a participant in the cooperative economy. Any adult can apply to join the platform as a consumer. The expectation is that admitted consumers are productive members of their community, i.e., are salaried employees, operators of a business, engaged in a formal volunteer program, enrolled as students in university degree programs, temporarily unemployed, retired, on parental leave, or unable to work because of some physical or mental impairment. Unless unable to, every consumer within employment age should offer some contribution to society. If the candidate is unemployed or only works part time, this prospective consumer should be able to apply for a vendor account in order to develop and offer products or services in lieu of having a full-time salaried job. The objective is to discourage free riding and laziness and ensure that all able consumers are also productive as part of their social responsibility. An individual who is not making an effort to be productive may end up being dismissed as an employee or may receive a low quality rating as a vendor, which would disqualify that individual from being a consumer or a vendor in the system. That being said, the notion of productivity should be expanded to encompasses creative writing, artwork, music making, spiritual guidance, and many other professions that may be considered sub-productive in the modern economic system despite being valuable to a non-materialistic society.

As part of the admissions process, prospective consumers should be screened with the aim of admitting those who are ethical and prosocial rather than opportunistic and greedy. For this purpose, candidates may be asked to complete a questionnaire that assesses their behavioral inclinations. The questionnaire would gather information about personality traits, attitudes, culture, religious beliefs, and social background to assess the expected behavior of the candidate. This information should only serve for making the admission decision, and once made, the information should be deleted rather than be retained by the system. Prosociality is not categorical, and it can have different manifestations. Therefore, it is essential to focus on its aspects that are most relevant for the functioning of the system and to set a threshold level of measured prosociality for the admission decision. The questionnaire is insufficient for screening candidates, however, because opportunistic candidates may behave opportunistically and provide false answers to the questions. Therefore, in addition to this evaluation, each candidate should be required to receive endorsements from at least two active platform members who can vouch for the candidate. This process is not merely symbolic but becomes relevant in the case of a violation of the platform's rules. Indeed, the screening and vouching processes are not foolproof, but they are worth pursuing if they can eliminate some opportunistic behavior by consumers. In addition, admitted consumers would sign a service contract in which they commit to disclosing correct information. Intentionally providing false information would be considered a violation of system rules. The ultimate objective is to screen out greedy individuals who are unlikely to exhibit prosocial behavior, which is essential for the functioning of the cooperative economy.

Another objective of the admission process is to gather information that enables the classification to income brackets. In this process, prospective consumers would be asked to provide information about their household size, marital status, and annual income, with the aim of estimating their available income and classifying it to the appropriate income bracket. In calculating income, the consumer would be asked to account for all sources of income including salary, pension, social security benefits, rent, interest, dividends, etc. If in a relationship, the consumer can decide to apply for a joint account, with dependent children in the household being acknowledged. If divorced, alimony payments would be considered as a source of income for the recipient and a deductible expense for the payer. Finally, the income tax in the relevant country would be applied when calculating the net available income per person in the household. At the conclusion of this process, each consumer can be assigned to the relevant income bracket based on the distribution of available income in the community and based on the number of household members. The detailed information would not be retained at the conclusion of this assessment. The consumer's account may be linked to accounts of other consumers in the household for combined purchases. Consumers would be asked to update their income data twice per year or in the case of a material change in their income during the year. Consumers would be randomly asked to validate their stated income with supporting documents. To ease the review process, consumers may be asked to have their employers validate their salary statements. Consumers who self-report to belong in the top 10th percentile of income can opt to be exempt from validation because being classified as a top-earner results in paying the highest prices for products and services.

Misreporting income information would be considered a violation of system rules, so if a consumer is found misreporting income, that consumer should be excluded from the system. In addition, any endorsement received from that consumer would be void. Hence, those vouchees who received endorsements from the delinquent consumer would need to seek alternate endorsers. Finally, those who vouched for the delinquent consumer would be notified about a violation. If they have vouched for several delinquent consumers, their status should be reviewed as well. Hence, the plan is to minimize the occurrence of violations by means of social pressure and ramifications. It is likely that enforcement of system rules would mostly be needed at the early stage of setting up the economic system. Once a critical mass of prosocial users is admitted, behavioral norms are instituted, and consumers' social responsibilities are fulfilled, there should be less need for control and enforcement because the inherent value of the system's rules would become more apparent to participants, and prosocial behavior is expected to be self-reinforced in the system. This is due to the accumulation of a critical mass of prosocial consumers and the fact that they know that all consumers have been subjected to the same rules and checks, which helps establish perceptions about the behavior of others as well as build trust and institute behavioral norms. Finally, based on the consumers' location, the system can identify nearby communities and allow the consumers to join a community of choice within their region.

In parallel to the admission process for consumers, vendors should go through a similar process to ensure that they meet standards and follow the system's rules. Endorsements from two other vendors that are already enrolled as active vendors in the system would be required. The prospective vendor would be asked to complete a questionnaire to assess the corporate propensity for ethical and prosocial behavior. Additional questions would evaluate the meeting of quality and sustainability standards. Vendors would be required to disclose their annual revenue and profit levels, which would be then compared to the maximum profitability levels imposed by the system. Misreporting would be considered a violation of system rules, carrying similar sanctions as those applicable to consumers. As part of the service contract that they will sign with the platform operator and as part of their social responsibility, vendors would commit to distributing their excess profits to consumers in the system. Additionally, vendors that operate as employers would commit to verifying the salaries reported by their employees who enroll as consumers in the system. This could simplify that process and ease the validation of consumers' income levels. Consumers would be asked to give consent to such validation of their employment and salary data. Indeed, the amount and type of information that prospective consumers and vendors would be asked to provide is greater than in conventional market platforms, but this is necessary given the unique functionality and nature of this platform, where transparency and honesty are vital. The proposed admission process is summarized in Box 5.2.

BOX 5.2 ADMISSION PROCESS

Consumers:

- Any adult who is a productive member of a community can apply
- Select a community based on the candidate's location
- Complete a questionnaire assessing prosocial and ethical inclinations
- Receive endorsements from two platform members
- Sign a service contract, committing to disclose accurate information
- Provide information on dependents and income to set income bracket and link to household accounts (information discarded, updated semi-annually)
- Random validation of stated income for consumers below highest income bracket
- Misreporting is a violation of system rules, resulting in (a) exclusion from the platform, (b) voidance of endorsements granted by consumer, and (c) notifying consumer's endorsers

Vendors:

- Any vendor can apply
- Select a community based on the vendor's location
- Complete a questionnaire assessing corporate propensity for prosocial and ethical behavior
- Complete a questionnaire relating to quality and sustainability
- Provide information on annual revenue and profit
- Receive endorsements from two platform vendors
- Sign a service contract, committing to distribute excess profit
- Verify the stated salaries of employees below highest income bracket
- Misreporting is a violation of system rules, resulting in (a) exclusion from the platform, (b) voidance of endorsements granted by vendor, and (c) notifying vendor's endorsers
- Reassess the status of endorsers of multiple delinquent consumers/vendors
- Relaxed control and enforcement after prosocial norms are instituted

5.2   PRICE SETTING

A primary process in the cooperative economy involves the differential pricing of products and services per consumers' varied income levels. Price setting can be designed as a two-stage process in which the price of a product or service is initially set for vendors and then for each consumer in the system. When setting the price for vendors, first, vendors categorize their products and services in the system, indicating the available quantity for sale and their asking price for the product or service. Subsequently, after finalizing the categorization, the system identifies all vendors that offer a particular type of product or service in the community. The baseline price for vendors is set as the average asking price across vendors. By having a consistent market price set for a product or service across all vendors in the community, the system enhances efficiency and minimizes possible supply or quality distortions that may arise as a result of varied prices. A platform service charge (a fixed percentage of that price) is added to the baseline price before calculating the price for consumers. To encourage vendors to lower their asking price, in assigning orders, priority should be given to vendors that submit a lower asking price for the product or service. Thus, vendors that bid with a lower price than their competition are selected to fulfil orders first. The potential drawback is the downgrading of quality, but quality can be monitored and promoted to avoid this problem.

The next step is to determine the price per consumer. This is more complicated given that we do not know in advance the income levels of consumers who place orders for a particular product or service. The system can use an algorithm to predict the frequency at which consumers at various income levels place orders, relying on patterns of past consumption by active consumers in the system. The primary principle is that the higher the available income of a consumer, the higher the requested price for the product, with high-income consumers subsidizing low-income consumers. When applying this principle, the total revenue received from consumers should cover the baseline price paid to vendors multiplied by the quantity sold, plus the service fee.

Because the calculation of price per consumer is rather technical, I elaborate on it with an illustrative example in the appendix (Box 5.3). In this appendix I provide an example of three vendors that offer a similar product with different asking prices. I show how the baseline price can be computed and how much revenue each vendor receives. I then consider a distribution of 300 consumers at ten different income brackets and illustrate the calculation of product prices for consumers in each income bracket for sequences of orders of 100 products, each given changing demand patterns. In that appendix, I conclude with a discussion of the balancing process that supports the adjustment of prices per period given the surplus or deficit created in the previous period as a result of deviation from the estimated demand pattern. The underlying idea is that demand is estimated based on the previous period, and if the actual revenue is higher (or lower) than expected in the current period, then the prices are adjusted down (or up) in the subsequent period based on the difference. Beyond relying exclusively on demand in the most recent period, there are alternative approaches for estimating demand, for instance, based on average consumption over longer periods of time. There are also various conditions, such as overdemand or oversupply of a product at a given point in time, that require attention. However, regardless of these conditions, the fundamental principle is that affluent consumers subsidize poor consumers based on their relative available income. Simulation and machine learning techniques can be used to refine the pricing algorithm and select the appropriate parameters, with the aim of enhancing the accuracy of the predicted demand pattern and perfecting the formula used for setting prices, as long as the underlying principle of proportional subsidization is kept. In the appendix, I elaborate on how to set the ratio of highest-to-lowest price per product. If this ratio is too high, high-income consumers may feel exploited and may reduce their consumption, while low-income consumers may be disincentivized to work and to increase their income. But if this ratio is too low, the subsidization of the low-income consumers may be insufficient to make products affordable to them. This ratio can be adjusted using machine learning to attract high-income consumers while ensuring sufficient subsidization. In the appendix I also discuss some solutions, e.g., cross-product subsidization, for situations in which there is oversupply or overdemand for a product.

Another possibility for improving the pricing process is to allow consumers to pay more than their requested price if they wish. There is value in allowing prosocial consumers to decide how much they wish to donate.[2] However, if all consumers pay whatever they wish, and some pay less than expected, then the system cannot use predictive algorithms to reach a dynamic equilibrium and guarantee that sufficient revenue is generated to pay vendors. In contrast, if consumers are allowed to pay any price above the requested price in their income bracket, this is likely to result in a surplus that can serve for lowering the price requested from all consumers in the next period via the balancing process mentioned above. By providing consumers with the option of paying more than requested, the system can achieve a more optimal solution that better fits the willingness to pay of prosocial consumers. This solution involves voluntarily increasing the price for some and lowering it for others within the same income bracket (for a summary of the pricing and transaction processes, see Figure 5.1).

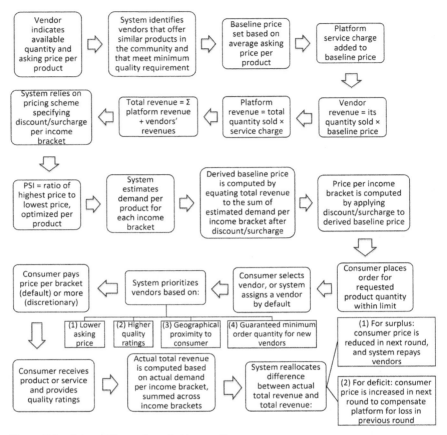

Figure 5.1 *Price setting and market transactions.*

APPENDIX (BOX 5.3) ILLUSTRATION OF THE PRICING PROCESS

To illustrate the calculation, let us assume three vendors that offer a similar type of apple to be sold through the system. Let us further hypothetically assume that Vendor 1 offers 20 apples for $1 each, Vendor 2 offers 50 apples for $1.5 each, and Vendor 3 offers 30 apples for $2 each. In total, there are 100 apples being offered, with the baseline price for a vendor set as the average asking price: (20 × $1 + 50 × $1.5 + 30 × $2)/100 = $1.55 per apple. For a service charge of 10%, the baseline price for the average consumer is set at $P_b = \$1.55 \times (1 + 10\%) = \$1.705$ per apple. Assuming that there is sufficient demand for the whole quantity being offered, the total expected revenue is $170.5, of which the platform will receive $15.5 in service fees, and the vendors will correspondingly receive (20 × $1.55) = $31, (50 × $1.55) = $77.5, and (30 × $1.55) = $46.5. Let us assume that there are currently 300 apple consumers in the system, and that their income distribution is as follows: [5, 10, 30, 50, 80, 60, 30, 20, 15, 0], with each number corresponding to a count of consumers in the relevant income bracket. That is, 5 consumers are categorized at the lowest 10th percentile of income in their community, 10 at the lowest 20th percentile, 30 at the lowest 30th percentile, 50 at the 40th percentile, and so on. Let us further assume the following price distribution for apples in the system: [−50%, −40%, −30%, −20%, −10%, +10%, +20%, +30%, +40%, + 50%], with each value indicating the extent of discount or surcharge consumers would need to pay based on their income bracket. That is, at the lowest income bracket, consumers would be offered a 50% discount on the baseline price, while at the highest bracket they would pay 50% extra of the baseline price. The general price per income bracket is therefore $P_b \times 0.5 \times (\frac{7}{9} + \frac{20}{9} \times k)$, where P_b is the baseline price and k ranges from 10% to 100%, corresponding to the income percentile.

The challenge is that we do not know which of these consumers will be placing orders for the available 100 apples. As a first approximation, we can estimate a demand pattern based on consumption in the previous period. Let us assume that for the previous 100 apples, the demand from each income bracket was as follows: [2, 8, 11, 16, 21, 25, 14, 3, 0, 0]. In this case, P_b is not equal to $1.705. Rather, P_b is derived based on the following formula for derived price based on total revenue and the distribution of consumers' income: $\$170.5 = 2 \times P_b \times 0.5 \times (\frac{7}{9} + \frac{20}{9} \times 0.1) + 8 \times$

$P_b \times 0.5 \times (\frac{7}{9} + \frac{20}{9} \times 0.2) + 11 \times P_b \times 0.5 \times (\frac{7}{9} + \frac{20}{9} \times 0.3) + 16 \times$

$P_b \times 0.5 \times (\frac{7}{9} + \frac{20}{9} \times 0.4) + 21 \times P_b \times 0.5 \times (\frac{7}{9} + \frac{20}{9} \times 0.5) + 25 \times$

$P_b \times 0.5 \times (\frac{7}{9} + \frac{20}{9} \times 0.6) + 14 \times P_b \times 0.5 \times (\frac{7}{9} + \frac{20}{9} \times 0.7) + 3 \times P_b$

$\times 0.5 \times (\frac{7}{9} + \frac{20}{9} \times 0.8) = (50 \times \frac{7}{9} + 24.6 \times \frac{20}{9}) \times P_b.$ Thus, $P_b = \dfrac{170.5}{93\frac{5}{9}}$

$= \$1.822446555$. Accordingly, consumers in the lowest income bracket will pay $\$1.82245 \times 0.5 \times (\frac{7}{9} + \frac{20}{9} \times 0.1) = \$0.91122$ per apple, consumers in the 2nd income bracket will pay $\$1.82245$

$\times 0.5 \times (\frac{7}{9} + \frac{20}{9} \times 0.2) = \$1.11372$ per apple, and so on, with the consumers in the 8th income bracket (the highest for this product) paying $\$1.82245 \times 0.5 \times (\frac{7}{9} + \frac{20}{9} \times 0.8) = \$2.32868$ per apple.

If in the current consumption period the distribution of demand across income brackets will be identical to that in the previous period, then the total revenue for the 100 apples will equal $170.5, which is sufficient to pay the vendors. In practice, the demand pattern is likely to vary, which can result in either a lower or a higher total revenue for the 100 apples. A balancing process is needed to reach equilibrium. By way of illustration, suppose that the actual demand pattern turned out to be [0, 6, 11, 14, 27, 23, 11, 6, 2, 0]. In this case, the total revenue would be $6 \times \$1.82245$

$\times 0.5 \times (\frac{7}{9} + \frac{20}{9} \times 0.2) + 11 \times \$1.82245 \times 0.5 \times (\frac{7}{9} + \frac{20}{9} \times 0.3) +$

$14 \times \$1.82245 \times 0.5 \times (\frac{7}{9} + \frac{20}{9} \times 0.4) + 27 \times \$1.82245 \times 0.5 \times (\frac{7}{9} +$

$\frac{20}{9} \times 0.5) + 23 \times \$1.82245 \times 0.5 \times (\frac{7}{9} + \frac{20}{9} \times 0.6) + 11 \times \$1.82245$

$\times 0.5 \times (\frac{7}{9} + \frac{20}{9} \times 0.7) + 6 \times \$1.82245 \times 0.5 \times (\frac{7}{9} + \frac{20}{9} \times 0.8) + 2$

$\times \$1.82245 \times 0.5 \times (\frac{7}{9} + \frac{20}{9} \times 0.9) = \$175.5624$. In this scenario, there is a surplus of $\$175.5624 - \$170.5 = \$5.0624$. Therefore, when estimating the prices for the next 100 apples traded on the platform, the actual demand pattern from the previous round [0, 6, 11, 14, 27, 23, 11, 6, 2, 0] will serve for the estimation, and to the extent that the same three vendors submit similar asking prices, then from the total revenue of $170.5, the excess $5.0624 will be deducted, and the prices will be calculated so that the total revenue from selling the apples reaches $\$170.5 - \$5.0624 = \$165.4376$.

On top of this amount, the excess $5.0624 will be added by the platform to the amount paid to vendors, thus balancing it with the previous period. In turn, if instead of a surplus there would be a deficit following the previous transaction, then the deficit amount would be added to the total revenue and hence increase the price asked from consumers in the next period, again reaching balance across periods. Of course, the composition and price quotes of vendors may vary, which could influence the baseline price.

In the above pricing example, the price formula was linear across income brackets. Another alternative is to make the prices proportional to the mean income level at each bracket. Even if we keep the simpler linear formula, there is the question of price range. In the above example, the highest price bracket was three times higher than the lowest bracket. Specifically, consumers in the $k = 100$th percentile paid 50% more than the baseline price, while consumers in the $k = 10$th percentile paid 50% less than the baseline price. Thus, the ratio of highest price to lowest price was $1.5/0.5 = 3$. Although the hope is that all consumers are prosocial, the tendency of affluent consumers to purchase products may decline as this ratio increases. Another potential drawback is that to the extent that the above ratio comes close to the income difference ratio, poor consumers may have no incentive to increase their income, whereas their tendency to purchase products may decline as this ratio decreases. The greater the expected prosocial behavior in the system, the higher the ratio that can be set. Hence, this ratio can be referred to as the Prosociality Index, or PSI. The PSI should be set at a level that is not too high, in order to attract a sufficient number of affluent consumers who do not feel that they overpay relative to their income. The PSI should be also sufficiently low to motivate employment among low-income earners who realize that the subsidizing is not sufficient to offset the income differences. Yet the PSI must be sufficiently high to provide meaningful subsidies to poor consumers. To allow flexibility, it is best to set a different PSI for each type of product or service and to rely on machine learning techniques to converge on the optimal PSI per product. The PSI can be also adjusted over time in response to changing demand patterns. At the outset, the PSI can be set at a relatively low level to attract affluent consumers to join the platform, and then be gradually increased as consumers gain more confidence using the platform.

Another contingency concerns the possibility for oversupply or overdemand. The price setting should work smoothly when there is a sufficient volume of transactions from consumers with various income levels. To the extent that there is an insufficient number of consumers placing orders per product, it is possible to cross-subsidize related products. For instance, suppose that there is a relatively small demand for apples and oranges. In this case, it is possible to determine that high-income consumers of oranges subsidize low-income consumers of apples. The question is to what extent apples indeed substitute for oranges. We can define a Cross-Subsidy Index (CSI_{ij}), which defines the relatedness between any pair of products i and j. When $CSI_{ij} = 0$, the two products are unrelated, and there should be no cross-subsidizing between them. When $CSI_{ij} = 1$, the two products are perfect substitutes, and there is complete subsidizing between them. For a $0 < CSI_{ij} < 1$, this index reveals the extent of relatedness, and thus the extent of possible cross-subsidizing between the two types of products. Each product will have its own price scheme, but the pricing of the two products will be related as indicated by this index, so that a high price paid for product i can be used to subsidize the low price paid for product j, and vice versa.

5.3   PURCHASE LIMITS

One of the key social responsibilities of consumers is their commitment to reduce consumption. Such a commitment is unlikely to emerge voluntarily in a community. To achieve that, a distinctive feature of the cooperative economy is the reliance on system-set restrictions on consumption as opposed to voluntary reduction in consumption. The former approach has not been typically used to battle overconsumption in the current economic system. In the cooperative economy, the subsidization of products and services could unfortunately increase the demand for them. As evidenced with the current economic system, affluent consumers enjoy greater purchasing power, and typically consume more. However, the application of subsidies in the cooperative economy can also increase the purchasing power of low-income consumers, who may then increase their tendency to consume. Given the distribution of income in the population, i.e., a greater number of consumers with lower income compared to consumers with higher income, the outcome of price subsidization may be further overconsumption of natural resources, counter to the objective set for the cooperative economy. To reduce overconsumption of natural resources, there is a need to impose purchase limits. The subsidization process makes products and services more expensive to high-income consumers, which creates a natural disincentive for them to consume relative to the price levels prevalent in the current economic system. These high-income consumers are likely to naturally reduce their consumption to an extent. Accordingly, purchase limits are mostly required for low-income consumers. This is also the case because the consumers in these income brackets would experience a sudden increase in their purchasing power after joining the system, which may spur consumption. Given the increased purchasing power of low-income earners, their purchase limits should be more restrictive.

The underlying idea is that purchase limits should be set based on what is reasonable for a consumer to consume per his or her household size. The question is how to determine what is reasonable, given that consumers vary in preferences for the products and services that they consume. Practically, one method is to set purchase limits based on the consumption habits of consumers at the intermediate income bracket. These consumers enjoy an average purchasing power that is barely influenced by subsidies. After accounting for substitute products and services, a limit can be set based on their observed consumption. For instance, if the average consumer consumes 60 apples per year, then the limit can be set at 25 percent above that number, i.e., at 75 apples per year. Some flexibility may be introduced if considering substitute products and allowing for overconsumption of one product at the expense of a substitute product, given their CSI.

The purchase limit can be applied consistently for all consumers at income brackets lower than the intermediate one. For consumers at higher income brackets, assuming no shortage, there is in fact merit in having them consume more apples, since this could increase the subsidization of low-income consumers, with the only remaining caveat being that of overconsumption of natural resources. To cope with this caveat, purchase limits should be imposed on consumers at all income brackets and be set at a level that is restrictive even to high-income consumers. Therefore, it is possible to gradually increase the purchase limits to those consumers from 25 percent up to 100 percent of the average consumption. Accordingly, the corresponding limits per consumer for each of the ten income brackets could be [+25%, +25%, +25%, +25%, +25%, +35%, +50%, +65%, +80%, +100%]. The expectation is that very few consumers would consume at the maximum level permitted because the limits are set above the consumption level of the average consumer.

How should these purchase limits be imposed? For the above example, the limit of 75 apples per year corresponds to 6.25 apples per month. Hence, a consumer that purchases 5 apples can be notified that s/he is approaching the limit, a consumer that purchases 6 apples can be informed that s/he has reached the limit, and a consumer who seeks to purchase more than 6 apples can be notified that s/he exceeded the limit, and only 6 apples would be approved for purchase. Some provisions may apply, e.g., it may be possible to borrow an extra amount at the expense of a substitute product or at the expense of next month's limit, as long as the annual limit still applies. The above example raises the question of whether the purchase limits should be set per purchase or at a monthly or annual level. There is some discretion in deciding how to impose these limits. For example, there may be a legitimate reason for a consumer to purchase a high volume from a particular product for a certain occasion. In this case, low-income consumers may be able to purchase the extra quantity for a non-subsidized price. Another possibility is to give every consumer some exemptions that can be applied when making a high-volume purchase. Yet another possibility is to apply a surcharge for purchases above the limit. Finally, it may be reasonable to limit food consumption based on total calorie value per person. These alternatives can be further studied with respect to their implications for the system's ease of use and for overconsumption.

Another important responsibility of consumers that should be imposed concerns a resale restriction. This is to avoid consumers leveraging the subsidizing process to profit from arbitrage in a secondary market. Therefore, purchases should be limited to personal use by the household members and untransferable via resale. For instance, the system should not allow a low-income consumer to purchase a product at a discounted price and then resell it to a high-income consumer at an intermediate price where both make a profit. In part, the limits on purchased quantity restrict the scope of such undesirable practice. But it is technically possible, so in the service contract such practice should be termed a violation of system rules, for which those involved in the resale transaction would be disqualified and excluded from the system. The question, then, is what can be done with purchased products and services that have not been used by consumers, given the sustainability objective and the aim to reduce waste. Although resale is forbidden, donations are welcome, so consumers can share their purchased products or services. In fact, the cooperative economy will provide a platform for donations by consumers and vendors to facilitate this practice. Furthermore, the system will provide a platform for barter to enable vendors to facilitate the exchange of unused products and services under certain conditions, which I discuss later. The notion of purchase limits and resale restrictions is atypical in electronic commerce, but with the aim of restricting overconsumption and abuse of natural resources, it is important to implement these restrictions. To be effective, the setting of purchase limits should be accompanied by educational programs that inform consumers about the undesirable consequences of overconsumption and the importance of reducing consumption.

5.4   QUALITY RATINGS

Whereas the pricing process provides vendors with an incentive to reduce prices, this should not come at the expense of quality. Quality ratings are essential for the functioning of the cooperative economy. I propose four types of ratings: product quality, delivery quality, vendor quality, and sustainability rating. The first three ratings can be submitted by consumers after receiving a product or service, while the sustainability rating can be based on external assessment. Consumers' quality ratings can rely on a standard five-star scale, with the average consumer rating serving as the score that is made visible to consumers for each product and vendor. This score can be made available for any vendor for which a sufficient number of consumer ratings has been posted. For instance, it could be determined that at least 100 ratings are needed to exhibit that score. Given that different products and services have distinct performance parameters such as taste, speed, or appearance, a subjective assessment by consumers should be sufficient for product quality.

Vendor quality refers to the overall quality of customer service provided by the vendor, including the vendor's responsiveness, handling of requests, and resolution of emerging issues with orders. This is independent of product quality, although product quality could reflect on the vendor rating to the extent that the advertised product features are inconsistent with the actual product features noted by consumers. The quality of delivery can be assessed separately because fulfillment and delivery will be mostly provided by independent third parties, which are separately rated. For that rating, quality means on-time delivery and the condition in which the product was delivered.

Additionally, each vendor should be assigned a sustainability score. To that aim, the system can rely on established metrics. Several such metrics are available to date. For instance, MSCI (www.msci.com) has developed a rating system that captures a vendor's resilience to long-term, industry material environmental, social, and governance (ESG) risks. Their rating indicates the extent to which the vendor has coped well with exposure to such risks relative to its industry peers. An alternative metric is S&P

Global Corporate Sustainability Assessment (CSA) (www.spglobal.com/ esg/csa/), which relies on industry questionnaires and provides a score ranging from 0 to 100. Another alternative is RepRisk (reprisk.com), which offers an ESG metric that leverages advanced machine learning in combination with assessments by trained analysts. Finally, Asset4 from Refinitiv (www.refinitiv.com/en/financial-data/company-data/esg-data) is yet another database offering ESG scores for vendors. Each alternative has some pros and cons, and the corresponding scores are not highly correlated. When comparing six different ratings, researchers reported an average correlation that ranges between 0.46[3] and 0.54.[4] Furthermore, the coverage of these metrics is limited to about 10,000 vendors, so they do not cover small vendors in some countries. Therefore, in addition to relying on these established metrics, vendors should be asked to complete a questionnaire that provides some basic information about their sustainability performance. Small vendors should also receive assistance from the platform operator and a group composed of established vendors that can serve as a community support forum for enhancing sustainability.

The vendor quality ratings, including the sustainability rating, can serve several purposes. The first purpose is to screen out vendors that do not meet the minimum set requirements. Failure to meet a certain score, e.g., 2 stars on the 1–5-star scale, may result in excluding the low-quality vendor from the system or at least from the business sector in which that vendor received a low quality rating. Vendors with a below-average score may be notified and asked to improve their sustainability policies and enhance their quality based on the feedback received from consumers and rating agencies. All vendors should receive detailed reports of their quality ratings by geography, consumer type, etc., benchmarked against competition, so that they can work on improving their quality performance. The second purpose of the vendor quality rating and sustainability rating is to provide consumers with valuable information about the vendors, which they can consider in their choice of vendor and purchasing decision. In that regard, it is important to acknowledge the numerous studies that reveal that consumers seek information about the sustainability ratings of vendors and are increasingly willing to pay more for sustainability-marked products. For example, the 2021 Global

Sustainability Study conducted by Simon-Kucher & Partners revealed that 85 percent of consumers have become "greener" in recent years, and that sustainability is an important purchase criterion for 60 percent of consumers, with 50 percent ranking it as part of their top five criteria. Moreover, 34 percent of consumers say that they are willing to pay a 25 percent premium for sustainable products or services.[5] Finally, another purpose of this quality assessment is to prioritize vendors that score high on quality and sustainability when the system automatically assigns orders for fulfillment by vendors, which is the default for low-income earners. In sum, quality ratings motivate vendors to improve their practices and their quality (see Box 5.4).

BOX 5.4   QUALITY RATINGS

1. *Product quality*—Average subjective assessment by consumers of the quality of a product or service provided by a vendor (e.g., on a 5-star scale)
2. *Vendor quality*—Average subjective assessment by consumers of the vendor's quality (e.g., responsiveness, handling orders, customer service, on a 5-star scale)
3. *Delivery quality*—Average subjective assessment by consumers of the delivery agent's quality (e.g., speed, packaging, on a 5-star scale)
4. *Sustainability rating*—An annual external assessment by rating agencies or a validated self-assessment by vendor of its sustainability performance

---

5.5   CONSUMER AND VENDOR PRIVILEGES

Having considered the admission criteria and the rules for setting prices and promoting quality, let us consider in more detail the privileges and responsibilities of, first, consumers and then vendors in the cooperative economy. In a nutshell, consumers, at least those with below-average income, benefit from subsidized prices. In addition to increasing their purchasing power, the system provides them with an opportunity to increase income by initiating a small business with guaranteed market access, and subsequently using the extra income to make purchases. High-income consumers can gain in happiness and self-esteem as well as enjoy flexibility in choosing vendors. For their part, vendors, including new entrants, can rely on orders assigned by the system based on objective price, quality, and location criteria, as well as enjoy a guaranteed volume of purchase orders.

The main privilege of consumers in the cooperative economy is the possibility for low-income consumers to enjoy enhanced purchasing power and thus pay less for products and services compared to the price levels in the current economic system. Another privilege is in enabling low-income consumers to create vendor accounts and start operating small businesses, which can increase their income. To the extent that low-income consumers are unemployed or underemployed, they should be encouraged to open a vendor account and produce products or provide services that suit their skills and expertise. The system can assist such individual entrepreneurs by providing them with practical guidance for starting their businesses as well as guaranteed minimum sales, to the extent that there is demand for the type of products or services they offer. This privilege can be made available to all new vendors. Nevertheless, individual consumers who decide to start a business should also receive discounted service fees, which could increase their income or make their prices more attractive to consumers. For instance, if the standard service fee is 10 percent of the baseline price, this fee can be reduced for a low-income individual, so that it is proportionally discounted in such a way that those at the 50 percent income bracket are still charged a 10 percent service fee, those in the 40 percent income bracket are charged an 8 percent fee, those in the 30 percent income bracket are charged a 6 percent fee, those in the 20 percent income bracket are charged a 4 percent fee, and those in the lowest 10 percent income bracket are charged only a 2 percent fee. The discounted service fee should be made available only to consumers who become individual entrepreneurs rather than to all other vendors, which should be charged the standard

10 percent service fee. Another benefit for a consumer that also operates as a vendor in the system is that this consumer can use the business income from transactions in the system for making purchases, as long as there is a clear separation between business purchases transacted at the baseline price and consumer purchases transacted at the subsidized price based on the consumer's income. Hence, the main benefit for a consumer-vendor is the available credit in the system.

But what privileges do high-income consumers receive? Referring to the research discussed earlier, consumers who contribute or donate more using the system's subsidizing process can expect to gain greater happiness. Such realization is supported by religious and spiritual beliefs that suggest that receiving with the aim of giving back and influencing others in one's community is most fulfilling. However, such donation is fulfilling only to the extent that individuals can afford it. Thus, the optimization of the PSI (see Box 5.3) should ensure that high-income consumers are sufficiently content with the set prices. Knowing that with every purchase they make they benefit many other consumers is of perceived value for prosocial consumers. To the extent that these consumers believe in karma or in other spiritual or religious principles of cause-effect or reciprocity, then they can expect that the universe will repay them for their generosity. The platform merely automates the process of giving, making it more straightforward. These consumers do not need to look for the street beggar; the needy are easily reachable on the platform. But the platform would provide some tangible privileges to those who contribute more, mostly as a token of appreciation rather than as a monetary compensation in the traditional sense.

One possibility is to identify high-income consumers as "donors," perhaps making this status visible on their consumer page. Nevertheless, the system should be designed in such a way that every consumer, not only a high-income consumer, contributes to consumers at lower income brackets, with those at the lowest income bracket having the option to donate in kind. Hence, all consumers can be considered donors. Furthermore, according to some religious beliefs, a donation is considered charity only if it is covert without expectation for personal benefit, i.e., true altruism. In that sense, having a visible "donor" status undermines the perceived benefit. Another privilege that high-income consumers who pay more than the baseline price could enjoy is their ability to choose a vendor to place an order with. Low-income consumers who pay less than the baseline price would be assigned a vendor by default based on the system's criteria, and while they can change that assignment, high-income consumers would be able to switch to their vendor of choice more easily.

This raises the question of automatic vendor assignment. In the case of multiple vendors that provide a similar product or service, the system would prioritize a vendor based on price, quality, and location. First, vendors that asked for a lower price compared to their competition would receive priority in receiving orders. There is a double incentive for such vendors to ask for lower prices. Besides receiving priority in order assignment, they can profit more within the permitted range because the set baseline price is higher than their asking price when they bid below average price. The lower their asking price relative to the baseline price, the higher their potential profit and the higher the priority that they receive in assignments, which creates an incentive for vendors to ask for lower prices.

Second, to be assigned orders, a vendor must meet minimum quality requirements, with the exception of new vendors that have not yet received sufficient quality ratings. New vendors and vendors that meet quality requirements would be guaranteed a minimum order quantity, assuming that there is sufficient demand for their product or service and that they can supply the requested quantity. The guaranteed minimum quantity would be set to facilitate competition. On the one hand, new entrants—typically small vendors—can gain market access by having that minimum order quantity guaranteed. On the other hand, the minimum quantity should not be too high in order to provide an incentive for vendors to compete for the remaining quantity for sale. Machine learning techniques can be used for finding that minimum quantity needed for enhancing competition. For instance, it could be decided that 25 percent of the annual quantity ordered is allocated to the guaranteed minimum quantity, which is then divided across all qualified vendors in proportion to the volume they sold in the previous period. New entrants with insufficient sales history could receive a minimum guaranteed quantity equal to 25 percent of their capacity. It could also be decided that regardless of their time of entry to the industry, small vendors would receive the minimum guaranteed quantity as long as they meet quality standards. This initial 25 percent could then be modified based on a machine learning algorithm in a way that increases competition, that is, favors new entrants while providing an incentive for vendors to compete on price and quality for the non-guaranteed order volume. The application of a minimum guaranteed quantity for new vendors also replaces investment in advertising, which is avoided on the platform.

Besides meeting minimum quality requirements and beyond the minimum guaranteed quantity, vendors with higher quality ratings should receive priority when consumers' orders are assigned to vendors. This quality criterion in assigning orders encourages vendors to enhance the quality of their offerings with respect to product quality, overall vendor quality, and the sustainability criterion. Finally, another criterion in addition to price and quality is geographical proximity. Vendors that are more proximate to a consumer should receive priority in assignments. This serves several purposes. First, connecting proximate consumers and vendors means greater potential for face-to-face interaction and acquaintance, which creates a sense of community. This sense promotes trust and enhances the expected prosocial behavior, while reducing the hazard of opportunistic behavior. Second, reducing the physical distance between vendors and consumers can reduce the order fulfillment time, and the downstream value chain can be managed more efficiently. For certain services, such as a hairdresser visit, proximity is essential, given that the consumer and vendor must physically meet. Finally, besides enabling a consumer to receive a service or collect the product from the vendor's site, and thus save on delivery charges, the shorter delivery distance reduces the overall distance traveled for deliveries, and thus creates less pollution due to carbon dioxide emissions, which harms the environment. This supports the sustainability objective of the cooperative economy.

A final question is how much weight should be given to price versus quality and distance when assigning orders to vendors. To answer this question, we can start with an equal weight, and then use machine learning and an optimization algorithm to find the weight composition that maximizes customer satisfaction, i.e., the weights assigned to product, vendor, delivery, and sustainability quality ratings in the system. In addition to the minimum guaranteed quantity to vendors, each vendor would need to specify its maximum available quantity for each product or service in order to ensure that when orders are assigned to vendors, the assigned quantity would not exceed the vendor's capacity. Vendors should be able to update their available capacity, which can be updated automatically based on assigned orders, bearing in mind that inability to fulfill orders in a timely manner could negatively impact the vendor's quality rating.

As noted, low-income consumers would be assigned a vendor by default based on the aggregate quality ratings, with the option of deselecting that default vendor. High-income consumers would be given the opportunity to select a vendor of their choice, which means that their choice might depart from the optimal combination of price, quality, and distance. Still, the privilege of having a choice in selecting a vendor would probably compensate for the loss in expected satisfaction associated with the automated choice. It is possible that consumers prefer a specific vendor as a result of a previous experience with that vendor or for another reason, so consumers should be given the option of repeated purchases from a previously contracted vendor. In any case, for high-income consumers, available vendors should be listed in order of priority based on their combined price, quality, and distance scores as well as based on their available quantity, so that high-priority options would be made more visible, with the first choice presented being the default automated choice based on the set criteria. Most consumers are expected to retain the default choice, but having the option to replace a vendor has an intrinsic value. Note that, whereas in the existing economic system, platform owners also prioritize vendors or self-preference their own products or service offering, in the cooperative economy, the platform's defaults and priorities serve the interests of consumers rather than those of the platform operator.

5.6 VENDOR AND CONSUMER RESPONSIBILITIES

The social responsibilities of vendors and consumers who wish to take part in the cooperative economy are translated to concrete commitments. These commitments include disclosing business information and complying with the profit restriction rule, so that excess profit is redistributed to consumers. Additional commitments include avoiding personal use of business purchases and meeting employment standards. In addition to the purchase limits, consumers, much like vendors, commit to the "rest rule," i.e., avoiding purchases and production or service provision for one day per week.

First, as explained above, vendors are subject to disclosure requirements at the admission phase. In addition, vendors are required to disclose their profits and revenues at the end of each fiscal year. The reason for this commitment is that the system applies a maximum profitability restriction on vendors. There are several possibilities for deciding about the maximum profitability allowed. One possibility is to impose a universal restriction on all vendors regardless of their industry or business. For example, such a restriction can be set at the rate of 10 percent return on sales (net profit margin, i.e., net income divided by total revenues). Nevertheless, some industries are asset-intensive while others are equity-intensive, and it is not obvious that the relevant measure should be return on sales rather than return on assets or return on equity. Furthermore, there is variation in the typical profitability across various industries. For example, in the United States, at the end of 2018 (prior to the Covid-19 pandemic), the average net profit margin in the auto repair and maintenance industry was 12 percent; in the construction industry, 5 percent; in hotels and hospitality, 8 percent; in the food and

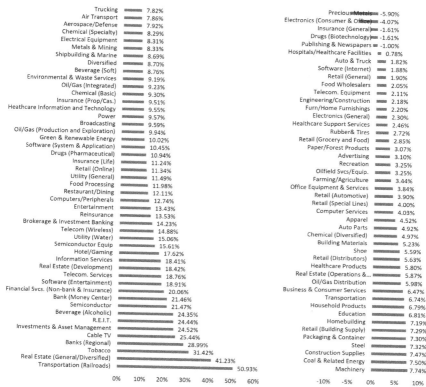

Figure 5.2   *Net profit margin by US industry.*

restaurants industry, 15 percent; in retail, 5 percent; and in transportation, 19 percent. Across all industries in the United States, the average net margin was 8.89 percent at the end of 2018. Hence, a limit of 10 percent profitability is only slightly above the cross-industry average profitability. Nonetheless, there is variance in profitability across industries, as revealed in Figure 5.2, as well as variance across countries.[6] Hence, it is possible to set the profit limit based on each industry's annual average per country, and then update this limit annually. In the long term, if the cooperative economy captures a substantial share of the economic activity in a country, it is likely to distort the observed average profit margins in that country, which could result in convergence on a particular level of industry profit. In this case, it would be possible to set the profit limit based on a cross-industry average within the country. Still, further research is needed to specify the optimal approach for identifying the reasonable profit level in an industry.

What happens when a vendor exceeds the limit specified by the system for the profit margin? In this case, the vendor should be required to donate the excess profit to consumers via the system. This can be done in several ways. One is to donate, during the following year, products and services whose value is equivalent to the excess profit; a second is to transfer funds equivalent to the excess profit to the platform; and a third is to donate part of the excess profit to voluntary organizations or another noble cause from listed options as per the vendor's choice.

In the first case, the value of the donated product or service should be determined based on the average asking price of vendors with similar products or services at the time of donation, as usually set by the system. For example, suppose that the vendor had an annual revenue of $10 million with a net profit margin of 12 percent. If the profit limit was set at 10 percent, then the excess profit is $10 million $\times$ 2% = $200K. The vendor can donate products valued at $200K (first option) or transfer the $200K to the platform to be redistributed to consumers (second option). A possible question is whether the excess profits should be redistributed to all consumers, only to those consumers who purchased products from the vendor in question, or to prospective consumers who will purchase products from that vendor in the subsequent period. Redistributing the excess profits to consumers who made the purchases in the previous year is most appropriate. Because they were overcharged. The reimbursement can be calculated as a percentage discount on subsequent purchases based on the relative amounts paid on the previous purchases from that vendor. Nevertheless, other redistribution methods can be considered. The system could also allow the vendor to donate up to 50 percent of the excess profit to charity organizations, voluntary associations, and other noble causes from a list of verified options (third option). While these donations do not directly benefit consumers on the platform, they do benefit society at large and thus serve the mission of the cooperative economy. There may be tax and inventory management considerations when the vendor makes the choice between the three options for repaying the excess profit. An interesting case of a firm that has already implemented a business model that applies profit restriction and value redistribution is Laka Bicycle Insurance, which does not charge a fixed sum, instead calculating its fee based on the collective claims, with a commitment to redistribute 80 percent of the total amount to pay claims. This motivates its customers to minimize incidents for the sake of the collective and to reduce their paid fee.

With respect to the second option for repaying excess profit, one alternative is for the platform to accumulate all the monetary transfers from vendors and then use the balance to provide discounts to all consumers, regardless of their income level, throughout the year, with the discounts allocated to all products and services so that the same percentage discount applies to all products and services. Of course, the actual consumption of all products and services can only be estimated based on past consumption, but to the extent that the actual discount amounts provided to consumers vary slightly from the available balance based on predicted consumption, the difference can be balanced out in the following year. Furthermore, the platform operator's profit is also subject to the same profit restriction rule, so excess profit from service fees should be redistributed to consumers at the end of each fiscal year. The implication of this profit restriction rule is that vendors have no incentive to set prices that maximize their profits. Rather, even if they seek to maximize their profit, they may aim not to exceed the set restriction, e.g., 10 percent return on sales.

To apply the profit restriction, vendors would be asked to disclose their revenues and profits even if the vendors are privately owned and not publicly listed. Such disclosure would need to be verified and confirmed by their independent accounting firms. This information should not be used other than to calculate the excess profit, so it would not be revealed to the public, although the vendor might decide to reveal this information. For instance, some vendors may hope to improve their reputation by publishing the amount refunded to consumers, although this also suggests that they may have overpriced their products and services in the first place. The profit restriction rule should be enforced. To the extent that a vendor refuses to transfer the excess profit to consumers through the platform, this can be considered a violation of system rules for which the vendor should be penalized by being excluded from the system. Alternatively, the platform may accept orders on behalf of the delinquent vendor and withhold payments until the excess profit debt is repaid by the received revenue.

A relevant question is how to handle a case of a vendor that generates revenues outside the system, using alternative marketplaces. In this case, it would make sense to calculate the revenues and profit only for products and services sold on the platform during the first three years of its platform membership, but then, after these three years, take into account the overall revenue and profit of the vendor. The motivation for this deferred restriction is to attract vendors to join the platform without creating a disincentive in the form of overall profit restriction, and once the vendors have substantial business transacted through the platform, extend the profit restriction. This can help achieve the mission of moving away from profit maximization beyond the boundaries of the cooperative economy.

Another question is how to manage vendors that also place orders for raw materials and inputs on the platform. In this case, the vendor is considered a business customer, with applicable rules that differ from those applying to individual consumers. In order to maintain fair competition among vendors in their respective industry, there should be no price discrimination when purchasing inputs. Hence, business customers should pay the fixed baseline market price plus the service fee for products and services that they purchase for their firms rather than receive discounts or pay surcharges based on their business income. Such purchases must not be used by the owners or employees of the vendor for personal use; otherwise, this could bypass the subsidization process and the consumer purchase limit. Personal use of products and services purchased by business customers is thus considered a violation of system rules and may result in excluding the vendor from the system. The advantage of being a business customer, unlike an individual consumer, is that there are no purchase limits applicable for business use. Nevertheless, being a vendor, the business customer is still subject to the profit limit rule, and thus has to redistribute its excess profit to consumers. All consumers including business customers are also subject to the resale restriction, and thus cannot resell purchased products or services for a profit. An exception is business customers that operate as importers or provide value-added resale services within their stated line of business.

Another unique responsibility of both vendors and consumers relates to rest. Consumers would commit to avoid consumption, i.e., purchasing, for one day per week. Vendors also would commit to avoid production or any other business activity for one day per week. Indeed, many vendors in most countries already follow this rule and do not operate for at least one day per week, but the objective is to reinforce this rule, so that employees receive at least one day of rest during the week. The choice of day could follow the tradition in the country in question. While this may facilitate social interaction in the community, some discretion may be left to the vendor or employee. The objective is to promote a work-life balance and enable individuals to devote time to activities other than work and consumption. Such mission is also promoted by various religions and state laws. As for consumers, this restriction facilitates rest, but also battles overconsumption. The rest rule should not be enforced actively, but consumers and vendors may receive notices when violating this rule, and the quality and sustainability ratings of the vendors may be affected. Furthermore, to the extent that a vendor violates employment regulations, it may be subject to enforcement by state authorities. A final rule that would be imposed on vendors after three years of affiliation with the system concerns employment terms, which I will discuss in detail later.

5.7 PLATFORM OPERATOR RESPONSIBILITIES

The platform operator in the cooperative economy, i.e., the Cooperative Economy Foundation, takes on several responsibilities and self-imposed restrictions that go beyond those taken by platform owners in the current economic system. These commitments include responsibility for developing, operating, and maintaining the system, while optimizing its parameters to serve societal goals. Additional commitments include abstaining from competing with vendors by offering its own products and services on the platform, while delegating order fulfillment, service centers, and banking services to third parties to the extent possible. Furthermore, the platform operator commits to avoiding any form of advertising or recommendations on the platform while protecting user data and maintaining transparency of business processes. It should also adhere to protective employment standards and restrict pay differences across its employees and the employees of vendors.

First and foremost, the platform operator is responsible for developing and implementing the economic system as per the rules discussed previously, e.g., the admission process with its various verifications and the subsidization process, among others. Various algorithms should be developed and deployed for determining parameters for the price subsidization scheme, consumption predictions, profit limits, minimum guaranteed quantities, etc. Minor changes in these parameters can greatly impact the behavior of consumers or vendors. Hence, the platform operator should commit to optimize the system parameters using means such as questionnaires, simulations, experiments, and machine learning, with the aim of improving the system performance with respect to the stated objectives, such as encouraging competition, minimizing economic inequality using distributed purchasing power, minimizing overconsumption of resources, etc. Thus, the expectation is that leveraging research, developing and applying algorithms, and continuously adjusting the system parameters can enhance the overall welfare of the various stakeholders.

One of the key commitments of the platform operator is not to engage in business activities other than those essential for operating the platform. Hence, the platform operator must not offer its own products and services to compete with vendors, and further, the current practice of self-preferencing must be void in the cooperative economy. A related restriction is that the platform operator must not offer its own fulfillment service and instead rely on existing or new providers of delivery and fulfillment services. Consumers should have several options for fulfillment and delivery. Given the community focus of the platform, one option is for consumers to pick up the product or receive service from the vendor's premises or physical store at no extra charge. Another is to use the vendor's own delivery service to the extent that such a service is being offered. Yet another option is to use the services of third parties, such as local delivery service providers, and as a final option there may be specialized fulfillment service providers that engage in aggregation, packing, and dispatching of orders that are composed of products purchased from multiple vendors. Their fulfillment centers can receive merchandise from vendors, consolidate, and ship it to consumers. Thus, unlike platform owners such as Amazon that operate their own warehouse and fulfillment centers, it should be mostly local third parties that provide such services within their community. Third-party delivery providers should operate as vendors in the system, and thus be subject to all rules applicable to vendors. This means that the price per delivery would be set based on the average asking price for a particular delivery service, e.g., for a given weight, size, and distance. Additionally, the delivery charges paid by consumers would be subsidized so that high-income consumers would pay more for delivery than low-income consumers. The delivery charges would be added to the product or service price plus the service fee that each consumer pays.

Another service that would be offered by third parties relates to support agencies. Because the digital system requires an Internet connection, a computer, or a smartphone, and some proficiency with managing computer infrastructure and electronic commerce transactions, it is probable that the poorest consumers might have no access to the required technological infrastructure or skills needed for operating on the platform. In addition, it is possible that even within richer communities, the elderly and some individuals who are handicapped or suffer from health or mental impairment might be unable to use the system. Therefore, it is important to offer service centers in which the infrastructure and assistance are provided to those who wish to use the system but are unable to do so independently. The platform operator would contract with service agencies that set up the infrastructure and provide the support services to the needy population. These services could also be provided remotely via the phone or another medium. The certified agencies would operate as service providers on the platform and comply with the rules applicable to vendors, e.g., quality ratings, a set baseline price per service unit based on average asking price, guaranteed minimum service orders, and redistribution of excess profit. Unlike other vendors, however, these agencies should be paid by the platform operator rather than by consumers, so that low-income and other deprived consumers can receive this service free of charge.

Although the platform operator should not provide fulfillment and support services, it may offer basic banking services to support transactions on the platform. Still, these services may be furnished by third-party digital banks to the extent that they can be seamlessly integrated into the system and meet reliability and regulatory requirements. Specifically, the provided services should enable consumers and vendors to open a cash account or link their external bank account to the system. This should facilitate transactions on the system, which can be managed electronically without needing to rely on credit cards or other forms of external payments. If consumers choose to receive their salaries on the platform's bank account and use this account for making purchases from vendors that are also set up with the platform, this can enable seamless transactions without requiring extra verification, credit card charges, or delay in consummating the transactions. The platform's cash accounts can be managed mostly in local currency, but some foreign exchange services may be provided if needed.

Another important commitment of the platform operator is to avoid any form of advertising on the platform. In addition, consumers should not be profiled and studied in order to understand their preferences and behavior. Accordingly, no product or service recommendations should be made by the platform, and no attempt should be made to bias, influence, or facilitate consumption. This is strikingly different from the alternative platforms in the modern economy that seek every opportunity to facilitate consumption and make profit at the expense of consumers and the environment, while restricting consumers' free choice. By avoiding advertising and recommendations, the proposed platform should enable consumers to follow their own style and preferences. By taking on these commitments, the platform operator in the cooperative economy would refrain from engaging in business practices that undermine the welfare of consumers and vendors.

There are several domains in which the platform operator's responsibilities exceed those typical of conventional platform owners. Given the sensitivity of the personal and financial information collected from consumers and vendors, even though most information is not retained, it is important to implement cybersecurity measures and follow strict data protection policies. Overall, the platform should meet high standards of data protection and privacy, which has been an issue of concern for established platforms. Cybersecurity is also essential to prevent hackers from accessing the system and exploiting the subsidizing process for their personal gain. The bank accounts of consumers and vendors administered by the system should also be protected.

Another domain in which the platform operator should accept higher standards concerns transparency. In addition to accounting and financial transparency, given the nature of the platform and the need to build trust in it, the system's algorithm should be available for review by authorities. This is to ensure and certify that the algorithm serves its stated purpose. The challenge is that currently authorities have neither the legislation nor the software experts to perform such reviews. The required legislation should be developed and personnel with relevant expertise should be hired by designated government agencies, with the aim that algorithm review will become a standard not only in the cooperative economy, but for all platform ecosystems.

Another responsibility of the platform operator is to adopt protective employment standards. Whereas employment legislation varies from one country to another, there have been documented cases of platform owners violating basic employee rights such as the right to rest, while other platforms, such as Uber and Wolt, have refused to recognize the status of their employees, treating them instead as temporary freelancers who lack basic employee rights. The proposed platform should recognize employees as organizational members. It should limit the work week to 40 hours and offer paid vacation and sick leave, and guarantee a pension, medical insurance, and all the employment terms that are currently available only in certain countries and offered to certain sectors of employers. The platform should also follow strict policies for preventing discrimination by gender, race, age, etc., with the aim of fostering plurality and equality. Most importantly, the platform should restrict pay differences across employees holding different positions. In 2020, it was reported that American CEOs were paid 351 times more than their workers, with 80 percent of CEOs in S&P 500 firms paid more than 100 times the median worker. The 351 pay ratio demonstrates an increase from a 61 pay ratio in 1989.[7] The platform operator should commit to maintain a pay ratio smaller than ten between the highest salaried employee and the lowest salaried employee. For those using the platform, purchasing power is balanced despite income inequality, so the pursuit of income equality by minimizing pay differences should not be perceived as drastic. It serves the same purpose, i.e., enhancing income equality and redistributing value.

Most important is the proposal that the platform operator would require all vendors that participate in the system and that have reached a certain size, e.g., 100 employees, to comply with the same employment standards and reduced pay differences as noted above. Recognizing that this may deter some vendors from joining the system, the service contract with vendors should impose this requirement only after three cumulative years of operation on the platform. Vendors would have three years to adjust their employment policies to adhere to these standards, and perhaps reduce the pay differences gradually. After three years, vendors are expected to have sufficient business transacted through the system to motivate their continued operation and adoption of the proposed employment practices. Here as well, the hope is that the proposed solution would promote societal values beyond the boundaries of the cooperative economy, as the vendors operate also—if not mostly—in other markets and on other platforms.

In addition to the responsibilities already noted, the platform operator is responsible for monitoring and enforcing the system's rules. The system rules are designed to facilitate prosocial behavior and deter opportunistic behavior. For example, consumers are expected to correctly report their income, while vendors are expected to correctly report their profits. Consumers are expected not to resell products that have been traded on the platform for an arbitrage, while vendors are expected not to use their vendor accounts to purchase products for personal use. These are but a few examples of opportunistic behaviors that need to be prevented in order for vendors and consumers to gain trust in the system and exhibit prosocial behavior. To that aim, the platform operator should maintain an audit unit that verifies information provided by system users and identifies suspected violations of system rules. Nevertheless, the hope is that following the launch of the platform and after few years of operation, norms of prosocial behavior transpire, and violations become less frequent. Once these norms have been established, there would be less need for controls and checks, because social pressure, self-governance, and mutual trust may be sufficient to maintain the prosocial behavior that is essential for the proper functioning of the platform.

5.8   BARTER AND DONATIONS

In addition to the two-sided electronic commerce market that will serve as the primary platform for economic exchange, the system will offer further opportunities for exchange between vendors and consumers, namely barter and donations. Barter refers to the direct exchange of products or services among individuals, without payment. For instance, one consumer can exchange five apples for four oranges belonging to another consumer. The platform will offer a barter market in which vendors or consumers can list their offerings and requested products or services, so that other vendors or consumers who possess the requested products or services can respond to these barter offers and perform the exchange transaction. The system would list all the current barter offerings by category, with a search function to facilitate exchange. To the extent that the system identifies a mutual match between the offer of one party and the request of another, it would make the relevant match visible to the two parties. For instance, if an accountant is offering her services and seeks office décor, while a carpenter in her community offers design and furnishing services and needs an accountant, the system can identify this match and flag it to both parties.

The barter platform would facilitate exchange by revealing the market prices for the exchanged products and calculating the suggested quantity for one product to be exchanged for the other. For instance, in the example of apples and oranges, the system can indicate that an apple is worth $1 and an orange is worth $1.25, so that the exchange ratio is 5:4. Of course, the actual price depends on the income levels of the two consumers, or the consumer in question in the case of an exchange with a vendor. For example, suppose the consumer who possesses the apples has a higher income, whereas the consumer who possesses the oranges has a lower income compared with the first consumer. In this case, depending on their respective income brackets, one apple may cost $0.75 to the low-income consumer, whereas one orange may cost $1.5 to the high-income consumer, based on the respective market prices in their income brackets. Therefore, in this example, the exchange ratio is 8:4 rather than 5:4, and to the extent that the parties agree to the exchange, the low-income consumer would receive eight apples for the four oranges, instead of five apples that would have been exchanged if the consumers belonged to the same income bracket. Clearly, the actual exchange is restricted by the quantities of fruits available to the parties and should be rounded to the nearest whole number in the case of an indivisible product. Adapting the value of the product or service per the income brackets of the exchange parties is essential to maintain the subsidization process and prevent arbitrage. If one party is a vendor, then the value of the consumer's product or service to that vendor would be set based on the baseline price, while the value of the product or service offered by the vendor would be set based on the consumer's income bracket at the time of exchange. Each party can agree to offer more for the set barter price, much like a consumer can decide to pay more than the requested price in the two-sided market transaction. The platform would charge the same service fee for this transaction, but it could be split between the two parties. If both parties have above-average income (or if the party is a vendor), a 5 percent fee would be charged to each party. If one of the parties is entitled to a service fee discount, such a discount should be applied.

The barter platform is less efficient than the two-sided market platform because consumers cannot purchase all products and services, only those for which they have relevant products and services to exchange. For this reason, when non-perishable products are involved, the system should extend the matching to include parties that are more geographically distant from each other. Despite the constraints, to the extent that the barter is carried out between consumers rather than vendors, e.g., two owners exchanging apartments for a one-week vacation, then in many countries this exchange is not taxable, so the parties can save on income tax compared to selling merchandise for money.

To avoid arbitrage, the barter system should be subject to some rules. One rule is that the exchange must be performed at the respective adjusted market price for each party, to avoid the case of a consumer purchasing a product at a discount and then exchanging it for a higher value. Second, consumers are only allowed to trade their own products and services and not products and services provided by others. Third, products and services that were received as donations cannot be bartered. Tracing the origin of the offered products or services in the system can allow the latter two rules to be enforced. For instance, the consumer may be able to select a product or service for barter only if it was purchased on the platform before, and thus paid for, traced, and logged. One of the key advantages of the barter platform is that it provides consumers an opportunity to dispose of unused products and available services, and thus reduce waste and overconsumption, while preserving natural resources. For example, instead of throwing away the unused apples and purchasing oranges, consumers may avoid both transactions by exchanging these items via the barter platform.

Another important platform in the cooperative economy is the donations platform. This platform allows vendors and consumers to donate their products and services to consumers that meet certain requirements as specified by the donors. This is also one of the primary platforms for donating products and services by vendors that made excess profit in the previous year. However, a vendor donation can be also a simple act of generosity regardless of previously earned excess profit. For instance, a supermarket or a restaurant owner may donate food items that are about to expire to the poor in their neighborhood. Consumers should be able to search in the donations section offerings that donors designated for their profile, and then complete a transaction by picking up the donated merchandise or having it shipped for a delivery fee per their income bracket. All donations should be given free of charge, and the platform should not charge a service fee for them either. Moreover, donors should be able to donate products and services even if not originally purchased on the platform. If no profile is specified by the donors, the system should automatically prioritize consumers at the lowest income bracket in a location proximate to the donor, and after a while, if the donation has not been claimed, the system would extend the availability to consumers at higher income brackets and at further distance. Finally, donated products and services that were not claimed would be moved to the two-sided market platform for purchase by consumers. Because these goods do not yield revenues to vendors, they should be assigned a zero price for the purpose of calculating the baseline price and corresponding consumer prices. This can lower the prices to all consumers and thus contribute to subsidization.

The donated product or service should still be limited in quantity and restricted to personal use. Furthermore, to avoid arbitrage, received donations cannot be resold by recipients on the two-sided market or barter platforms. To avoid free riders and laziness, one last requirement would be that any capable consumer who receives a donation should commit to offer a donation in return, within a year. The donation can be minimal, perhaps even of symbolic value, but nevertheless required. For example, a low-income consumer who receives some unused food items from a restaurant may commit to volunteer time for helping in a nearby hospital. This requirement can also help deal with the shame that low-income consumers may feel when receiving donations in kind, instead allowing them to perceive themselves as givers. This pure pay-it-forward practice is expected to reinforce prosocial behavior among those in greatest need, who may otherwise be tempted to behave opportunistically. One of the key merits of this donation platform is the minimization of waste and overconsumption. Because vendors and consumers that donate and receive donations may also operate on the other two platforms, the pay-it-forward process embedded in the donation platform will likely support prosocial behavior in these other platforms. Finally, the expectation is for this prosocial behavior to spread beyond the cooperative economy and benefit society at large.

5.9 FUNDRAISING AND MARKETING

The cooperative economy's platforms offer a comprehensive solution that requires substantial investments in research and development, operations, and marketing. The question is: how will funding be raised and marketing carried out? As noted, the platform operator is responsible for avoiding shareholder influence, and thus traditional funding sources such as venture capital investments and the stock market should not be considered. The platform operator should instead seek donations from international organizations such as the United Nations programs, the European Research Council, and the National Science Foundation. Other sources may include research grants and university donors. Private donations are also welcome but do not provide any privileges. One primary source that does carry privileges is crowdfunding.

Crowdfunding has become an important source of funding for entrepreneurial projects and charities. It involves funding a project by raising funds from a large number of individuals who each contribute a relatively small amount. Crowdfunding websites include Kickstarter, Crowdcube, Indiegogo, GoFundMe, RocketHub, SyndicateRoom, Crowdrise, Mightycause, SeedInvest, and NextSeed, among many others. The most attractive crowdfunding websites should be selected for fundraising. A minimum donation may be set without a maximum per donation. In return for their donation, donors would receive an invitation to join the platform without the endorsement requirement. Donors would still need to go through the remaining requirements of the admission process. Jointly, they would form the founding group of consumers and vendors. Hence, the platform can gain funding and an initial pool of users using the same process. The assumption is that individuals that identify with the cause and are willing to donate funds without any benefit other than an invitation to join as consumers or vendors are, by definition, prosocial.

Although stock ownership by investors should be avoided, the proposal is for the platform operator to distribute shares to consumers, vendors, and employees in order to formalize the relationship between the Cooperative Economy Foundation and its stakeholders. Each stakeholder group would together own 25 percent of the shares, with the platform operator holding the remaining 25 percent. Thus, each stakeholder group would receive an equal share in the platform. Within each stakeholder group, all shareholders would own one share each. Hence, every customer, vendor, and employee would receive one share after one year of active engagement with the platform. The share would be valid as long as the holder of the share is actively involved with the platform, i.e., has engaged in transactions on the platform in the past year and has not been dismissed because of departure or a violation of system rules. The share would be distributed at no cost and have no face value, because it is untransferable and non-tradable on the stock market. This is to avoid the shareholder control that is typical of the current economic system. Furthermore, to prevent takeover by traditional investors, the stakeholders would not be able to sell or transfer their shares. Finally, these shares would not provide decision rights, to avoid overruling of the principles on which the Foundation is instituted.

Although the shares would not provide the consumers, vendors, and employees with direct influence on decision making, the platform operator would provide annual reports to these stakeholders. The platform operator would also hold consumer, vendor, and employee conventions to receive feedback and input from these stakeholders about their needs and expectations. Additionally, the operator may ask for votes from a particular stakeholder group on issues that concern them and for which feedback from this stakeholder group is essential. Most importantly, once a year all holders of shares would be asked to evaluate whether the platform operator adheres to the system rules and indicate whether they are aware of a systematic violation of these rules by the platform operator. To the extent that there is sufficient evidence of such a violation, the stakeholders would assemble a review board to assess the evidence and may decide to dismiss the platform operator subject to a majority vote by all shareholders. In addition to these privileges, the allocation of shares provides a sense of ownership to these stakeholders, i.e., those actively involved in the daily operations of the platform. The ownership of each consumer, vendor, and employee would be equal within the respective stakeholder group. Each would have a voice that can shape the platform's operations but is insufficient to guide the operator in a direction that deviates from the principles upon which the Cooperative Economy Foundation is founded.

The centralized organizational structure of the Foundation is essential for the entrepreneurial effort and the scaling up of the cooperative economy. However, once the platform has grown to potential capacity and demonstrated smooth operation in some communities, it would be advisable to switch to a franchise model, like McDonald's, Burger King, 7-Eleven, or Ace Hardware, allowing qualified entrepreneurs in their local communities to take a leadership role in managing the local platform operations. The candidate entrepreneurs would be elected with a majority vote from active holders of shares in their community, and their term in office would be limited and subject to renewal. The elected franchisees would be responsible for meeting all obligations of the platform operator in their community and would be subject to periodical inspection by the Cooperative Economy Foundation, which they must pass if they wish to retain their franchise. Overall, the above stakeholder privileges and imposed restrictions on fundraising and the distribution of ownership demonstrate that the cooperative economy is a project for the community by the community. Once the franchise model is implemented, this will become clearer.

In addition to relying on crowdfunding for identifying the initial pool of consumers and vendors, marketing efforts for the platform should be directed to consumers and vendors that are most likely to benefit from the platform and to promote prosocial behavior. With respect to consumers, pilot platforms can be set up in communities that are most likely to be cohesive and exhibit prosocial behavior. Such communities may be organized around specific congregations and spiritual groups. By leveraging the established social norms and belief systems in these communities, it would be relatively easy to guarantee sufficient prosocial behavior to support system operations. Based on the early experience in implementing the system in small cohesive communities, it can be extended to other communities that will recognize its merits, and over time, as its parameters are optimized, it will gain in efficiency. Once the pilot program is completed and the platform scaleup is extended to larger communities, the platform operator may target philanthropists, thought leaders, and celebrities who would agree to join the platform. Advertising with their consent that these typically affluent consumers have joined the system would make it easier to attract additional high-income consumers. Even though some of these early joiners may do so for a claim to fame and to promote their reputation or brands, this can still serve the purpose of populating the system with donors who demonstrate prosocial behavior by being willing to subsidize low-income consumers.

Marketing efforts should be also directed to vendors. Initial efforts can concentrate on small businesses, entrepreneurs, and local vendors, who suffer a competitive disadvantage relative to large multinationals when seeking to access markets. The platform can provide them with guaranteed sales, which is an attractive value proposition for them. Furthermore, by operating locally, these vendors serve proximate consumers, so that their social embeddedness in the community increases the likelihood of observing prosocial behavior due to established social sanction and control processes. Once the small vendors grow their business and the larger vendors notice the volume of transacted business on the platform, they are likely to join as well, in part to enhance their reputation as contributors to their community and to society at large.

The details in this chapter are essential to demonstrate that the notion of the cooperative economy is practical rather than merely theoretical. Nevertheless, these concrete ideas are preliminary and should serve as a basis for further refinement, followed by experimentation and empirical investigation that can provide a proof of concept.

NOTES

1 Schlagwein, D., Schoder, D., & Spindeldreher, K. (2019), "Consolidated, systemic conceptualization, and definition of the 'sharing economy,'" *Journal of the Association for Information Science and Technology*, 71(7), pp. 817–838.
2 E.g., Lin, K.J., Savani, K., & Ilies, R. (2019), "Doing good, feeling good? The roles of helping motivation and citizenship pressure," *Journal of Applied Psychology*, 104(8), pp. 1020–1035.
3 Gibson, R., Krueger, P., Riand, N., & Schmidt, P.S. (2020), *ESG rating disagreement and stock returns*, European Corporate Governance Institute, ECGI Working Paper in Finance No. 651/2020.
4 Berg, F., Koelbel, J.F., & Rigobon, R. (2020), *Aggregate confusion: the divergence of ESG ratings*, MIT Sloan School Working Paper 5822-19.
5 Business Wire (2021), "Recent study reveals more than a third of global consumers are willing to pay more for sustainability as demand grows for environmentally-friendly alternatives," October 14, www.businesswire.com/news/home/20211014005090/en/Recent-Study-Reveals-More-Than-a-Third-of-Global-Consumers-Are-Willing-to-Pay-More-for-Sustainability-as-Demand-Grows-for-Environmentally-Friendly-Alternatives.

6 Damodaran, A. (2021), "Net margins by industry," New York University, http://pages.stern.nyu.edu/~adamodar/.

7 Hess, A.J. (2021), "In 2020, top CEOs earned 351 times more than the typical worker," CNBC, September 15, www.cnbc.com/2021/09/15/in-2020-top-ceos-earned-351-times-more-than-the-typical-worker.html.

CHAPTER SIX

Conclusion and an invitation

DOI: 10.4324/9781003336679-6

6.1 PRIME TIME FOR ACTION

My kids and I have played the board game Monopoly since they learned how to count. Sometimes it took a couple of hours, sometimes a couple of days, but the outcome was always the same: one player holding all the money, cities, houses, and hotels. Last summer, we played the new version of the game with an electronic bank and credit cards. My kids, now young adults, decided to collude and prevent me from purchasing the most attractive cities, the train stations, electricity, and water companies. How did it end? The same as always. Monopoly is a stylized model of our modern economic system. It may take years or even decades before a few entrepreneurs or financiers capture dominant incontestable positions, but the outcome is inevitable, with the concentration of wealth and power taking over. Once, my younger daughter lost patience and pushed away the gameboard, sending all the money notes flying into the air. After our last game, my older daughter complained that I had made her favorite game her most hated one; she swore not to play it again. The unfortunate reality is that it is not possible to terminate, amend, or effectively regulate our economic system. We have tried, but we failed. We voiced our discontent but have continued to play the game and order on Amazon. The essence of the problem was first noted in the 1980s. The idea of greed as the oil that lubricates the economic machine is not new. What is new are the platform ecosystems with their sophisticated algorithms, artificial intelligence, and machine learning, which honed this economic system to perfection and have enabled opportunistic behavior to transpire more swiftly, to be better rewarded, and become more harmful to everyone but a few. Nowadays, greed can be found in the local restaurant or shoe shop, not only in Wall Street hedge funds.

I started this journey by discussing the flaws of our current economic system, which has evolved and mutated from traditional capitalism to a ruthless economic beast. There is nothing wrong in value creation and capture. But there is much to be concerned about when the quest for profits becomes the primary purpose and is pursued at all costs.

The immediate implication is the concentration of wealth and income that leaves too much in the hands of a few and too little in the hands of many. While the ultra-affluent travel on their high-emission yachts and private jets, economic inequality brings an increasing proportion of the population to the verge of hunger and despair. It shortens life expectancy and leaves few expectations from that life, with no hope of reversing the vicious cycle whereby the rich become richer, and the poor become poorer. Attempts to break this vicious cycle have fallen short, with increasingly regressive taxation shifting the burden from corporations to families, multinational firms that systematically evade tax, an ineffective public welfare system, and weakened labor unions.

The vicious cycle fueled by greed is also propagated by network externalities that are typical of platform ecosystems. Competitors, complementors, consumers, and employees are all in the grip of platform owners, who monetize transactions to their own benefit and at the expense of consumers and other stakeholders. Amazon, Apple, Google, Microsoft, and Meta, among other knights of the Internet era, have become conquerors that dominate emerging and traditional sectors of the economy. They operate as gatekeepers that use exclusionary tactics to drive out competitors; they dictate unfavorable terms and exploit their complementors; and they lure consumers with enhanced value propositions, only for these consumers to later discover that they have incurred increasing switching costs, limited options, reduced quality, and higher prices that harm their welfare. Whereas the individuals owning the platforms have become the world's richest, many employees lost privileges and job security while experiencing worsening employment conditions. Efforts to harness the platform owners rely mostly on legislation, regulation, and antitrust enforcement. Yet such regulation is not suitable for coping with digital market platforms that enhance product availability and offer their services to consumers for free. The US House Judiciary Committee has prompted an aggressive approach, threatening to severely restrict and even break up the Big Tech firms, whereas the EU has opted for a lax approach of self-regulation. Neither is likely to be effective in chasing the moving target of nimble platform owners who can easily outmaneuver and outsmart the regulators, who in turn are slow to adapt and react, understaffed, and unequipped for the digital reality. Severe structural measures are likely to leave consumers worse off while paving the way for a new generation of dominant platform owners, who will learn to avoid the mistakes of their predecessors using preemption and deception.

Of particular concern is the Big Tech firms' accumulation and exploitation of sensitive user data. In the name of profit making, these firms have harvested personal information from numerous sources to construct a psychological profile of their consumers. They have leveraged big data analytics, artificial intelligence, and machine learning not only to predict preferences and choices, but to direct and divert consumer behavior for the purpose of maximizing their gains. This has deprived consumers of free choice and left them exposed to manipulation while polarizing public opinion and fostering social divide. Users have been used, often left with no choice but to concede their personal data, yet rarely do they know how that data is being used. Regulation such as the GDPR has had little impact on the critical data privacy and protection violations by Big Tech firms, which have managed to lobby and restrict regulation or use it to their advantage, while small firms and start-ups struggle under its administrative burden.

With the self-interested pursuit of profit and utility, firms have leveraged and abused natural resources, while individuals excessively consumed beyond the capacity of the planet. Although population growth can be blamed in part for overconsumption, it is mostly consumption by the affluent and the growth in GDP that explain this trend. Food is wasted by some while others are challenged by hunger, with the world's animal population halved in the past three decades. We consume to satisfy emotional desires rather than real needs, but this consumeristic culture does not result in happiness. We consume at the expense of others and especially at the expense of future generations, with little concern for this social dilemma. Overproduction and exploitation of natural resources follow overconsumption, destroying and polluting the soil, air, and water, along with their wildlife habitat. Some firms strive to be environmentally friendly, but most have done so for the sake of profit making, while greenwashing to extract the green dollar bills. The

United Nations' SDGs set aspirations for restoring sustainability, yet their goals occasionally conflict and often fall short of steering action. The focus has been on production efficiency, but overconsumption is the real challenge. Furthermore, recycling processes and environmentally friendly substitutes to harmful products are costly and may generate a rebound effect. Calls for slow consumption, voluntary simplicity, and a sufficiency-oriented lifestyle have remained mostly unanswered in the face of superfluous consumption. Firms, governments, and consumers share interest in maintaining unsustainable economic growth. With their careless consumption, consumers bear responsibility for the tragedy of the commons. It is within their power to reverse overconsumption if they change their behavior, but unlike firms and governments, they cannot easily engage in coordinated action. In fact, when assuming their role as employees, they cooperate with their employers to maintain economic development and livelihood at all costs. Without the active efforts of consumers, the current trend of overconsumption would persist regardless of the efforts of other stakeholders. Therefore, the cooperative economy calls for the social responsibility of all stakeholders, including vendors, consumers, and employees.

Finally, globalization has facilitated and reinforced the illnesses of the economy. It has brought economic growth and wealth to some at the expense of others, and made capital owners and multinational corporations more powerful, while unskilled employees and the least developed countries saw no gain. The wealthy individuals and nations that benefited most from globalization are responsible in most part for the overconsumption and abuse of natural resources and their consequent environmental damage. Moreover, globalization has made it difficult for governments to devise independent policies that serve society and has promoted a uniform consumeristic and materialistic culture that weakened traditional social structures. It has increased global efficiency while making the supply chain interconnected yet fragile, with possible ripple effects. Much like the broader economic system, globalization cannot be easily undone, and policymakers fail to see any remedies for its ramifications.

The root cause of the grand challenges imposed on society by the economic system is not self-interested search for profit but the fact that such quest overrides societal values. In this quest, values such as equality and care for the other and for the environment have been forgotten. The economic system admires and rewards greed and reinforces opportunistic behavior. The few that are kind to others tend to be exploited and penalized for their deviant behavior, which thus remains rare. This is despite more than half the population not being greedy but rather conditionally prosocial. The problem is that the modern economy ensures that the corresponding condition for exhibiting prosocial behavior is never met. Regulators, politicians, activists, and researchers who have sought to solve societal grand challenges have an insufficient toolbox to cope with the powerful yet elusive platform owners. Indeed, some of my colleagues recently concluded that "we should abandon utilitarian approaches and embrace morality and self-governance at both the individual and organizational level in order to overcome the profit-making logic that dominates much of corporate action in today's capitalist systems."[1] The big question is: how this can be achieved? What are the incentives for self-regulation? Public regulation and law enforcement are ill equipped for the digital era and are too slow to identify and react to violations. Most current remedies apply a band-aid to the bleeding system, whose problem is not with its superficial skin, but with its DNA. It is time to admit that we have failed to fix this economic system. We spent too much time attempting to fix it, while we should have focused on figuring out how to breed a new economy with a DNA that subscribes to a different set of priorities.

Societal values should come first, with profit after. This simple new order contradicts the very nature of our current economic system. Given its motives and self-reinforcing processes, the current system cannot go through a metamorphosis and accept this new order. Instead of trying to convince or force the system to accept this alien logic, we should reject the system that has failed to serve society and build a new system around this new logic—a system that gives priority to the fair distribution of value rather than to the creation and capture of value by the fittest.

Constructing an economic system around societal values is more straightforward than reprograming the current economic system, which has evolved to serve the profit-seeking aims of some capital owners at the expense of all other stakeholders. Now is the right time for this endeavor, before all the money notes are sent flying into the air. Instead of investing trillions of dollars in a mission to Mars, so a few selected individuals can escape the annihilation that humanity has brought on itself, such funds should be invested in healing this planet. Do you really believe that once the first colony is established on Mars, it would not bring with it the flawed values and practices of the economic system that put Earth at risk? This colony will probably proceed to exploit the natural resources of Mars for the sake of profit making, eventually needing to seek yet another host planet to repeat history. There is no more suitable planet for humankind than the planet in which it has naturally evolved. It is better to invest in the cooperative economy to improve the lives of billions on this planet than to invest billions of dollars to save a few thousand "lucky" individuals who are likely to infect the host planet with the flaws of the modern economic system.

This is perhaps the time to remind us that the board game Monopoly evolved from the Landlord's Game, whose creator, Lizzie Magie, introduced it in 1904 to illustrate the merits of an egalitarian economic system that benefits all players. The game served to mock the ruthless monopolies and show how imposing a single tax and offering equal opportunities and higher wages could make everyone a winner.[2] These old rules have been long forgotten and replaced with the cutthroat rules we are familiar with today. It is time to revert to the earlier rules of the game.

6.2 FROM EXPLOITATION TO COOPERATION

The cooperative economy replaces the fundamental driver of behavior and cures many of the illnesses of the modern economic system. The primary objective of the cooperative economy is to fulfill societal values, such as economic equality, sustainability, and well-being. This contrasts with the profit maximization or utilitarian motive in the current economic system. The most critical difference between the two systems, however, is the substitution of greed and its consequent opportunistic behavior in the current economic system with prosocial behavior as the dominant behavior that guides exchange in the cooperative economy. The strategy of firms and individuals in the current economic system is to create and capture value at others' expense. In the cooperative economy, there is still emphasis on value creation, but instead of focusing on increasing one's share of value, the system ensures a fairer distribution of the value created among members of the system. The cooperative economy also differs with respect to its market span. Whereas the current economic system relies on the global market to optimize the location of activities and enhance value chain efficiency and the variety of products and services, the cooperative economy is organized around communities, and thus contributes to social cohesion.

The cooperative economy and the current economic system are both semi-open. However, the current economic system excludes the needy, who may receive some social benefits but cannot effectively participate in economic transactions. In contrast, the cooperative economy provides opportunities for all participants while striving to exclude greedy participants who fail to follow its principles. Interestingly, in the current economic system, return on capital is far greater than any other compensation or earning, so consumers, small vendors, and employees subsidize affluent platform owners, who avoid paying their fair share of taxes. The cooperative economy is designed to reverse this process by using price discrimination, so that high-income consumers subsidize lower-income consumers. In fact, the cooperative economy rebalances the distribution of ownership and power in the system, so that the platform operator merely engages in the provision of its platform services, while stakeholders such as consumers, small vendors, and employees have greater opportunities and voice. This contrasts with the current economic system, in which platform owners enjoy concentration of wealth and power both horizontally relative to competitors and vertically relative to vendors, complementors, and consumers. Furthermore, entrepreneurs and new entrants fare better in the proposed cooperative economy, in which they have guaranteed market access with a minimum sale volume and a cushion protecting them from failure. This enables them to overcome the network externalities underlying the competitive advantage of incumbents in the current economic system, thus generating healthier competitive dynamics.

One of the main faults of the current economic system is the unconstrained superfluous overconsumption that strains natural resources. The cooperative economy seeks to restrict such consumption by incorporating reasonable purchase limits as per need. In addition to these restrictions, in the cooperative economy, sustainability goals are measured and enforced, unlike in the current economic system, in which they are often declared but rarely guide corporate behavior. Moreover, whereas the current economic system jeopardizes data privacy and manipulates purchasing behavior and consumer behavior at large for the sake of profit making, the cooperative economy neutralizes such undesirable practices and offers users free choice, not only in consumption but also in employment. Furthermore, in the current economic system, which is driven by profit maximization, vendors have incentives to reduce cost and quality, whereas the cooperative economy provides incentives to increase quality while reducing prices. This system also ensures proper employment conditions and restricts pay inequality, besides setting prices based on income. This contrasts with the current economic system, in which price discrimination is based on willingness to pay.

In addition, the current system relies exclusively on a multisided exchange market, with voluntary donations and barter being sporadic and having limited impact. In contrast, the cooperative economy embeds these alternative platforms and facilitates their operations, which enables even low-income consumers to actively engage in economic exchange. Furthermore, in the current system, firms leverage technologies to predict and guide consumer behavior and support exploitation. The cooperative economy can leverage similar technologies to screen new members, set prices, and allocate orders to vendors, as well as to trace and neutralize rule violations that undermine cooperation. Additionally, the governance of the cooperative economy gives more voice to communities and offers equal rights to stakeholders such as consumers, vendors, and employees as opposed to detached shareholders who drive decisions in the current economic system. In both economies, the platform owner or operator controls operations, but over time, in the cooperative economy the plan is to distribute ownership rights on a regional basis to elected capable operators, so there is no need for intervention by antitrust regulation and enforcement. Furthermore, the algorithms are transparent, and there is no attempt to outmaneuver competitors, vendors, consumers, and regulators as in the current system. Finally, while the current economic system relies to a great extent on capital raised in the stock market, in the cooperative economy, funding is raised via crowdfunding, grants, and donations.

In sum, there are striking differences between the cooperative economy and the current economic system, not only in their underlying logic but also in their operations and implementation (see Table 6.1). These differences reveal why it is difficult to steer the current economic system

Table 6.1 *Comparison of the current economic system and the cooperative economy.*

	Current Economic System	Cooperative Economy
Objective	Profit and utility maximization	Serving societal values
Dominant behavior	Opportunistic	Prosocial
Strategy	Value creation and capture	Value creation and distribution
Market span	Global	Multi-community
System boundaries	Excludes the needy	Excludes the greedy
Subsidy recipients	Affluent capital owners	Low-income consumers

Table 6.1 Cont.

	Current Economic System	Cooperative Economy
Platform structure	Horizonal/vertical concentration	Service function, stakeholder involvement
Competitive dynamics	Incumbent network externalities	Entrant guaranteed sales and cushion
Consumption	Superfluous	Reasonably restricted
Sustainability	Often declared, rarely pursued	Measured and enforced
Individual choice	Data mining and misguided behavior	Free consumption and employment choice
Profit making	The sky is the limit	There is a limit
Price setting	Based on willingness to pay	Based on income
Barter and donations	Voluntary and rare	Built-in system
Employment	Unprotected, severe pay inequality	Respectful, reduced pay inequality
Role of technology	Supporting exploitation	Supporting cooperation
Governance	Owner-controlled, shareholder-driven	From centralized to decentralized, stakeholder-driven
Operations	Maneuvering	Transparent
Funding	Stock market	Crowdfunding and donations

in such a new direction or borrow some of its principles when building the cooperative economy. Although some social capitalistic states in Europe have managed to accommodate some of the values of the cooperative economy, at least to an extent, it is still difficult to dissect the profit-seeking DNA and transplant the missing elements in the current economic system. The freedom that comes with the decision to build a new system is a virtue that can enable this system to succeed where all prior efforts have failed. It is easier to give birth to a new economy than to destroy, amend, or rebuild an inert system. At least, this is what we have observed with the ongoing efforts to fix the current economic system.

6.3 OVERCOMING THE PITFALLS

Although the proposed cooperative economy seems utopian, it can be practically implemented. This is not to say that it will not encounter some challenges. The main challenge is in converting opportunistic behavior into prosocial behavior. To achieve that, the system screens out greedy individuals while penalizing opportunistic behavior. Nevertheless, it offers an implicit incentive to those who seek to exploit others by creating an opportunity for an arbitrage, which is otherwise limited in the current economic system. In particular, by providing false information about income, a consumer may be able to purchase cheaply and resell at a higher price. These practices are forbidden and penalized, yet they might occasionally occur. The challenge is that the system is very sensitive to opportunistic behavior. Once such behavior is observed, it can discourage prosocial behavior, which is essential for the functioning of the cooperative economy. The concern is that the network externalities inherent to the system reinforce opportunistic behavior, and beyond a certain threshold, the economic logic of prosocial behavior may fail. For that reason, every effort should be made to exclude greedy consumers and promptly eliminate opportunistic behavior. This is especially critical at the embryonic stage of the system, in which building trust is paramount. Once the system has evolved to support routine operations and the norms of prosocial behavior are established, it will be easier to discourage opportunistic behavior and ensure that even if it occurs sporadically, it does not transpire to challenge the logic of the system. Much like prosocial behavior is penalized in the current economic system, opportunistic behavior should be penalized in the cooperative economy. At the steady state of the system, once prosocial behavior becomes pervasive and stable, it will be sufficient to rely on trust and social pressure as opposed to verification, control, and enforcement to reinforce prosocial behavior. Participants in the cooperative economy should not feel compelled to behave in a prosocial fashion, but rather realize the intrinsic value of the system. By achieving a balance between safeguards and inspiration, the cooperative economy can avoid the risk of becoming dystopian.

It is also worth noting that not every entrepreneur can become a platform operator in the cooperative economy.[3] Given the unique nature of this economy, stakeholders must build trust in the platform operator. The very basic level of trust is calculative trust, whereby the parties build expectations about each other's behavior based on applicable laws and contracts, under the assumption that each behaves rationally and would not violate this trust given the specified penalties. In turn, relational trust is built based on experience in past interactions of the parties once they become familiar with each other's behavior and can build expectations on that basis.[4] In the case of the Cooperative Economy Foundation, calculative trust will be built based on its design principles as well as by leveraging transparency, e.g., subjecting the algorithm code to review by trusted state authorities. Over time, the calculative trust will give way to relational trust by building on the experience that stakeholders have gained using the platform. Given the broad application of system rules and the fact that users know that the same rules apply to all, it is expected that they will gain trust in each other because they trust the system, which will facilitate exchange transactions. Such trust is also likely to emerge given the community focus of the cooperative economy and the opportunity for engaging in social interactions that create embeddedness in the community.[5] Moreover, it is more straightforward to build trust when the parties follow prosocial behavior than when they behave opportunistically. In that sense, to the extent that prosocial behavior is prevalent and observed, it is also likely to be reinforced.

Related to this is the challenge of leadership. The proposed system has built-in safeguards such as reliance on transparent algorithms and non-compete clauses that can prevent corruption by the platform operator. However, given the profit restriction and the immense responsibility of the platform operator, one could wonder if in each community we can hope to find the right leadership to take on the role of the platform operator. My answer is affirmative. To the extent that we expect a sufficient number of prosocial individuals to take part in the cooperative economy, we could also expect some of these individuals to take on more social responsibility and become involved as platform operators.

This directs attention to the concern of whether there will be a sufficient number of prosocial individuals to support the operation of the cooperative economy. The short answer is yes. Experiments suggest that about half of the population are conditionally prosocial, meaning that to the extent that they observe that others behave in a prosocial fashion, they will follow suit. It is more important to ensure that early adopters of the system will be prosocial than to build scale fast. As long as incoming members are prosocial, network externalities are likely to reinforce such behavior and support further scaling up of the cooperative economy. Furthermore, because the natural career path is characterized by increases in salary and wealth over an individual's lifetime, recipients of price subsidies are likely to become donors as they progress professionally. This reinforces the pay-it-forward pattern, which is a stronger form of prosocial behavior driven by one's own experience and sense of gratitude. Over time, these network externalities and the crystalizing norm of prosocial behavior are likely to help align the behavior of the few participants who exhibit opportunistic behavior with that norm. Furthermore, these dynamics can also ensure that to the extent that opportunistic behavior is observed, it is unlikely to negatively impact the conduct of prosocial consumers at large. Finally, given its shift from a global economy to a community-based exchange, the cooperative economy need not suppress the current economic system at a global scale. It is sufficient for it to reach dominance in the communities in which it is implemented. Once the cooperative economy captures a substantial market share, platform owners in the current economic system are likely to follow suit and adopt more prosocial practices that benefit their stakeholders in an attempt to win back their lost market share. Hence, in addition to regulation and legislation, it is market pressure that would bring about a behavioral change in the global economy.

The notion of a community is central to the cooperative economy, but the question of how a community should be delineated can be revisited. In order for a community to foster prosocial behavior, members must feel that they belong to the community and identify with its values and norms, which may be characteristic of various communities including virtual communities of like-minded individuals who share certain interests. However, beyond fostering prosocial behavior, physical proximity and interaction are essential for minimizing delivery times, travel, and waste of physical products and resources, and thus serving societal goals. Hence, it is advisable to have each consumer belong to one physical community, but perhaps have affiliations with multiple virtual communities that exchange digital products and resources, without undermining the benefits of physical communities.

A remaining question is whether the cooperative economy can prosper given the prevalent human nature, or rather is an optimistic form of impractical spiritualism, God forbid. To that I reply that if the current economic system had the right spirit in it, there would have been no need to introduce the cooperative economy. Indeed, a certain level of shared beliefs in retribution, solidarity, and mutual responsibility are essential, but once infused in the system, the cooperative economy reinforces them. Our experience with the current economic system has taught us that self-interested behavior does not serve the ultimate interests of society and humankind. For the cooperative economy to materialize, this realization should be followed by a change in behavior.

Is it possible to make people prosocial or to convert greedy individuals so they become more prosocial in their community? As discussed, in addition to being a relatively stable human trait, prosocial behavior is shaped by norms, culture, institutions, and religious beliefs. Hence, to the extent that these factors change, they can influence the tendency to become prosocial versus opportunistic. Nevertheless, institutions, cultures, and religious beliefs are rather persistent and do not tend to change frequently or drastically. That being said, we live in a dynamic era. Drastic measures are taken, institutions fall, beliefs are put into question, and norms evolve rapidly. In part, this is due to the state of the current economic system, which is unsustainable and self-destructive. As we observe during this unfortunate period, extreme economic inequality leads to social unrest and to the uprising of those who are unwilling to accept deprivation. Overexploitation and abuse of natural resources lead to shortages, inflation, and an inability to maintain a decent standard of living, as well as to regional conflicts concerning the use of such resources. Global warming facilitates natural disasters that leave many in despair. Opportunistic behavior and overexploitation of stakeholders dilute social cohesion and facilitate distrust, which undermines economic exchange. Overall, the current economic system is not sustainable, and its collapse is likely to bring economic loss, challenge institutions, and make many question its underlying logic and become less materialistic and, perhaps, more spiritual. Added to these is the wind of war that surrounds Europe with Russia's invasion of Ukraine. War leads to destruction, economic collapse, stagflation, and despair while encouraging solidarity within communities. This is another force that, much like the other fundamental changes that characterize our time, can make some people more prosocial. In that sense, whereas the emergence of the cooperative economy does not entail the demise of the current economic system, the eventual demise of that system is likely to prompt vendors and consumers to join the cooperative economy and accept its alternative logic. Hence, there is no reason to wait for the current economic system to reach its end of life, for the next pandemic to emerge, and for war to bring destruction. Rather, the cooperative economy should be ready to admit the prosocial individuals who are left without an alternative or decide to desert the current system.

6.4 A CALL FOR ACTION

When I presented my preliminary ideas in seminars and conferences, some of my colleagues approached me and asked whether, in introducing such revolutionary ideas, I was not concerned about my academic reputation. My answer was that it is because I am concerned about my academic reputation that I pursue these ideas. It is indeed safer to join a trend than to initiate one. But if we keep waiting for someone to bring change, change will never come. It is probably the last call for a change in direction. The current economic system is short-lived. A new system should be built while we observe the sunset of the current one. Building a new economic system is not an easy task, but the foundations and practical guidance are provided here. The first step would be to refine the economic model and to test it. I therefore call upon my fellow researchers—those who always ask to serve as the devil's advocate. Why won't you serve as the angels' advocate for once? To those who say that these are not new ideas, tell me why similar ideas have not materialized. To those who say that these ideas are too radical, tell me why they would not work. To those who say that I am wrong, prove it. Design experiments, collect data, and help identify boundary conditions and optimize parameters that can perfect the cooperative economy. Researchers should study the conditions under which individuals tend to exhibit prosocial versus opportunistic behaviors in the cooperative economy; they can isolate the optimal Prosociality Index that motivates high-income consumers to donate while not disincentivizing low-income consumers' contributions to society; they may identify the profit margins that would encourage corporate entrepreneurship while striving for economic equality; they can test alternative pricing formulas and various methods for value redistribution, and develop algorithms for effective prediction of consumption patterns. Numerous related research questions have yet to be answered.

I extend a call to system engineers, computer scientists, programmers, and those with expertise in algorithms, artificial intelligence, and machine learning. Both well-trained professionals and graduate students: you have used your skills to help the Big Tech firms grow and prosper. You have been well rewarded, but are you proud of your creation? Do you prefer to fight with David or with Goliath? Would you not want to design and develop a system that serves societal values rather than drives value into the already deep pockets of a few shareholders? If you are up (or app) for the challenge, join the Cooperative Economy Foundation and make a difference. This call is not limited to computer scientists and information technology experts. The Cooperative Economy Foundation will need experts in all functional domains, ranging from product and service design to finance and accounting, business development, legal, supply chain management, operations, and human resource management, among many others. This is a call for duty that is a privilege.

I extend a call to affluent sponsors, financiers, and donors. Setting up a new economic system requires a major upfront investment. Unlike other investments, this one will not bring you an immediate material return. You will receive no shares but will take a share in creating a system that benefits humanity and our planet. Instead of donating to the deprived and needy, help them become less needy by contributing to the creation of a more egalitarian and just economic system. With its self-reinforcing logic, the system should continuously create and distribute value, but it still requires a kickstart. If you are not among the fortunate who have a fortune, but would like to donate to this worthy cause, you can take part in crowdfunding campaigns and sign up as a prospective consumer or vendor.

I extend a call to regulators, government officials, and leaders of international and national programs with relevant interests and aligned goals. Instead of chasing the rabbit and crafting regulation that seeks to prevent yesterday's breaches, focus on designing legislation and enforcement capabilities that serve the future economic system, e.g., by calling for transparency and inspection of algorithms and by setting up dedicated units to that aim. Associations and programs that sponsor research and development projects should be open to proposals that challenge long-held assumptions and offer radical solutions as the cooperative economy does. Given its unique nature, the cooperative economy may not be well aligned with regulation that makes strong assumptions about the motives and practices of platform owners. Legislators should focus on the underlying logic rather than on appearance, on the outcomes rather than on actions per se.

A final call is extended to all readers. If the ideas presented here resonate with you, and you believe that this could be the right solution to some societal grand challenges, then when the time comes, join the cooperative economy as a consumer or vendor, and take part in economic exchange that benefits society beyond the benefits to oneself. Check for updates on cooperativeeconomy.net.

Let me conclude by noting that in introducing this system I am merely a messenger who put together in words what many believe in heart that is just: a platform that serves society rather than society that serves a platform. The roots of this system are as ancient as humanity, and its logic is simple and natural. It is the modern economic system that is overly complex, convoluted, and deceptive. What I suggest is not creative destruction, but construction that adheres to the laws of creation. By following these laws, we can restore our confidence in economic systems, distribute rather than concentrate value and wealth, have corporations serve society rather than the other way around, reverse the trend of overconsumption and heal our exploited planet, respect all stakeholders and their choices, and rebuild communities around societal values. Solving societal grand challenges is within reach, but the journey starts not with a new economy but with humankind: less consumeristic, opportunistic, and utilitarian; more prosocial, egalitarian, and humane. Let it begin.

NOTES

1 Aguilera, A., Aragon-Correa, J.A., & Marano, V. (in press), "Rethinking corporate power to tackle grand societal challenges: lessons from political philosophy," *Academy of Management Review*.
2 Pilon, M. (2015), *The monopolists: obsession, fury, and the scandal behind the world's favorite board game*, Bloomsbury USA.
3 For elaboration on the desirable characteristics and commitments of platform operators, see Weber, E.P., & Khademian, A.M. (2008), "Wicked problems, knowledge challenges, and collaborative capacity builders in network settings," *Public Administration Review*, March/April, pp. 334–349.

4 Poppo, L., Zheou, K.Z., & Li, J.J. (2016), "When can you trust 'trust'? Calculative trust, relational trust, and supplier performance," *Strategic Management Journal*, 37(4), pp. 724–741.

5 Granovetter, M. (1985), "Economic action and social structure: the problem of embeddedness," *American Journal of Sociology*, 91(3), pp. 481–510.

INDEX

Page numbers in *italic* denote figures and in **bold** denote tables.

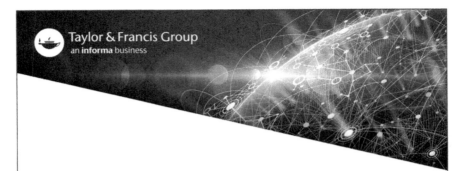

Printed in the United States
by Baker & Taylor Publisher Services